8-13-80

Too Deep for Tears

Too Deep for Tears

Lucy Freeman

with Jenny and Rosette Spinoza

HAWTHORN / DUTTON
New York

Contents

Preface

This book presents, for what is believed the first time, a mother's story, then her daughter's, of the relationship between them that led to the daughter's emotional breakdown. What happened occurs to some degree in the lives of every mother and child.

The mother blames herself for what went wrong. Most of the therapists she consulted insisted her daughter's illness was her fault.

But the book is not accusatory. It portrays the intertwining of tragedies in the lives of a sensitive, intelligent woman and an equally sensitive, gifted daughter, neither able to understand or cope with what was happening to them.

It became mother and daughter against the world—finally the terrifying world of city and state mental hospitals. As one therapist put it: "I heard beneath their words the painful screams of both mother and daughter and tried to ease the pain as best I could."

The book has the quality, it is hoped, of a psychological detective story. Who was the villain in this case of what August Strindberg called "soul murder"? Society? Mother? Daughter? Every therapist who inflicted inhumane, cruel treatment or gave inept help? What was the villain's motive?

Perhaps there were several villains acting in conspiracy. Or no villain at all, if there is understanding of the nature of the crime.

Lucy Freeman
New York City, New York

cAcknowledgments

My deepest thanks to Dr. Karl Menninger for suggesting that this book be written; to Joan Nagy, formerly executive editor at Hawthorn Books, for her artistry in helping shape the manuscript; to Beth Backman, former senior editor at Hawthorn Books/Dutton, and Marian Skedgell, senior editor at E. P. Dutton, for their skillful help in the editing; to Alan J. Haber, editorial assistant at E. P. Dutton, who helped with the many editorial tasks; and to Shirley Burke, literary agent, for having faith in the story of Jenny and Rosette Spinoza.

Thanks also to Dorothy Bloch, Dr. Robert Cancro, Dr. Aylin Radomisli, and Dr. Walter A. Stewart for giving their interpretations of the relationship between mother and daughter that appear in the final section. And to Adrian Petrescu, director of the Romanian Library in New York.

Last, but not least, my gratitude to Jenny and Rosette Spinoza for their understanding of and dedication to the work when in progress and their willingness to bare the truth of their lives so others might be spared pain. Jenny has dedicated the book "to my beloved daughter Rosette and my sister Berta."

I

Jenny

I

Before Rosette

My God, what did I do wrong? I love her more than life itself and yet I have inflicted deep suffering on her. What I have done is tragic beyond words.

I only wanted her to find the happiness I never had. I tried so very hard to do my best but I only caused her deeper pain. Not out of malice or meanness but ignorance. Not knowing what to do, which way to turn.

Why did I hurt her?

Where did it all start?

I have lived on three continents—Europe, South America, and finally North America, ending in the city of New York. It is a long way from my birthplace, Khotin, in Romania (it was spelled Hotin before it became part of the Soviet Union).

Khotin stands on the Dniester, a wide, beautiful river that runs north and south, flowing into the Black Sea, in my day separating Romania from the Soviet Union. This section once lay in the province of Bessarabia, formerly belonging to Czarist Russia but given to Romania after the treaty of Versailles. Today it is part of the Soviet Union.

When I lived there, its five thousand inhabitants consisted of Russian peasants and poor and wealthy Jews. Bessarabia never accepted Romanian occupation and I often saw officers and soldiers quartered there to keep peace.

Like many ancient European towns, Khotin was two cities in one. The "old" city stretched out beside the Dniester and poor Jews, including tailors and shoemakers, lived along its dirty, narrow streets. The "new" city, away from the river, boasted wide, clean streets, palatial parks and large houses, the homes of the wealthier inhabitants. We lived there, as did my mother's father, Mendel Sadovnick, the Rabbi of Khotin.

Centuries before, the Turks occupied the province of Moldavia of which Bessarabia was part. They built a tremendous fortress in Khotin, high on a mountain, pointing its guns toward the steppes of Russia on the other shore of the Dniester. As a child, I played in the fortress, racing over the old stones thick with grass. An air of mystery floated out of the many secret passages, legends woven of love affairs consummated within.

During the summer I swam in the Dniester, following the custom of the older people—the boys bathed nude in one area, and half a kilometer away the girls ran naked into the river. The older, more religious folk swam in their underwear, then sat on the shore under a sheet to dry. Once in the river, boys and girls would swim toward each other as the adults shrieked at them to separate.

One day when I was eight, I nearly drowned. I wanted to see how far I could walk. All of a sudden my foot slipped, I must have fallen into a hole. The water closed over my head. Somehow I lifted up my body, struggled for air, then caught onto a rock and pulled myself out of the water. Many times in later years when I felt I could bear no more pain, I regretted I did not drown that day, go down to oblivion in the clear blue waters of my beloved river.

My mother, one of four daughters, was also born in Khotin. She went to medical school for two years, then, to earn money for further study, decided to tutor Jewish children, most of them denied admission to the local schools where the Jewish quota was limited. At the age of twenty-two, she was hired by my father's parents to teach his sisters in their home at Rishcon, about a day from Khotin by horse and carriage.

There she met my father, Mark Altman, named in honor of Rishcon's rabbi, Mark Zail. Even as a boy, my father had an affinity for the printed word. In high school he fell in love with the world of books. He learned to read in French, Yiddish, Hebrew, Spanish, Portuguese, and Russian, so he could acquire knowledge from more and more books.

He grew up in the midst of pogroms. The Romanian peasants looted the stores, broke the windows of houses owned by Jews, sometimes set them afire. One night they stormed my father's house, smashed all the furniture. His mother hid her children in the barn, ordered them to keep silent.

My father hated the military, spoke of war as a "crime" and generals and army heroes as "assassins and delinquents." He became interested in socialism. As he was reading in bed at three o'clock one morning, the door to his room opened. His father, a man with a ferocious temper, walked in. He saw his son reading Karl Marx, struck him on the head with the cane he always carried, hurled him to the floor, and tore the hated book to pieces.

The next morning my father left home, hatred in his heart for his bigoted father, a wealthy Rishcon landowner and moneylender. My father journeyed to Lipcon, the birthplace of his father, grandfather, and great-grandfather, to live with his older brother, Moishe, who also thought their father a tyrant. But after running out of money while studying in Odessa, my father cooled down enough to return to Rishcon, make up with his father, and get a job teaching.

One night he walked into his father's mansion, saw my mother, who had just been hired as tutor, and fell in love with her. She was very pretty with blue-gray eyes, brown hair, and an alabaster complexion. His father forbade him to marry her, wanting a wealthier daughter-in-law. But my father, always the rebel, again defied his father. He left home at the age of twenty, this time to marry my mother, two years his senior. They honeymooned in Vienna, then lived for a while in the large house of my mother's father, the Rabbi, and his second wife. (His first wife had died when the four daughters were quite young.)

Within a year my mother was pregnant. Her first child was a boy. They moved to Odessa, then decided to go back to Rishcon and live on a small estate my grandfather was giving my father so he could earn a more profitable living than by teaching school. My grandfather desperately wanted my father to become wealthy like himself.

World War I had just erupted and the military had taken over the railroads so my mother and father were forced to travel by horse and carriage from Odessa. It was a two-day journey in the middle of winter. My little brother caught pneumonia and died before they could get him to a doctor.

My mother felt so devastated by the loss of her baby she tried to kill herself by swallowing iodine. Doctors managed to save her by instantly pumping out her stomach. My father, who kept a lifetime diary, wrote of this day: "My wife became so depressed over the death of our child that she attempted suicide. I barely saved her. My idyll came to an end and, bereft of hope, there was very little left of my love. I said, 'Rosa, our love has ended. Let's get a divorce. There is no use going on this way together.' Rosa cried. It inspired pity in me, but pity is not love."

They remained together however. Two years later, on the night of November 10, when the snow was already ten inches deep and falling steadily, my mother, once again pregnant, felt labor pains. She asked my father to run for the midwife. He put on his high black boots and heavy overcoat and ran out the door. A branch of a tree on our front lawn swept off his glasses and they fell to the ground. He could hardly see without them so he started a long search in the snow. In the meantime, I was delivered by an illiterate maid instructed by my mother.

My mother gave birth to a second daughter, Berta, when I was eight. She was an exceptionally beautiful baby with platinum hair, a tiny tilted nose, and large gray-blue eyes. She always kept close to mother, followed her around the house clinging to her skirt. I loved Berta, though I was usually too busy with school, my books, and my friends to pay much attention to her.

We shared a one-story house with the owners, an old man and his wife, who seemed peaceful people. They occupied three rooms and we had three. A fruit orchard a block long, with peach, apple, and plum trees, stood to the rear. Flowers of many colors bloomed in spring and summer in the front garden. Every April 1st, I climbed the Khotin mountain to search for violets under the snow to carry home to mother.

In one of our three rooms, my mother and father slept in twin beds on monogrammed sheets. The expensive blond wood furniture had been bought in Vienna on their honeymoon. The living room served as sleeping quarters for Berta and me. We slept on sofas, one at each end of the room, and kept our few dresses, coats, and hats in an armoire. The living room also held the table at which we ate and at which we read nights by the kerosene-lit, Russian cut-glass lamp of brilliant colors, a perpetual rainbow cluster. There was a fireplace to keep us warm in winter. I thought it a friendly room.

My father's younger sister Fanny, one of the two mother tutored, moved in when I was about nine. For three or four months at a time my father taught school in distant towns and when he was gone Fanny slept in his bed. As soon as he came home, she shared Berta's sofa.

I thought my father a handsome, dignified man. He stood six feet tall and slender. His face was cleanshaven; he had a wide, generous mouth and intense blue eyes. His glasses gave him an academic look. He dressed meticulously and his blond hair was always carefully combed, not a strand out of place. He would sometimes take me with him when he lectured; I would sit in the front row, proud to be the daughter of the most intellectual man in Khotin. Every poet, novelist, and dramatist who visited the area wound up at our house talking to my father, a man of energy and liveliness.

My mother, who was short and by this time plump, was an aristocratic, stoic woman who spoke slowly and thoughtfully. She seldom raised her voice in anger. Though once, when I disobeyed her she screamed, "I wish you were dead!" Another time she shouted, "May your children do to you what you are doing to me!" Several times she wailed, "Why do you bleed me this way?" I felt hurt she could say such hateful things. My father told me she came from a "very disturbed" family, that one of her sisters had spent time in a mental hospital.

There were moments I did deserve her wrath. I enjoyed reading in the seclusion of the fruit garden, lying on the green wooden bench or underneath an apple or peach tree. Sometimes she would call but I would not answer, knowing she wanted me for some irritating chore. I was voracious for the printed word, devoured every classic in the library more hungrily than I did sweets. The librarian would look at me in wonder as I returned two books and say, "You just took them out yesterday!" Like my father, I was excited by ideas. I inherited his imagination and blond hair but my mother's gray-blue eyes and short stature.

The most cherished memory of childhood is of my mother sitting before the fireplace each evening reading to Aunt Fanny and me the latest installment of the romance serialized in the daily newspaper, which I would have rushed to the store to buy. My father, when he was home, read Jewish poetry or composed his own stories, usually allegories.

As I grew up, Romania was caught in the increasing momentum of a political and economic revolution that shook the world on November 7, 1917, not only for the famous "ten days" but the years to follow. Many an afternoon I sat on the grassy slopes of the Khotin mountain watching men and women on the far side of the Dniester harvest wheat and corn. A new world was being formed on the Russian border of the river and I wondered if it were a world where Jews, victims of Romanian pogroms, would be considered equal to all other men.

When I was ten, my parents asked what I wanted to be. I said, "I want to build bridges." Why did I wish to become an architectural engineer? Perhaps one of my fantasies was to build a bridge across the Dniester and escape to what I thought the freedom of a brave new universe.

Even at ten I realized there was something wrong with a society filled with so much hate. The Jews hated the Gentiles, the Gentiles hated the Jews. The Romanians hated the Russians, the Russians hated the Romanians. Men hated women, women hated men. I watched the peasants work all day in the fields, then dance at night, the men swigging vodka from bottles, beating their wives when they reached home. The book that influenced me most as a girl was Gorky's *The Mother*, about a woman beaten by her husband, then her son after the husband died. But when her son started to read books and became a member of the Communist Party, he stopped beating her, wanting a more humane world. I thought, There must somehow, somewhere, be an answer to the misery people suffer.

Khotin was very anti-Semitic. The Jews drafted into the Romanian army were given the dirty jobs, whipped, even killed, if they rebelled. Many a young Jew facing army duty tried to cross the Dniester to the safety of the Soviet Union but usually was caught and executed. These were the days a professor of law, A. C. Cuza, encouraged youth groups to act in the service of Nazi Germany, organizing the National Christian Defense. The democratic forces of Romania finally overthrew what had become a Fascist government, joining the Allies and declaring war against Germany on August 23, 1944.

The first time I saw a swastika I was on my way to school one very cold morning when the snow was deep. Usually I walked eyes lowered as some of the streets were not paved. This day I happened to look up, saw a white house on whose door had been painted in black a large sign I did not understand. The street was deserted so early in the morning but I waited until several adults I knew came along and called their attention to this peculiar drawing. In fearful voices they referred to it as a ''swastika.''

After the October Revolution, as the Kerensky government tried to take over Russia, the Romanian peasants occupied Bessarabia, now allied with the Russians. The Bund of Kishinev, a social, political and cultural organization, which accepted the Romanian occupation for the price of cultural autonomy, opened a network of Jewish schools in the cities and small towns.

My mother was appointed director of the first Jewish school in Beltsy, a city of 60,000 in Bessarabia, where we lived for a time. My father, though he did not possess the correct credentials, was considered a teacher and was allowed to help mother in an unofficial capacity. He fought for the education of the poor as culture spread over Bessarabia in new libraries, evening schools, and newspapers that brought the latest information about the Soviet Union, Lenin, the revolution, the counter-revolution, and the ongoing pogroms.

My father joined the socialist movement. He wrote in his diary: ''I felt as if I was getting married for the second time, joined to the proletariat and their new party.'' He lectured, composed articles for newspapers, attended conferences. In 1920 he was invited to teach and direct cultural events in Britchev, where he spent much of the next few years and we saw little of him. He returned to join us in Beltsy in 1925.

Shortly after this, he met a young woman, Rebecca Goodman, of whom he wrote in his diary: "She is very coquettish, she goes from man to man . . . from bed to bed . . . beautiful, loving, and warm. She is burning like fire, attracting men to herself like the glowing light draws butterflies. She insists on coming with me to my lectures."

In 1928, when we were living once again in Khotin, the boy King Michael, just a child, with a Committee of Three ruled Romania as a dictatorship. That year the government announced there would be elections for Congress—a token gesture to the growing number of workers and peasants clamoring for representation in the government.

My father, by then a noted socialist, ran for the Romanian Congress on the workers' platform. He wrote in his diary: "Everyone is nervous but not I! Imagine . . . a congressman . . . isn't that something! I amaze myself! Not only will I be a writer, a leader of the Jewish race, but also a congressman! Among the Gentiles! Now my destiny leads directly to Bucharest. Now I'm ready for high society . . . now I'll conquer the world!" My exuberant father was thinking in exclamation points, which were soon to be reduced to mere periods when his party lost the election.

The government then issued an indictment against all losing candidates, charging them with treason. But because my father's father had influential friends, my father was given a chance to escape the charge provided he leave the country. His father sent him 20,000 lei to finance his flight. We were all anxious as to where he would go, hoped he would take us with him.

One night I watched him write a letter as he sat at the square wooden table in our living room. My mother walked into the room.

She asked worriedly, "Mark, to whom are you writing?" Her grammar was perfect, even in conversation.

"My cousin, Moishele Altman," he said. He felt close to this cousin.

Mother looked over his shoulder. As she read his words, her hand flew to her mouth to stifle a scream. She said to my father pleadingly, "Oh no! Oh no! Please don't do that to me."

"I must," he said firmly. "You've got to get accustomed to how it is."

I learned how it was a few days later. On a bitter cold March day of 1929, my mother, my little sister and I stood at the railroad station staring up at my father. Not believing what he intended to do.

By his side stood a woman almost twenty years younger, her vivacious face wreathed in smiles—Rebecca Goodman, the coquette who insisted on accompanying my father to his lectures, and who also had been a student of my mother's. Long blond hair flowed to her shoulders, her blue eyes sparkled. Her cheeks held the rosy glow of Russian women, who never need rouge, a result of battling the icy chill so many months of the year.

My father was forsaking all of us for the new love standing next to him. And for a new country—Brazil.

He was forced to leave Romania to escape arrest and imprisonment by the government, this we understood. But we did not understand why he did not take us rather than the young woman with whom he had apparently fallen in love, who seemed bursting with happiness at the thought of voyaging to the other side of the world with a man who was abandoning his wife and two small daughters.

My mother stood with sadness on her face, in startling contrast to the joy my father showed, obviously looking forward to an exciting life. We said nothing, the time long gone for words of despair or recrimination. We kissed father goodbye. There were no tears, just stony looks that denied feelings of anger and of grief.

The coal-powered train chugged noisily out of the station, disappeared into the mountains. We three females, my mother, myself, then eleven and a half, and Berta, three and a half, walked in silence back to our small white house.

My father's desertion precipitated a second crisis. Mother had been supporting us by teaching in the government school. But now, because of my father's anti-government politics, she received a letter saying she was fired. Our rent had been paid six months in advance but she had saved scarcely a cent beyond 500 lei earmarked for the second year of my gymnasium tuition. I was one of a few Jewish children permitted to attend the Khotin high school, where classes were to start on September 16.

Mother could have sought financial help from her father, but she felt too ashamed to tell him of her husband's desertion. She was not close to her stepmother.

Each morning mother would sit in the front garden, wait for the postman. As he passed he would say, "I have no letter for you today."

"Please look again," she would beg.

It was weeks before she received a letter from my father, saying he had arrived in Rio de Janeiro, the capital of Brazil. At first I missed him, then forgot about him. Or perhaps denied the loss, thinking, What good does it do to long for him?

I watched mother grow more and more depressed. I suspected she might be expecting another baby for she visited the doctor several times and when she came home looked as though she had been weeping. Her weight had plummeted to ninety pounds; often she refused to eat. We had little money, our meals were usually a potato with a small pat of butter.

Sometimes mother would say to me, "Please go into the garden, I have something to discuss with Fanny." In our small quarters it was difficult to find privacy. I felt hurt, banished from intimate talk. Once I put my ear to the closed door, then told myself, "This is too undignified," and flounced into the flower garden.

Four days before I was to start the second year of gymnasium, the evening of September 12, I was lying on my sofa, deep in Schiller's *The Thieves.* I wore one of the old dresses in which I slept. I did not enjoy the luxury of owning a nightgown.

My mother walked into the room. She wore a blazing red wool blouse she had made. Neighbors thought her flamboyant because she liked bright colors and cut her hair short. Even I was surprised at how daring she had become, as though trying to keep up her spirits.

But now tears glistened in her eyes. I felt uncomfortable, I had no patience with the tears of adults.

She came over to my sofa, sat down. She started to embrace me, to kiss me. I pushed her away, said impatiently, "Let me read."

I believed my mother loved us though she rarely showed it openly. Neither she nor my father kissed or hugged us. Such aloofness was the custom in that day when parents seemed to be afraid to display loving feelings for children. Because of this unusual display of affection I should have been warned something was wrong with mother.

The next morning I woke to a shining sun. It was Friday, the 13th. In three more days I would be back at my beloved school.

Suddenly I became aware of an unusual early morning sound—loud voices just outside my window. Without even washing my face, I ran out of the house. I found myself in the midst of neighbors milling around in our garden, talking in excited voices. I pushed through them.

Then I caught a glimpse of my mother. She was stretched out, still and quiet, on the green wooden bench, wearing her long white nightgown. Autumn flowers framed her head and body.

I ran to Aunt Fanny, who was talking in whispers to a neighbor. I asked, frightened, ''What's happened to my mother?''

Aunt Fanny looked at me with horror on her face. She said, ''Your mother did something terrible.''

I sensed whatever mother had done was unspeakable so I did not ask what it was. I could not bear to look at her masklike face but noticed her abdomen was swollen. I wondered again if she were pregnant.

I walked slowly into the house, threw myself on the sofa, burst into tears. I did not know exactly what my mother had done but thought it must be catastrophic. Aunt Fanny opened the front door and came over to me. She said, ''Your mother swallowed a mixture of iodine and ammonia. She tried to kill herself.''

''Is she dead?'' I asked through tears.

''No. We're arranging to take her to the hospital. I want you to stay here and care for Berta.''

I was glad Aunt Fanny lived with us, thinking, What would Berta and I do without her? I remained in the house all day with Berta who, as always, kept very quiet. I held her close, spoke to her continually to comfort her with words. Two of my closest friends, who were identical twins—only their mother and I could tell them apart—came over to give us solace. When their mother, a dentist, and their father, a teacher in our high school, arrived to pick them up, they said they hoped my mother would recover from her suicide attempt. I had never heard the word "suicide," thought of it, in my naïveté, as a disease from which some recovered, others died.

Even though I was not particularly religious, after the twins and their parents left, I kneeled and prayed, "Please God, don't let my mother die." I took after my father, who never was very convinced there was a God.

I boiled two potatoes for our supper, gave Berta my pat of butter. I put her to sleep on the sofa, waited anxiously for Aunt Fanny. I did not even light the lamp but sat silent in the dark. Aunt Fanny walked in about ten o'clock. She looked pale and tired, said only, "We have to get up early in the morning so you'd better try to get some sleep." I was afraid to ask how my mother was and Aunt Fanny did not say another word.

In the morning she wrote out a telegram and asked me to take it to the post office. It was addressed to mother's two cousins in Beltsy and said: "Rosa died, funeral Sunday."

I realized my mother was never coming home from the hospital. It took me years to accept her death. I kept believing she would show up any moment, that what happened was a nightmare from which I would wake.

When I returned from the post office, Aunt Fanny told me, "Your mother wouldn't let the doctors use a stomach pump, so this time they couldn't help." My mother had been saved when she tried to kill herself after her first child died, but when her husband abandoned her, she refused all chance to live.

Aunt Fanny also said, "Your mother's last words were, 'See that Jenny gets an education.'"

I asked, "Did she take the poison late at night or in the morning?"

"We don't know," said Aunt Fanny. "She may have lain in the garden all night."

I remembered with a pang how, earlier in the evening, I had pushed mother away when she wanted to hug and kiss me. I have never forgiven myself for this. A million times I have wished I had been thoughtful enough to return her caresses, listen to her few words of self-pity. I have been haunted the rest of my life by the thought it would have made a difference if only one person had comforted her, taken her in their arms, kissed her tear-covered cheeks.

The next morning Aunt Fanny wrapped a black armband around my sleeve and one around hers and we walked half a mile to the hospital, leaving Berta with a neighbor. At the hospital we were directed into a bare room, the only thing in it a body on the floor covered by a black sheet. Aunt Fanny said, "Stay here while I make arrangements."

Alone in the room, I stared at the black sheet, wondered if this body could be my mother. I wanted to raise the sheet, peek at the face, but was too frightened. I felt like crying but the tears would not flow. I had to be like stone or I would lose control.

Since there was no chair, I stood perhaps an hour, bewildered, afraid, lonely. I wished my mother were near to hold my hand, tell me what to do, what to think. I had lost my closest friend, my only friend. I could not understand how she dared leave me even though I was aware she had been unable to face my father's desertion of her for a younger woman, the loss of her job and all income, possibly the birth of another child. And, as I now realize, losses inherent in the deep depression she suffered, emanating from the early death of her mother (and could her mother also have committed suicide? I sometimes wonder).

Aunt Fanny eventually appeared, saying with a look at the black sheet, "They're taking the body at once to the cemetery so we'd better start there."

We had no money for a horse and carriage so we walked the two miles to the cemetery where the burial was to be held early that afternoon. After we arrived, a guard directed us to the outskirts, where a newly dug hole, earth flung to one side, indicated an expected grave.

I found the courage to ask Aunt Fanny, "Why is my mother not to be buried near all the other people?"

"In our religion, those who commit suicide have to be buried on the edge of the cemetery," she explained.

I stared at the hole in the ground prepared to receive mother. I thought it barbaric for her to be sleeping there alone through the icy Russian winters, no bodies near to give comfort.

Several relatives arrived—one of my father's brothers, Joseph; mother's older sister, Ana; the two cousins from Beltsy. Mother's father, the Rabbi, in his seventies, was too old to come, Aunt Fanny said. I wondered if he were too ashamed of his daughter for taking her life.

When two men lowered the wooden coffin into the hole, I felt like hurling myself in with my mother so I could be with her always. As they packed the dirt around the casket, I turned away, choked back sobs.

My father's brother gave us a ride home in his carriage, saving us the long walk. He and Aunt Fanny talked in low voices about my father's leaving us and mother's tragic solution to her sorrow. It took me years to realize my father was on his way to achieving what *he* wanted—to be an intellectual and fight for the freedom of "the people"—but as far as his family was concerned, he was a very selfish man, interested only in his whims and wishes, unable to assume responsibility for a wife and two small daughters.

I wondered who would now take care of Berta and me. Aunt Fanny had never worked a day in her life and, as I later found out, she did not have the emotional strength to come to our rescue. Who else was there? Our father had gone to a far country with a mistress, forever, as far as we knew.

Because we had no money for the next six months rent, the owners of the house, now not so peaceful, evicted us. The blond wood dressers and twin beds from Vienna stood strewn in the street, rotted almost at once by a heavy rainstorm. I was aghast at the wanton destruction of the furniture mother had so loved.

"What will we do?" I asked Aunt Fanny.

"I don't know," she said.

Then mother's sister, Ana, the one who had been in a mental hospital, offered to take Berta to live with her and to keep me a few weeks until I could find another place. Aunt Ana was a strange lady; one evening she glared at me, pointing a finger at my nose, and said accusingly, "You're very spoiled—*you* killed your mother!" I was horrified, wondered if she were right, if I *had* killed my mother by being "spoiled" and refusing to kiss and hug her when she needed me.

Aunt Fanny, who was staying with us, made up her mind to go to America, where two of her brothers were doing well in the fur business. It was obvious no one wanted me.

I did not care. I would look out for myself.

I thought of a plan. It meant giving up my mother's cherished dream that I graduate from high school but that could wait. First, I had to keep alive.

I packed my two dresses, underwear, and heavy sweater in a small valise. Then I kissed Aunt Fanny, Aunt Ana, and Berta goodbye. Berta clung to me as if she never expected to see me again. Aunt Fanny slipped mother's gold wedding ring on my finger. She also gave me mother's silver monogrammed set of spoons, knives, and forks.

"If there's anything else you want, I'll send it to you," she said.

"A picture of my high school." If I were never to see it again, at least I would have a photograph of the place where I might have achieved my mother's dying wish.

Aunt Fanny also gave me enough money for the four different coaches I would take to reach Rishcon—my destination.

I had rarely seen my grandfather. He was such a distinguished, important man he had no time to visit his grandchildren. My grandmother had occasionally come by carriage to our house but then had eyes only for her six-foot son. As a child, I had lived in Rishcon where my mother and father taught school but remembered nothing of the town.

My father had told me his parents owned a mansion where a sparkling chandelier lit the dinner table, the source of its glow kerosene. There was no electricity, no running water in the homes, no paved roads in Rishcon, a far smaller place than Khotin.

When the fourth and final carriage deposited me in Rishcon, I asked a stranger where the Altman house was located. He looked at me in deference, said it was only a few blocks away—the town had only four main streets, you could never get lost.

I had never seen a home so large outside of the castles in fairy-tale books. It was like a palace, a terrace around it instead of a moat.

I walked up to the carved black-wood door, knocked gently. No one came. I pounded on the door.

I waited, it seemed like half an hour. Then I pounded again.

Finally my grandmother, Etti-Feige Altman, opened the door. She had not seen me in years. She did not recognize me.

She asked, "Who are you?"

"I am your granddaughter, Jenny, and I have come to stay," I announced.

My grandfather was not there. He had died three days after my mother killed herself, from a heart attack following a large meal. My grandmother, literally, offered me his bed.

I slept in her room in a twin bed which, like its counterpart, was made of solid silver. In either her bed, or his, she had conceived sixteen children, ten of whom had lived. She met my grandfather the day they were married; it had been "arranged." On their wedding night, he told her, "I will reign over you."

And reign he did. In his presence she trembled in terror. In those days Jewish women were not allowed a thought of their own. She never dared ask for a penny but would "take" money out of his pockets at night, a practice of which he was undoubtedly aware, his method of giving it to her.

She was a strikingly beautiful woman with gray eyes, quite plump but with a dignified air. She looked motherly, which was reassuring to me. She did not know how to read but would memorize words. On holy days, she would run her finger along the lines of the Bible as though reading but fooled no one.

She covered her hair with a babushka, wore a wig to schul on the sabbath. She was in awe of and afraid of God. Each Friday she would ask me who in town had been sick, pack baskets with soup and chicken, and say, "Take this to their homes, the carrots in the soup will be good for them."

"Oh, Grandma, it's so far," I would complain—the poor lived on the other side of town.

"Go! Go! God will reward you for this mitzvah," a good deed.

Several years before there had been a robbery at the mansion. My grandmother's jewels, including priceless strings of pearls, along with thousands of dollars and hundreds of I.O.U.s belonging to my grandfather, who loaned money to individuals and banks, had been stolen from the safe. The guard supposed to protect the valuables had collaborated with the thieves, letting them in the house one night. Aunt Fanny told me how the noise had wakened her and she raced into her father's room to see three robbers beating him. She flew to a window, threw it open, screamed to the countryside, "Help! Help! They're killing my father!" The men of the town came running in the underwear in which they slept, carrying brooms as weapons. They streamed into the house and the robbers fled. The townspeople had saved my grandfather's life even though they thought him somewhat of a Shylock. Eventually he managed to recover the I.O.U.s but the thousands of dollars in cash and my grandmother's jewels vanished forever.

My father's grandfather, an uneducated man who barely knew how to read, had become one of the richest men in Rishcon, acquiring $80,000, in those days a small fortune. My father's father increased his inheritance by buying up large estates under assumed names, because Jews were not allowed in "old" Russia to own more than one estate. Every Sunday the hundreds of peasants who worked for him in the fields of wheat surged into the large back yard of his mansion where he stood at a window in his "office" and paid them weekly wages. As he prospered, he would say to his family, "For everything you need luck."

You did if you were a Jew in those days. My grandfather and his family managed to survive the many pogroms carried out by the peasants against the Jews. They were instigated by the Romanian government, which eventually confiscated all my grandfather's land except his personal estate.

I witnessed a pogrom one Sunday when several wagons driven by peasants dashed through the main street. My grandmother ordered me into the house, closed the windows and shutters, barricaded the doors. I later learned the young Jewish tailors in town took up sticks and went out to fight the attackers. I had heard a pogrom meant beatings, looting, burning of houses, and raping of young girls, but that day no one menaced us.

Once my grandmother had owned four cows that gave milk only for her family, supervised four cooks to bake bread from the wheat of nearby fields and roast on the coal stoves the chickens and geese fattened on the estate. She still had money to live on but refused to spend any of it to buy me a new winter coat or shoes as I outgrew my old ones.

When my lone pair of shoes practically lost their soles, I wondered how I would get new ones. Then I said to myself, Don't complain, Jenny, look how lucky you are, nobody to tell you what to do, you have complete freedom.

My grandmother did give me a few pennies each day to rise from my solid silver bed at four in the morning, often in temperature of 30 degrees below zero, and bring in the wood, start the fire, put up the samovar for tea, run to the bakery three blocks away for fresh bread, set the table for her, myself, her daughter, my Aunt Gitl, her husband, Moishe, and their two children, who lived with us. I felt happy to be part of a family, useful to someone.

My grandmother sometimes indulged in *Habar*—bribery. She told me when her children were young she would pay them to eat green vegetables and, later, not to smoke on the sabbath. She paid me to go with her every Friday at one in the afternoon to the town bathhouse, which had running water. We would bring our own soap and towels, undress, put our clothes on a bench set before the tubs. She would bathe first, then I would slip in her bath water, wash my body and hair. We saved money by my using her dirty water. I did not mind. I was grateful to her for taking me into her home.

Perhaps I just happened to show up at a propitious time; she had just lost her husband and may have welcomed a replacement. Or perhaps she thought it her duty to give me a home and did so graciously. I was a cheerful, willing-to-please young lady of almost twelve who tried not to get in anyone's way. I desperately needed someone to care whether I lived or died. I felt more attached to Aunt Fanny, even though she had not been able to take care of me. She did send a photograph of my high school. And when she reached America, she wrote me of life there and, later, of her marriage to a man in Michigan City, Indiana.

I had hoped to go to high school and get a diploma but I had to go to work. My grandmother would not pay for school or new clothes. I liked to embroider and when I learned there was a seamstress in town with the same first name as my mother, I went to see her. This enterprising business woman turned out to be only fifteen years old. She ran a miniature factory of four employees in the living room of her small house.

I introduced myself as the granddaughter of Israel Altman. I said, "I know how to embroider. Will you hire me?"

"I can use you," she said.

Each morning after breakfast I swept the huge Russian carpet of many colors that covered my grandmother's elegant living room, dusted the ornate furniture, including eight black leather chairs on each side of the long, mahogany dining table—there had once been sixteen children at that table. My grandfather's chair, at one end, was like a throne and studded with copper nails. Behind it, a mammoth fireplace kept the room warm in winter. The high walls held colorful murals painted by artists brought from Odessa.

And now, after I finished my early morning chores at eight o'clock, I set off for Rosa's house a few blocks away. There I would work, eat lunch and supper, both meals consisting mainly of boiled potatoes dipped in a meat stew.

My grandmother was embarrassed because I had become a seamstress. The inhabitants of Rishcon were divided into the rich and the working class, the latter made up of bakers, shoemakers, tailors, carpenters, and seamstresses. My grandmother looked down on the working class, thought it a stigma her granddaughter was a member of it.

But I never enjoyed myself more. As I embroidered dresses for the rich ladies of Rishcon, I exulted in every stitch. The five young women, all slightly older than I, accepted me as one of them. We became lasting friends; in a sense they were my new family and I no longer felt so alone. After work they invited their boyfriends to Rosa's house, where we would sit until midnight, roasting potatoes in the fireplace and discussing what was happening in the world. We took turns reading aloud the classics. I read once again, in Russian or Romanian, books I had borrowed from the Khotin library, the works of Tolstoy, Gorky, and Dostoevsky. When we bought a newspaper, one of us would read it to the others, as my mother used to read to me. A few of the girls and boys remembered my mother as their teacher when she lived in Rishcon after her marriage. My grandmother did not seem to mind my coming home late at night. I told her I was getting an education at Rosa's house similar to school.

The most exciting event of the day was the arrival of the postman.

He sometimes brought a letter from a relative in North or South America. My grandmother would ask me to read letters from her two sons in the United States and occasionally one from my father in Rio, asking about me.

One day, to my amazement, I noticed a pink envelope addressed to me. It proved my first love letter, sent by a sixteen-year-old boy, the son of a Romanian army captain stationed in Rishcon. I was thirteen, and to me he was an older man, but I thought him the most handsome one in town, with his blazing blue eyes and ringlets of blond hair. He had a reputation as a delinquent, reportedly having seduced, even raped, several fourteen-year-old girls.

Knowing my grandmother would be furious if she found the letter, I searched for a hiding place. My eye fell on a lamp with a round carved glass shade that she claimed was her favorite possession. I placed the letter in the neck of the lamp, intending to leave it there temporarily. As I tried to remove my hand from the tiny opening, it stuck. Trying to free it, I shook the glass shade. It slipped and crashed to the floor, splintering into fragments.

At that moment, my grandmother called out for me, no doubt alarmed by the noise. Frightened at the disaster I had caused, I ran to the barn, hid there, ignoring the many calls of my grandmother and aunt. Finally they found me. I burst into tears.

"I broke your glass lamp," I said to my grandmother, expecting a beating. But to my surprise she kissed me and said, "I know it was an accident."

My mother would not have been so understanding, but then my mother would not have owned such a costly item.

I received a second letter from this boy asking me to meet him in a park at the edge of town that Sunday evening. I consulted Rosa as to whether I should go and she urged me to meet him. I arrived at the park to find him sitting on a swing. He jumped up, offered me his seat. He told me he thought me the prettiest girl in Rishcon. I was thrilled to hear any boy, but especially this boy, pay such a compliment. But when he tried to kiss me, I backed away. I said, "I'm not that type of girl." He smiled as though to say, Well, I thought I'd give it a whirl, and took me home. Thus began and ended my first romance.

The next two years passed swiftly as I saved money, intending to use it for my education. My father wrote he had become editor and columnist of a Jewish newspaper in Rio. He said he also traveled as a lecturer, espousing the cause of socialism. I suddenly yearned to see him. It had been four and a half years since he left us at the Khotin railroad station.

I wrote asking if I might come to Brazil, explaining I had saved money for the fare. I was ecstatic when he replied he would welcome a visit from me and my sister. My grandmother encouraged me to go, knowing how much I missed him.

Aunt Ana, with whom Berta was still living, agreed to pay her way and to help make out the papers we would need for traveling. She made no attempt to keep Berta, perhaps thinking four years was enough for her share. My grandmother kissed me goodbye, tears in her eyes, as though she would miss me. I was sorry to leave her; I had become very fond of her.

I set out for Khotin by horse and carriage to pick up Berta, now seven. I was reversing the route I had taken four years before when I feared what my reception would be and felt anxious. But now my mood was joyous. I was on my way to see my sister once again and reunite with my fugitive father.

Before Berta and I left for the first leg of our journey, a train trip to Le Havre, I wanted to visit my mother's grave once more. I walked two miles to the cemetery, as I had done four and a half years before.

I knelt at my mother's grave with its tiny stone on which her name was engraved. Blades of grass sprouted over the stone, almost covering it. That part of the cemetery was unkempt; there were no paths, no trees, no flowers—the shadowy home of outcasts who had died by their own hand. I thought of mother as deserted even in death, wondered how I could travel across the world, perhaps never to return, leaving her forever abandoned in this sorry cemetery. Overcome with grief, I cried as I had not cried the day she was buried.

I thought I was alone in this miserable spot and was startled to hear a man's voice ask, "Who is buried in this grave and why is it so isolated from the rest of the cemetery?"

I looked up, saw a young rabbi. I said, "My mother is buried here because she killed herself. She's not allowed in the regular part."

He seemed unmoved, asked coolly, "Do you want me to say a prayer?"

"Yes, would you please say a prayer?" I was grateful.

"Do you have money to pay for the prayer?" Brown eyes bored into mine.

I said apologetically, "No." It had all gone for my trip to Rio. I felt ashamed I didn't even have pennies for a prayer for my mother. I closed my eyes as they filled with tears. To this day I do not remember if his heart melted and he said a prayer, though if he did, it was a very short prayer, for when I opened my eyes he was gone. It later became the obsession of my life to return to this little cemetery to see my mother's grave once more before I died.

Berta and I left Khotin by horse and carriage on July 31, 1932, arrived on August 1 in Chernovtsy, a large city in northern Romania, Austrian in culture. The city was commemorating with demonstrations and anti-war speeches the day World War I started. From there we caught a train to Paris. For a little girl of seven and a young woman of almost sixteen, the trip across Europe was like a journey through fairyland. We sat holding hands, fascinated by the scenes of wooded beauty that flashed continuously before our eyes.

My grandmother had sewn 500 lei in the lining of my coat so we could pay for food. But I was ashamed to tear open the lining and we did not eat for two days. When we reached Switzerland I led Berta to the dining car, both of us famished.

A tall, imperious waiter sat us at a table covered by a cloth as white as the snowcapped mountains outside the window. We shared the table with a man and a woman drinking champagne. The waiter placed a large basket of bread and a mound of butter before us, also filled two empty glasses with water. Then he strode away.

I looked at the menu, printed in French, which I could read, and whispered to Berta, "These prices are very expensive. Let's just eat the bread and butter and drink the water."

In record time we devoured every crumb in the basket, every trace of butter on the plate, drank every drop of water in the glasses. Then we stood up to leave.

The waiter walked over and asked, "Aren't you going to order?" "We've had all we want." I tried to sound firm.

He looked at the empty bread basket, the empty butter plate. He said, "You'll have to pay for two meals," and wrote out the dinner check.

Embarrassedly, I ripped open the lining of my coat, pulled out the money. He took a large share.

In Paris we raced in a taxi from one railroad station to another as I peered out the window, entranced by the wide streets, the green parks, determined one day to return for a long stay. After reaching Le Havre, we boarded the French transatlantic ship on which we were to sail third class. We were assigned a tiny cabin that held two double-deck bunks. We shared the cabin with a fat Jewish woman who stole ten dollars from me. I let her keep it, afraid to accuse her.

The trip across the Atlantic took twenty-six days and each hour was exciting. I hungrily drank in everything around me. A French sailor shared with me his philosophy of life, which included providing adequate food and drink for everyone on earth. I went from passenger to passenger, listened to their dreams. I took notes on paper the French sailor gave me, thinking someday to use them for a book. I also intended to write my friends in Rishcon and Khotin, with whom I had promised to keep in touch "as long as I live."

We were not allowed on the second or first class decks so the only passengers I saw were impoverished people from Eastern Europe, some ignorant and illiterate, all frightened of what awaited them in a new land. The children, once they felt at home on the ship, played with each other in the sun. The French cuisine was nectar to these poor people who joyously shared the bottle of wine placed on each table. In my innocence I wondered why their greatest hope was to become rich. Years later I realized that people the world over want material things, a powerful wish no society, no philosophical doctrine, can take away.

From the moment we left Aunt Ana's house in Khotin, I was seized by the fear I might lose Berta. I took her little hand and did not let go until we arrived in Rio. Throughout Europe I feared she might somehow wander off the train when it stopped and not knowing the language of strange countries never find her way back to me. Even on the ship I kept her close, slept next to her in the top bunk, which barely held one person. I did not leave her alone on deck for a second, in case she might be swept into the ocean. This was the first time I was aware of the devastating fear of losing a loved one. A fear so intense it drives every other thought out of mind.

My father had written he would meet us at the pier. As the ship pulled up to it, I recognized his tall, thin figure, waved wildly. We ran down the gangplank and into his arms. He hugged us as though no time had passed since he left us in Khotin. I thought, Mother, mother, if you had only waited, he might have come back or we would have eventually joined him as I am now doing.

He took us to his small apartment, the upstairs two rooms of a house owned by an Italian tailor. He gave Berta and me his double bed; he slept on a sofa in the living room. There were no kitchen facilities so we ordered coffee and rolls from the café next door. He confided that Rebecca Goodman, the young woman for whom he had deserted us, left him almost the second she stepped on South American soil, to marry a very wealthy man. I thought, Serves him right for what he did to us.

Each morning he went to work at his newspaper office, to return at six in the evening, leaving Berta and me in the small apartment with nothing to do all day. He did not earn enough to send me to high school, which I had hoped he would do. Since all my savings had been spent on the fare, I decided to go to work to support Berta and myself.

He did provide us with a social and cultural life. He took us to the Jewish community center. There I met a friend from Rishcon named Tuba, "pigeon" in English, who asked, "What are you going to do?"

"I have a job with a dressmaker," I said. "But as soon as I can, I want to go to high school."

I had asked my father if I might seek work and he approved. He even bought me a new pair of shoes to go with the two dresses friends in Rishcon had made for the journey.

One morning I got up very early and dressed in the dark. My father woke, came into the room, and asked, "Where are you going?"

It was Sunday and I was meeting Tuba to prepare for a picnic. But I did not feel like explaining. Or perhaps I was trying to get even with my father for leaving us.

"That's my business," I snapped.

He walked over to me, slapped me hard across the face. This was the only time I recall he ever struck me. I burst into tears, feeling mortally wounded even as I knew I had provoked the slap.

At the Jewish community center I met a young medical student whose parents owned a factory and lived in a modest house on an island near Rio. He took an interest in the motherless Berta. He suggested she live with his mother and father, saying, "They've been looking for a little girl to adopt now that I've left home. They'll love her and take good care of her."

My father and I met his parents, they fell in love with Berta, and she seemed at home with them. My father agreed to pay a weekly sum for her care. I was reluctant to leave Berta with strangers. But the young medical student kept insisting, "Let her go. She'll have a far better life than you can give her."

So once again Berta and I separated. I also left my father, to share an apartment with a new friend, a girl I met at the Jewish community center. My father seemed as unconcerned as ever about the fate of his two daughters. I suppose each of us does the best he can. It was my unfortunate luck, and Berta's too, to have such an emotionally infantile father. Since I believe many people are not psychologically fit to be parents, perhaps I should not be too harsh on him.

In his way he cared for Berta and me. He visited Berta often in her new home, invited me to his lectures and to the house of Rebecca, with whom he was still friendly, who had a son. At least he was near and I knew I could see him whenever I wished.

But I soon lost him again. His articles on socialism so antagonized the Brazilian government that he was asked to leave the country. This was 1936 and he decided to go to Paris, where he had always wanted to live.

He wrote me from France: "For three days I walk like enchanted on the streets and boulevards. I visit all the museums and, of course, the Louvre. Paris is the last school for maturing. It is true it is a little late in my life for another rebirth, but it does not matter, one does not have to die a foolish old man, a pseudo-intellectual, semi-mature."

I remained in Rio for two years, two very difficult years. I earned only five dollars a week, which went chiefly for rent. Sometimes I was left with two pennies a day for food. I would walk up to the man in the fruit store and say, "I'd like to buy a banana."

"One banana?" He would look at me in surprise. Who bought one banana in Brazil?

The second penny went for a cookie at night. I think I ate only three hot meals during one six-month period.

Finally I decided, with Berta secure in her new home, there was no reason to starve in Rio. I would join my father in Paris, get my education there. For the fare, I sold my mother's gold wedding ring and the silver monogrammed forks, knives, and spoons that I had carried with me from Rishcon. To this day I regret having parted with them. They were all I had left of my mother in a material sense.

This time I sailed across the ocean alone. But I was not alone in Paris. I had kept in touch through letters with some of the boys and girls I had known in Khotin and Rishcon who had gone to Paris to live. When I arrived, they received me like a sister, gave me a temporary bed and board, loaned me money. They knew where my father was living. I looked him up and he seemed happy to see me but, as always, could not help financially.

I rented a room in the home of a childless couple. As I did not have the papers to work in France, I could only unofficially help out a friend who taught me how to sew on buttons and iron sweaters, paying enough so I could afford rent and food. After six months I moved into the apartment of a friend from Rishcon named Ruhele. She was such an exacting housekeeper even the curtains shone. The two of us slept on a sofa that divided into two beds.

I enrolled in evening courses at the Workers University even though I did not have a high school degree. I wanted to learn more languages. Today I speak eight—Russian, Portuguese, Spanish, French, Romanian, English, Yiddish, and Hebrew. It takes me three months to fully learn a language.

Shortly after I arrived, war broke out in Spain. My father left France to volunteer in the Spanish Loyalist Army. He was turned down because of his age and returned to Paris. In spite of his emotional immaturity, he was a fighter. He could have submitted to his dictatorial father, as most of his brothers did, and lived as a rich man's son from the profits of a large estate and the loan business. But he had a "cause." He wanted to help the poor become educated and he championed what he believed social and economic justice. From him I have received the heritage of courage in the face of tyranny.

The next four years were thrilling as I walked the streets of Paris, learning every corner of the city. I haunted the museums, went to concerts when I could afford them. Professors from the Sorbonne taught at our university and I also attended lectures all over Paris. But my education was more than intellectual. I could not escape the impact of the growing rush of refugees from almost all the countries of Europe, given the right of asylum by France. Men, women, and children from the oppressed Fascist nations, especially Spain, streamed in, needing medical and financial aid.

I learned the grim meaning of the word "Fascism": war, the destruction of European culture, civilization, and peoples. During the war in Spain I lived from one news report to the next. Ruhele, involved in helping the Loyalists, would invite hungry young refugees to our apartment several times a week. They would sit on the floor, eat meat and potatoes, mostly potatoes, and talk with us until dawn.

One of my close friends enlisted in the International Brigade and was killed almost the moment he stepped on Spanish soil. Many of our young German and Italian refugee friends enlisted in this brigade, never to return. I think of them with love, they were among the most decent, dedicated persons I have known. They taught me much about unselfishness. About the giving of one's life to save the lives of others. About real humanity.

One evening at a lecture at the university my eye was caught by a handsome, slender young man in a brown turtleneck sweater. He seemed to be staring at me and after the lecture walked over to introduce himself.

His name was Manuel Spinoza and he came from Caracas, Venezuela. He was in Paris to study architecture. I told him briefly about my background, that I had lived two years in Rio.

He asked if he could walk me home. I said yes, attracted by his soft-spoken, gentle manner and frankness. And by his very straight dark hair, large expressive black eyes, and shy smile. We spoke of the war in Spain. His father, who died when Manuel was a boy, was born in a province in the north of Spain once noted for its warriors. Manuel said, "The Loyalists must win this war. Otherwise Fascism will take over the world. Hitler and Mussolini are using Spain as a testing ground for their arms and their strength. If they win, they will unleash the most terrifying war humanity has ever seen. The industrialized democracies are allowing Hitler to arm because they hope he will march eastward and destroy the Soviet Union. To them, this is the greater enemy."

When I spoke, Manuel listened with empathy, as though thinking over my every word, as my mother would do. I expressed doubts Hitler would invade other countries. Manuel said, "Read *Mein Kampf*. Hitler means every word. He will destroy the Jewish race out of a psychotic hatred."

Manuel knew firsthand the cruelties of a despot. Six years before, when he was eighteen, Venezuela had a monster of a dictator, Juan Vicente Gómez, as president. He had an illness that required constant blood transfusions. Children of the poor mysteriously disappeared in large numbers, believed murdered, drained of their blood, used to save the life of Gómez. When two children of a wealthy French citizen vanished, the father threatened to create a scandal and the children were returned at once. They said blood had been taken from their bodies.

Fearing reprisal, Gómez forbade assembly in public places of more than four persons. One day, when Manuel was a student at the University of Caracas, he unthinkingly became one of a group of eight students talking on a street corner. The police arrested them as conspirators against the government. They were dragged to La Rotunda, a prison from which, it was rumored, few returned alive.

Manuel, along with thirty-eight other students and four professors, was held incommunicado for four years in a cell, ball and chains around his ankles. He was not allowed to see a lawyer, not given a trial, not even a hearing.

When his mother asked what had happened to her son, police told her they did not know. But she found out and every day took a home-cooked meal to the prison. The guards ate it—Manuel never received a morsel. She died while he was imprisoned, of heartbreak, he said. While in high school, Manuel had found a substitute father in a Dutch Jewish dentist he admired. Manuel had a respect for the Jews I have never seen in any other Gentile, perhaps because of his love for the dentist.

The four professors made a college out of the prison cell. They taught the young students all they knew. Manuel called the prison his "university." When Gómez died, a more liberal president, López Contreras, freed the students and professors. Manuel decided to become an architect and headed for Paris, only to encounter new savagery. Refugees from Germany described the horrors of concentration camps, refugees from Italy, Mussolini's cruelties.

When Spain lost the war, I felt as if I had lost a child. I now agreed with Manuel that this heralded a holocaust such as mankind had never seen, that millions would perish because of Hitler's fanaticism and sadism.

I had lived in Paris four years when, in 1939, Hitler marched into Czechoslovakia. It became apparent he would next invade France and Belgium. Manuel said, "We've got to leave."

He and I had become very close. He was two years older, the age of my brother who had died before I could know him. Manuel and I were not sexually involved, for in our group it was understood there would be no sex except between a young man and woman who fell in love and married. I found Manuel very attractive physically and we thought alike, sometimes almost telepathically. As he spoke I would think, This is precisely how I would have put it. I trusted him, something new in my life when it came to a man.

One night he said, "Let's go to Venezuela and get married. I can find work there."

Neither of us was mature enough for marriage, I knew. My idea of a husband was someone who would care for and protect me. My grandfather Israel was such a man, mean as he had sometimes been to my father. He was faithful to his wife, supported her in lavish style. He had never deserted his children, rescued them when they were in trouble. I believed that to love meant to assume responsibility for loved ones. Like my uncles in Rishcon who worked eighteen hours a day to take care of wives and children.

Manuel did not have a skill but dreamed only of becoming an architect. Yet I respected him as a thoughtful, compassionate human being. There was a delicate quality about him, a frailty, as a result of the physical deprivations suffered in the prison where he received little nourishment for four years of his youthful life.

But frail or no, he was offering me a way to save my life. Knowing the terror the Fascists had inflicted on Spain and Czechoslovakia, I finally believed Hitler was out to kill all the Jews of Europe and I did not want to die in a concentration camp.

So I said, "I will go with you to South America and marry you."

I asked my father if he was not afraid to stay in France and begged him to come with us. He said, "Hitler will never dare invade Paris."

He remained in his dream city, watching his friends depart one by one. When the Nazis marched into Paris, they rounded up all the Jewish intellectuals. They arrested my father along with Michel, a friend of mine. Michel's wife bought his freedom. My father no longer had a father who would pay large sums to rescue him. At last he had to face the enemy alone and penniless.

He was shipped to Auschwitz. The Nazis starved him for eighteen days, not giving him even a crust of bread before they ordered him to the gas chambers. He never had the chance to see the brave new world he envisioned so eloquently in the final words of his diary. Aunt Fanny gave the diary to me. She had received it from her brother Joseph when he visited the United States in 1939, meeting her briefly in New York. He had seen my father in Paris before he was arrested by the Nazis and my father asked him to keep the diary. Aunt Fanny had been saving it for me.

My father had written just before his death:

"My fifty years of life, my fifty years of wandering and searching, my happiness and suffering, have opened my eyes to the fact that I . . . a little man . . . am nothing but a small link in the chain which is called society and humanity. . . . I tremble. I see the dream to save the world, almost messianical. I wonder what kind of world will it be? When will the true salvation come? Will there be a new man? Who will put the finishing touches on the design in the human tapestry?"

He had no way of knowing—I am glad he did not—that his mother, at the age of seventy-three, was murdered by the Nazis when they pillaged Rishcon on their march to Russia. When I learned this, I cried for hours, remembering how she had been the one to give me shelter and affection when no one else cared.

But now a handsome young man was saving my life—literally. He was also offering love and marriage. It seemed as though at last the fates were trying to be kind.

II

The Love of My Life

"Don't you dare open your mouth in public," Manuel ordered. He was afraid my slight accent would give away the fact I was Jewish.

So I kept silent as I sat at the ship's dining table with the officers, who spoke German. And I maintained the silence as I looked each day at the swastika flag the German *Kapitän* used to mark the map, showing our progress across the Atlantic.

It had not been easy to book passage for South America. When Manuel and I went to the steamship companies we learned that thousands of rich Jews from all over Europe were desperately trying to flee to North and South America. Not to the United States, though; President Roosevelt refused to open the door to refugees.

Manuel and I had tried every line without luck. Then I suggested sailing on a German ship that left Antwerp for Panama. Once in Central America, we could make our way to Caracas.

Both Manuel and my friends, fearing for my safety now that Nazi anti-Semitism was overt, warned that the German officers on the ship might arrest me and send me to a concentration camp, or throw me overboard. I insisted it was worth the risk. I pointed out that with my snub nose, light brown hair, and blue-gray eyes I did not resemble the stereotype of a Jew.

We found a cargo ship that took twenty-six days to cross the Atlantic. To pass the time, Manuel, a mathematical genius, tried to teach me trigonometry. It was a hopeless task for figures are my bête noire. He insisted on buying first-class tickets and since I owned only one skirt and two blouses, I looked like a waif beside the few other first-class passengers.

I think the German officers guessed I was Jewish but they did nothing about it. When we landed at Panama, Manuel and I found space on a German freighter bound for Barranquilla on the coast of Colombia. From there we went by bus to Bogotá. Manuel had money for only one fare to Caracas. It was odd, I thought, that he had spent so much for first-class tickets on the cargo ship. This was part of his inability to plan ahead, as I was to learn.

"You stay in Bogotá, Jenny," he said. "I will go to Caracas, work a few weeks as draftsman with a friend who is an architect and send for you as soon as I have enough money for the fare and our wedding."

I rented a room in the home of a Colombian family and again found a job sewing. It took eight months for Manuel to send for me though we kept in close touch by letter. We were married at once in Caracas at a civil ceremony attended by a few of Manuel's friends. I suppose I should have felt guilty marrying a man outside my faith but my renegade father had little respect for organized religion and I had absorbed his skepticism.

Caracas, founded by the Spaniards and named after the Caracas Indians, was set atop one Andes mountain, with another, Avila, rising behind it. We were about an hour's drive from the ocean. The temperature was usually 8o degrees, summer and winter. The country's picturesque Angel Falls attracted thousands of tourists each year.

Our first home was one large room on the ground floor rented from the family who owned the house, allowing us to use their kitchen and living room. Manuel was taking architectural courses in graduate school, hoping someday to have a firm of his own. He did not make enough money as a part-time draftsman to support us. So I went to work in a factory that produced polo shirts and men's underwear. I learned to be a cutter, a craft usually only men acquired, the most important job in that factory of more than three hundred employees.

When the owner of the factory, the richest Jew in Caracas, invited me to his home for dinner, I thought it was because of my new dexterity as a cutter. But he pointedly told me that the few Jewish women in Venezuela did not demean themselves by working in factories.

"Find a more respectable job," he suggested.

"Am I fired?" I asked anxiously.

"Of course not," he said. "I just want to help you improve your position in life. You can stay with me as long as you wish."

"I like what I'm doing," I said.

He shrugged his shoulders, no doubt thinking me stupid. But I enjoyed my work even though I had to lift bolts of material weighing fifty pounds from the floor to the cutting board. And part of me exulted in doing a man's job as successfully as a man.

I was also happy at the thought that Berta and I once again lived on the same continent. I wrote Berta—I have written her at least two letters a week all the years of our lives—saying I hoped we would see each other soon. And I wrote Aunt Fanny in Michigan City describing my escape from the Nazis and my marriage.

With what he earned, Manuel paid for his education and clothes. I paid the rent, bought the food. We could not save a penny. I felt as though I lived on an island in the middle of the Pacific, so scarce was culture in Caracas. I made a few friends—I have always made friends easily no matter where I lived. One was the daughter of a general whose brother had been seized and taken to La Rotunda, but he had not been as fortunate as Manuel and was murdered there.

Manuel and I lived together fairly harmoniously as the months passed. He was easy to be with. He would listen with his chin propped on the palm of his hand. He never argued, just reasoned.

One night he asked me to cook dinner for a few of his friends. I prepared a pot of what he requested—black beans, which I had never cooked before. They were delicious, he suggested, served with rice topped with a fried egg or slices of fried banana.

I noticed the guests took large portions of the black beans but then left them on their plates.

I called Manuel aside, asked, "Why are they not eating the beans?"

He said, "Jenny, if you threw them against the wall they'd bounce back. You didn't cook them long enough." Everyone roared but reassured me I would learn.

During the third year of our marriage I discovered I was pregnant. We were now able to pay for a six-room house with two patios and a room for a maid. I wanted a child, though I wondered if Manuel could take care of a family, emotionally and economically. I had married a man much like my father—charming, brilliant, but irresponsible when it came to domestic life. Both men wanted to be eternal students. At least Manuel was not physically strong so he could justify not working very hard.

In preparation for the baby I crocheted blue booties, sewed blue and white dresses, for either boy or girl, though I really wanted a girl. I have kept the booties and the dresses in a box, dainty reminders of my baby's first days.

I went through a very difficult childbirth on April 10, 1942, Good Friday, at the Red Cross Hospital, the finest in Venezuela. I spent eight hours in the delivery room, enduring excruciating pain. I had worked until eight and a half months pregnant and damaged my bladder picking up those heavy bolts. But when the baby was born, I thought her worth all the agony.

She was a beautiful little girl. While carrying her, I felt she was part of me, something that would always be precious. And with her birth, I thought life would never be the same, that something miraculous had happened. Manuel came running as soon as he heard the baby was born. We stared at her for hours, fascinated by her fragile face, her delicate hands, every new movement. We named her Sylvia Rosa, after Rosa, my mother.

I thought Manuel would find a full-time job so I could stay home and care for my baby. But he did not want to give up his graduate studies. After a month I returned to work—just as my mother did following my birth—and left my baby in the care of a series of maids, as my mother had done with me.

I read books on how to feed a baby, instructing me to give Rosette my breast every three hours. I kept to this regime though wondering if it were wise because at times she would cry as though starved when I ignored her screams. I nursed her in the morning and the maid would bring her to me during the day, every three hours, across the street at the factory. We had chosen a house near the factory so I would not have a long trip twice a day.

Even though Rosette might be sleeping, I gave the maid instructions to wake her every three hours. Rosette protested this feeding schedule. When she was four months old, she went on a hunger strike. She turned away from my breast. Upset, I took her to the doctor, crying as I sat in his office holding my baby in my arms. Like most doctors, he was a very busy man; he quickly examined her, and told me to start feeding her by bottle.

But then she refused to take the bottle from me or the nursemaid of the moment. I spent my two-hour lunch period running home, coaxing her to swallow a few sips of milk, just enough to stay alive. I went through the same process in the evening. When she could eat, I cooked a squab every day, costly but nutritional, added it to soup and spent two hours getting her to swallow a few spoonfuls. Manuel insisted she was a small eater like he was and did not seem worried.

I toilet-trained her completely, including bowels, at six months, believing this the proper time. I did not remember at what age my mother toilet-trained me, but I think it was equally early.

It was not easy to find a good maid and during those early years of Rosette's life there may have been some who did not take proper care, who may even have struck her when she cried. Or left her alone in the crib all day, giving little or no affection. Every time I started to leave the house she would cry as though her heart were breaking.

When she could talk, she begged, "Mommie, don't go! Don't go!" I could hear her cries until I turned the corner, tears filling my eyes. I thought, But what else can I do, the three of us have to eat and be sheltered.

On Sundays Manuel and I would take Rosette to parks, one on the site of La Rotunda where Manuel had been so cruelly incarcerated. As Rosette sat in her stroller, passersby would stop, admire her beauty. She had her father's large black eyes and black curly hair. Her face was heart-shaped, piquant, her expression alert and lively as though she were ready to take in all the wonders of the world.

She learned Spanish quickly, though she was slow to walk. When she was two, and still having feeding difficulties, I decided to stop work and take care of her. There would be no more maids in the little white house with its two patios. I spent the entire day with my daughter and she soon started to eat more, gain weight. We would visit the parks, I would run after Rosette from swing to swing, both of us laughing joyfully. When we arrived home in the late afternoon of a hot summer day, we would fall asleep, she cuddled in my arms.

For eight months I did not work, the happiest time of my marriage. We managed somehow to scrape through on Manuel's meager salary and my savings. No longer were my days haunted by my child's pitiful cries each time I left her. No more hours spent staring at the factory clock, waiting for the moment her little arms would reach out to me in love.

Adept at building things, Manuel created a pink bedroom set for her, complete with rocking chair, bureau, and a colossal crib, five and a half feet long. He also bought her a black cocker spaniel, Pipo. She would sit in the pink rocking chair playing with the little black dog. I watched her discover new sensations, new images, helped her explore new experiences.

But in my life good things do not seem to last. Manuel was not a well man. He occasionally suffered fainting spells and his appetite became poor. He was not ambitious, money meant little to him. We lived in a country where a man without skills could not earn a living. I was forced to go back to work though my motherly instincts warned that Rosette needed me all day at this time of her life.

Gradually I realized I no longer had a marriage, perhaps never did. Manuel and I were intellectual companions; ours was far from a passionate relationship. We got drunk on words and ideas, not wine and primitive emotions. I thought perhaps his four years in prison had accustomed him to sexual deprivation. He seemed almost apathetic when it came to making love.

I often felt lonely as I ate by myself in the evening for Manuel ate his heavy meal of steak and *arrepa,* corn bread, in the morning, skipped lunch and often had supper out for he attended graduate school at night. We seemed to have lost the compatibility we shared before the birth of Rosette. I thought maybe he resented a child because of the added burden, financially and emotionally.

He was very depressed about the war, which was not going well for the Allies. He insisted, "If Hitler wins, we're all doomed." He made me feel the end might be near. I felt a new panic, wanted to be with someone near and dear.

I wrote Aunt Fanny of my conflicting feelings. She responded, "Child, come to me, you and little Rosette. I will take care of you." Her invitation seemed like going home to a mother when you were frightened to death. I thought both my child and I would have a better chance of surviving any possible holocaust in this part of the world living with Aunt Fanny, who had taken care of me as I was growing up and without whose help I do not think I could have survived the day of my mother's suicide.

Aunt Fanny could now take care of Rosette while I worked and earned money, eventually to get a house of my own. After all, we had taken her into our home when her father had thrown her out because she wanted to marry a man he thought worthless.

One night I went to a lecture—I enjoy lectures the way some people enjoy movies, others, cards. The speaker eloquently described how Abraham Lincoln and Thomas Jefferson brought democracy to the United States of America. He concluded by praising President Roosevelt, under whom, he said, the highest democracy was being achieved.

At that moment I fell in love with the United States of America. I decided I must move there. I would be one of the lucky few to live in this paradise called the U.S.A.

If I moved, the distance between Berta and me would increase. But we had not seen each other during my six years in Caracas, though we kept in touch through our weekly letters. She was now eighteen and had been on her own since my father died when payments to the Rio family ceased. She worked as a secretary to support herself and attended classes at the university in Rio. Neither of us had been able to afford a trip to see each other. The chances were more likely she would visit Aunt Fanny and me in Illinois than that she would come to Caracas.

Manuel did not stand in the way of my decision to leave. He did not even plead with me to stay. I had the stronger personality, I was the dominating one, even though I was in awe of his ability as a philosopher and his political consciousness.

He took us by limousine to the Caracas airport, holding Rosette tenderly in his arms. She was now three and a half and spoke Spanish like a young veteran. We were all quiet. I was reminded of the silence on the day I saw my father off at the Khotin station. Only now I was the one breaking up the family. But not for another love. For a freer way of life.

Manuel later wrote, "I watched your plane disappear into the clouds and knew my life would never be the same." I was sorry we could not make a go of it. Perhaps we were too different—a Catholic from Caracas who had been in prison between the ages of eighteen and twenty-two, and a Jewess from Bessarabia who had been on her own since the age of eleven and a half.

As the plane lifted into the sky I thought of a scene the night before as I packed. Manuel had come into the room, looked at me sadly.

"Must you go?" There were tears in his eyes.

"I have to," I said gently.

"Why, Jenny? Why?" He was pleading, for the first time.

I could not tell him I felt we had given the marriage a fair chance, that love had gone out of it. That I wanted someone who could pull his weight financially. There was something humiliating in having to support myself, my husband, and my child. By leaving, I was regaining a very important feeling—self-esteem.

I didn't want to hurt him. So I said, "It's for the best, Manuel. We are separating while we are still good friends."

There had never been an angry word between us. Nor was there ever. I always spoke of him to Rosette as a warm, kind, decent man who loved her dearly. And I never lost my gratitude for his caring enough to save my life.

Rosette and I arrived in Miami on November 15, 1945, just after the Allies won World War II. On my request to enter the United States, I had written I was born in Romania, which early in the war had collaborated with Germany. So I was deemed an enemy and had to wait until war ended before I could join Aunt Fanny in Michigan City via Miami, then Chicago.

One of my regrets as we headed north was knowing we would face climate almost as cold as Romania. As we stepped off the plane at Chicago's airport, I shivered at the first touch of winter in almost seven years.

I immediately recognized Aunt Fanny—though I had not seen her since I was eleven—from the photographs she had sent me over the years. Now forty-five, she had had her nose straightened, looked stunning, with her softly waved dark hair and flashing blue eyes. By her side stood her husband, Samuel Shapiro. He was a tall, handsome man with a craggy face.

They drove us to their home, about an hour east of Chicago. The chill day was gray, and compared to the sunny skies of Caracas and Miami, the scene was depressing. But both Aunt Fanny and Uncle Sam, enchanted by Rosette, seemed happy we were there. Aunt Fanny appeared to love Rosette as she had once loved Berta.

They lived on the second floor of a two-family house. They gave us their bedroom and slept in the living room on a Castro convertible. They bought a pink baby bedroom set, two lovely dolls, and a white fur coat for Rosette.

The two of Aunt Fanny's brothers who preceded her to America were now millionaires, involved in the fur business. Uncle Sam managed one of their stores in Michigan City. Aunt Fanny never suggested I seek help from my father's brothers nor did I want to ask for one penny. I thought, I will make it on my own, I am no beggar.

When I realized Uncle Sam did not earn a large salary, I knew I had to get a job to pay for food and the room Rosette and I shared. At the end of our first week I took the train to Chicago and found work in a factory in the center of the city where I was to sew linings in coats. In two hours I learned to operate a sewing machine and was offered $120 a week, a superb salary in 1945. I joined the International Ladies Garment Workers Union.

I could have moved Rosette and myself to Chicago but apartments were scarce, you had to buy the owner's shabby furniture at ridiculous prices and I did not want to spend all my savings or my salary now that I was completely on my own, in case of emergency. I also needed a small amount for evening classes at a high school—I was determined to learn English.

It was too taxing to commute every day to Michigan City so I rented a small room, actually an unheated porch, in a boarding house on the south side of Chicago, where I slept during the week, returning to Rosette on weekends.

She picked up English as she listened to Aunt Fanny and Uncle Sam. One Friday I walked in on a touching scene—Uncle Sam sitting at the kitchen table holding Rosette on his lap as Aunt Fanny fed her. Aunt Fanny called Rosette "my sweetheart." She told me, "Rosette is beautiful, from the top of her head to the tip of her toes."

Then all at once, within a few weeks, our welcome wore off. Aunt Fanny was what I call "crazy clean," with a compulsion for neatness and order. If Rosette dropped a toy on the floor, Aunt Fanny looked as though my child had committed a crime. I felt guilty if a crumb escaped my hand to fall on the tablecloth, I was afraid to dirty a washcloth or towel. We had obviously become a nuisance. I had made a mistake in accepting their bedroom. Rosette and I should have slept on the sofa in the living room, nobody should be asked to give up their bedroom. Though Aunt Fanny loved us in her way, we were not directly of her flesh and blood but two strangers in her home, one a small child who had to be cared for and indulged.

Aunt Fanny said to me one night, "Child, America is a big land. Go out and find yourself a home."

I could hardly believe my ears. After practically pleading with me to give up my home in Caracas to live with her, she was asking me to leave. She had even borrowed $300 of the $2,000 in savings with which I had arrived. She sent it to her brother in Israel so he could buy a small business. She never paid back one cent and I was too proud to ask for it.

I faced the disillusioning fact that Aunt Fanny was a very undependable woman who could not live up to her word. Rosette and I would have to make it on our own. I would have to find someone to take care of her—it would be no different from life with Manuel. When Uncle Sam suffered a severe attack of ulcers, requiring an operation, I thought this the opportune time to make the break. I packed and Rosette and I left for Chicago and my porch room.

Uncle Sam had told me to call his sister to help find a nursery. She suggested one run by the Daughters of Zion where Rosette could stay day and night while I worked and attended classes three evenings.

After learning English I was determined to get my high school diploma at long last.

Rosette was accepted at the Daughters of Zion nursery. I was asked not to visit for three weeks "to give her a chance to get used to the place." This was our first long separation and one she had to endure among strangers whose language she did not understand. A child of three and a half has no concept of time. The three weeks must have felt like eternity.

Though forbidden to enter the nursery, every night after work at the factory, I sat on the steps listening to the voices of the children, hoping to hear Rosette. When the three weeks ended, I stood excitedly in the waiting room as she walked down the stairs toward me. I ran to pick her up, held her to me, cried hysterically. She seemed unmoved, as if she had forgotten who I was. She sat quietly on my lap, saying not a word. I wondered if she were punishing me for abandoning her.

But during our first weekend together—I was permitted to take her with me for the weekend—she came alive. We slept on the small sofa in my room, she snuggling close. When I brought her back, the nurse had to tear her from my arms. I told Rosette, "Darling, you have to stay here for now. Soon I'll be earning enough money so we can live together."

Too many things were happening to her too fast. She did not know enough English to communicate with the other children or the nurses, who probably had little time to show kindness or affection. I sensed in my heart the scheme was wrong but I had no choice. Each Monday morning when I returned her to the nursery, she would cling to me, we would both cry. I would leave for work, thinking, How can I do this to her but what else am I to do?

One Saturday I took her to a toy store to buy a small, inexpensive doll but she became fascinated by a large doll with glistening blond curls and opaque green eyes dressed in a Dutch costume. She wanted it desperately even though I told her we could not afford it. She started to cry loudly, as though I had beat her.

I walked away, leaving her in front of the counter. After taking a few steps, I turned, saw a woman approaching her. I heard the woman ask, "Why are you crying?"

"Because my mommy does not love me," Rosette said.

I recalled that at the age of six I had wanted an apothecary jar made of bronze. I was a spoiled child, the only child for eight years, and when refused this request by my mother, who then dragged me out of the store, I lay down in the middle of the street and banged my head in fury against the sidewalk.

My mother had said to me, "I'm leaving you right here," and walked away.

I had stood up quickly and run after her. Rosette had not run after me but remained in front of the doll, feeling hurt and unloved.

One Sunday afternoon I brought her back to what she called the "lousy nursery." She would not let go of me. I told her gently, "Sweetheart, eat your supper. I'll wait for you right here."

Her sturdy little legs trotted away to the basement dining room. As soon as she disappeared, I raced off. I felt ashamed to lie but knew she would not have left unless I promised to stay.

Every Monday I counted the hours until Friday night when we would be together. I did not know a soul in this second largest city of the United States, I had only Rosette. I carried her in my arms from the nursery to my little room—our home. There I hugged her, kissed her, played with her, fed her, then went ·to sleep with her. In the winter we could not spend much time outdoors because of the cold, though it amused her to tramp through the snow. Sometimes we sat through a double feature of Western films just to keep out of the cold. The movies were a help in learning English. On Monday mornings I got up when it was still dark, fed her, carried her in my arms to the bus we took to the nursery.

She was a graceful child and I registered her for the free Saturday ballet lessons at the Jewish People's Institute. You cannot start too early to become a ballerina and she was nearly four. Through Aunt Fanny I discovered that my mother's first cousin lived in a large house in the near north side, the elegant part of the city called the Gold Coast. I phoned and she and her husband invited us to dinner. Their adopted daughter, Julia, had a piano and no sooner did Rosette see it than she climbed on the stool and started to play with the keys, entranced with the sounds. Julia generously shared not only her piano but her toys.

One day I picked Rosette up at the nursery and took her directly to

Julia's house. Rosette was wearing a dress three sizes too large and looked like a waif. Julia's mother said, "Jenny, *nothing* will ever undo the damage of raising Rosette in a nursery. You *must* take her out and live with her."

I burst into tears, knowing she was right. I thought of using the few dollars I had saved in case of emergency to pay for a larger room so Rosette could live with me, wondering who would take care of her during the day.

On her fourth birthday I brought a chocolate cake and a pale blue cotton dress trimmed with lace—on which I had spent half a week's salary at Marshall Field's—to the nursery. But Rosette refused to eat the cake or put on the dress.

I asked, "Precious, what *do* you want for a present?"

She turned those wide black eyes on me, said sadly, "Mommie, please take me home and don't ever make me come back."

I had just received a letter from Berta saying at long last she planned to visit me and take courses in English and anthropology for six months at the University of Chicago. While attending the university in Rio she had met a young anthropologist named Kurt Mendes, who fell in love with her and proposed. But before she married, she wanted to study English, which she barely spoke, and learn more about her fiancé's profession so she could help him with his work. She asked if she could stay with me.

That inspired me to look for larger quarters. Answering an ad, I found a religious old woman who wanted to rent one of her two bedrooms and share her living room and kitchen. The price was right and I accepted. I marched to the nursery, took Rosette away. She had been there eight months. I registered her in a nearby day nursery.

When Berta arrived, it was a holiday for all of us. I loved her as if she were my first daughter. We had not seen each other in sixteen years. She was twenty-three, very beautiful, good-natured, and spirited, with an inborn poise like my mother's. She reminded me of mother almost every second, in looks and manner. We spent the first days and most of the nights talking. I would get up more tired than when I went to bed. The three of us slept in a double bed with Rosette in the middle.

Life in the new apartment was pleasant, our only enemies the bedbugs we fought daily. Berta would read to Rosette evenings, then they would lie in bed and listen to classical records. Berta was an excellent cook and we all gained weight. I was happy my sister and daughter loved each other at first sight, a love that has lasted.

Her courses ended after six months and Berta returned to Rio and her fiancé. I made plans for Rosette to enter the first grade of public school. In Chicago the schools did not serve lunch, which meant I would have to leave my job every day at noon, pick up Rosette one hour away, feed her, and return to work. This was impossible in the hour allotted me for lunch.

I was still going to Aunt Fanny for advice, as I had when a child. She told me that a cousin, Blanche, lived in a place called Brighton Beach, just outside New York City. Aunt Fanny suggested I write to Blanche and ask about schools there.

Blanche answered right away, saying that the public schools in her area served hot lunches. She also said that the New York schools were the finest in the country, and if I wanted to move east, she would arrange for me to live in her building.

Her letter made up my mind. My daughter would start her education in the finest of public schools *and* get hot lunches so I could hold a job. I was certain I could find work in the city's garment center since I was now skilled at machine sewing. I would miss Aunt Fanny and Uncle Sam. Though I saw them less and less, it was reassuring to know they lived within an hour's ride. But I had lived without Aunt Fanny for years. And maybe it was time for me to really be on my own.

Rosette and I arrived in New York on September 1, 1948, in 100-degree temperature. We took the train, which left us at Grand Central Station. From there we got a subway to Ocean Parkway in Brooklyn. Blanche had sent her address and I found her at home. She led us to the two-room apartment—living room and kitchen—her landlord had leased us. It was across the street from the boardwalk and the Atlantic Ocean.

I found a job in a factory in Manhattan sewing linings in coats. Blanche, who was very religious, suggested I register Rosette at the Rambam Yeshiva, a private Jewish school on Kings Highway, thirty minutes away. A special school bus would pick her up at eight in the morning, return her at five in the afternoon. Blanche was a friendly woman, twenty years older than I, and I was grateful for her help in getting settled.

I registered at Washington Irving High School in Union Square for class once a week to get the regents credit required by New York State before I could be admitted to a college, though I had my high school diploma from Chicago. For that one night away from home, I paid a girl to babysit with Rosette.

We were to live in Brighton Beach for the next fourteen years. This was by far the longest period I ever stayed in one place up to that time in my uncertain life. Our first real home in the United States was an airy apartment on the ground floor in the front of the building. A court-yard stretched outside the L-shaped living room. Though we faced the street, the apartment was quiet. Five years later we were to move to a one-bedroom apartment on the third floor from which we could see the ocean.

Our first piece of furniture was a discarded mattress we found in the basement. I took a day off from work to look for a bed, table, and two chairs. I also bought a second-hand piano. Not very practical but I knew Rosette wanted a piano more than anything else after sharing Julia's. It was worth every hard-earned dollar to see the pleasure on her face when the piano arrived. I made cotton draperies of roses on a blue and white background for curtains and matching slipcovers for the two chairs.

Rosette soon made friends with the children in the building, played with them on the boardwalk and beach. Uncle Sam mailed her a dollhouse and a sequined ballerina doll. I washed and starched Rosette's dresses so she would be the most stylishly clad child of the ninety-nine families in the building.

After I received regents credits, I enrolled in evening classes at Brooklyn College, heading for my B.A. degree. My major was Romance Languages—Spanish and French. When my work ended at four, I rushed home, gave Rosette a bath, fed her, left her with the babysitter, raced to the college three nights a week, and arrived back at the apartment exhausted at eleven-thirty. I failed to get my degree at first because mathematics defeated me and I flunked science and astronomy.

The first summer, not knowing what to do with Rosette while I worked, I sent her to Camp Kinderland in the Catskill Mountains near Liberty, New York. I learned of the camp from Rosette's best friend, Vicky, a girl she met at the Yeshiva school. Vicky's mother, Jeanette, a widow, became my close friend as we visited our daughters at camp every weekend.

Jeanette and Vicky lived about half an hour away by subway. I was shocked at the relationship between this mother and daughter. Vicky talked back, something I would never allow Rosette to do, as it had not been permitted in my home. Jeanette would scream, ''Why can't you be well behaved like Rosette?'' and sometimes slap her daughter.

I insisted Rosette continue her ballet lessons and, this time paying for it, once a week took her to the Metropolitan Opera building in Manhattan. Exhausted from work and evening classes, as well as keeping house and caring for a seven-year-old, I managed somehow to wake every Saturday morning at six and get us both ready to be at the opera house by nine. I was one of forty mothers who watched in pride from a balcony as their children danced until noon. When I was pregnant I had daydreamed of a baby girl with beautiful features like Manuel's, not plain like me, who one day would appear onstage as pianist or ballerina. When Rosette started to draw and paint at the age of six, I hoped she might also become an artist. I lived only for her, dedicated my spare time to making her childhood pleasant and productive, believing in this way she would achieve everything I had not.

After ballet class we both went to art school where we took classes in basic drawing. On my salary of fifty-five dollars a week, a comedown from Chicago, I also paid three dollars weekly for piano lessons for Rosette. But I did not begrudge one cent spent on her. I felt she was blossoming in every respect. She had an amazing memory, quickly recognized the names of paintings, artists, symphonies, writers of classic literature.

She did so well in school she was allowed to skip the second grade. On Rosette's seventh birthday Berta wrote me that her love for Rosette was ''endless,'' she thought of Rosette as her daughter too, and even if she were to have children she would love Rosette more. She ended with the trenchant and touching line, "You and I never were children. We were born and immediately afterwards became old."

One day I said to myself, My mother was not born in a sweatshop, I was not born in a sweatshop, and I am not going to die in a sweatshop, and decided to go to business school and study bookkeeping. On graduating, I promptly found a job as assistant bookkeeper in a dress company in the garment center, a far more pleasurable way to earn a living than sewing linings into coats. From now on I would sew only for pleasure.

In Chicago I had asked for and received a divorce from Manuel and now thought of going out with other men. I did not want to live like a nun. Jeanette and I dreamed of dates on Saturday nights. Sometimes Rosette would sleep over with Vicky as Jeanette and I shared the expense of a babysitter so we could go to the movies.

I was in my early thirties, the prime of life, and very lonely. I hoped to marry a man who would support me and adopt my child, love her. The women my age in the building were all housewives who had never worked. I envied them, wanted the security of marriage and a man of my own.

One night Jeanette said grimly, "Women like us are doomed. We'll never find a suitable husband because we have a child."

I was shocked at this open rejection of Vicky even as I wondered if unconsciously I felt Rosette an obstacle to my remarrying and, like Jeanette, had begun to reject my daughter. Later I wondered how much influence Jeanette's cynical attitude had on me. I might have acted differently if my friends had been well-adjusted mothers who loved and enjoyed their children.

Instead of registering Rosette for another year at the Yeshiva school, I took her to P.S. 253, within walking distance. I put a key on a ribbon around her neck so she could get into the apartment when school ended, though she usually played with friends until six, when I arrived.

She was still far ahead of children her age in reading and writing, as I had been as a young girl. Blanche told me, "I have never seen a child so gifted and so good."

Rosette went through the fourth and fifth grades at P.S. 253. She wrote a composition in English class titled "The Person to Whom I Owe All My Life Is My Mother." It said: "My mother was born in Eastern Europe. Since she was very young she was holding a job during the day and going to school at night. My mother is both a bookkeeper and a stenographer. She can read, write, and speak six languages which would enable her to speak to three-quarters of the population of the world. Right now, she works and keeps home very nicely, at the same time."

I felt she was as proud of me as I was of her. We had both survived difficult days. From the time she was three and a half, because we had only one room we slept in the same bed. In Chicago it was a double bed, in Brighton Beach, a sofa that split into two sections. I was always so tired I would drop off to sleep the moment my head touched the pillow. Once in a while Rosette would have a nightmare, wake me, and I would comfort her. I rarely had nightmares, could not even remember dreams—who had time?

When the summer ended, Rosette entered sixth grade at P.S. 253. She started to suffer severe attacks of asthma. One day I left her home alone in bed during an attack. Blanche brought her food, said to me that night, "You could be a murderer for leaving your child by herself when she is so ill. She might go into convulsions and die."

But I was afraid to take time off for fear I would be fired and then what would we do? Rosette was absent from school many days that fall. But in spite of it she forged ahead scholastically. I came home one day to find her jubilant. She had scored 142 in the Stanford-Binet Intelligence Test. As a result she was eligible for the Special Progress Program in Cunningham Junior High School, P.S. 234. This was located on Kings Highway, four subway stops away at Avenue U. Her promotion meant she would go through seventh and eighth grades in one year, then enter the ninth grade.

Her teacher warned me that because Rosette had skipped from the first to the third grade, she would now be two years younger than the children in her class and might be under severe pressure to keep up with them. I wondered if I should insist she stay in the regular class. But I decided she might lose interest in her studies if not given the chance to use her intelligence in the class for gifted children.

One night a classmate at Brooklyn College asked me to go with her to a party to raise money for Adlai Stevenson, who was running for President. There I met the first man to whom I felt attracted since coming to the United States. He was an industrial engineer named Seymour Schwartz, nice-looking, intelligent, and articulate, two years younger than I.

He asked if he could drive me home. Then if he could come in for a cup of coffee.

Rosette was asleep in the bed we shared. I did not flick on the light for fear of waking her. Seymour and I tiptoed into the kitchen. I closed the door, made coffee. We talked in whispers.

Suddenly he walked over to me, took me in his arms, kissed me on the lips. I felt warmed, happy. He slowly unbuttoned my blouse. He kissed me tenderly on my shoulders, my breasts. After many years, once again I felt what it was like to want a man.

Suddenly the door to the kitchen was flung open. Rosette stood there. As she took in the scene, her eyes widened in horror. She said not a word, turned and fled.

My cheeks burning in shame, I asked Seymour to leave. Then, buttoning my blouse, I walked into the living room. I lay down next to my child. I put my arms around her, tried to find words to lessen the shock of what she had seen.

"I'm not an old woman and sometimes I need affection," I explained. "I've been alone, working hard, for many years. And after all, if I remarry, you'll have a father."

She pushed me away, said, "You disgust me!"

I did not know what more to say. I felt immoral, guilty, in spite of my fine speech, as if I had betrayed my daughter. Two years before I had told her where babies came from and the reason for menstruation. I did not want her to be frightened when it occurred—I had learned about it not from my mother but from girlfriends in Khotin. I also told Rosette she should remain a virgin until she married, that sex without marital love left a deep sense of guilt. And after all this preaching she had caught me acting like a prostitute—I was intending to have sex with a man I met that evening.

The next morning Rosette's first words were, "Was I dreaming or did something terrible happen last night?"

Again I tried to put into words how I felt but she would not listen. She did not want an explanation. I felt defeated.

From that night on, Rosette seemed to change toward me. I felt as though somehow I had lost my child. For days she would not let me kiss her or hug her, as though I were dirt. I realized this was the first time she had seen me in the arms of a man showing passion and it must have revolted her. Perhaps another girl of eleven, where there was a father in the house, not just she and her mother, two against the world, would have accepted the scene more casually. But to Rosette it was shattering. She probably thought she had lost me forever.

Seymour called, I let him visit that evening, and he brought a Monopoly set, hoping to make peace. Rosette, blocking out what she had seen the night before, played the game with us. Later Seymour and I walked along the ocean. He said he wanted to know me better with the thought of getting married. But I would have none of him, ashamed of what I had subjected Rosette to, ashamed also of my wanton behavior. After a few desultory dates, we stopped seeing each other.

Rosette started her second year at Cunningham Junior High, now in the ninth grade. We left together each morning on the same subway. She would get off at Avenue U. I continued to 34th Street in Manhattan. She seemed to have undergone an abrupt change in personality. She became apathetic and sluggish around the house, refused to do chores or go to her art, ballet or piano classes. She spent all her time daydreaming, reading magazines or listening to music on the radio. She gave up her friends, saying they were at other schools, had different interests.

I was now a bookkeeper for a nationally known lingerie firm. It was a relief to leave behind the daily racket of sewing machines sounding in my ears like machine gun fire. After school, Rosette sometimes took the subway to my office to practice typing until it was time for me to leave. I encouraged her, thinking the ability to type might come in handy. I also believed she would benefit from the discipline of an office and learning to get along with co-workers. The office personnel thought her friendly, courteous, and helpful.

One of the two millionaire owners of the business, I will call him Victor Lehrman, was a bachelor of fifty, fifteen years older than I. He was six feet tall with white hair, slightly balding, and a ruddy complexion. He smoked cigars continually. Though no Adonis, he had a warm personality. He and I had flirted casually in the office during the two years I had worked there. He said he liked my beguiling smile and soothing voice.

He bought the *Herald Tribune* but read only two sections of it—the stock market reports and the obituaries. He would walk into the office every morning and greet us in his deep, manly voice, "Guess who died?"

One day he noticed Rosette at my typewriter. I introduced her as my daughter. From then on, as I was working, he would occasionally take her to a coffee shop, buy her an ice cream soda.

One Saturday morning the phone rang. It was Victor. He asked, "Are you free tonight?"

"Yes." I wondered what he had in mind.

"Can I pick you and Rosette up and take you to dinner?"

"That would be very nice." I gave him our address. He lived in an apartment in Far Rockaway, half an hour's drive away.

Blanche was having coffee with me and I told her excitedly about my date, the first in a long time. She said, "I'll keep Rosette for the night. You don't want to take her along."

When I walked out of the apartment and into Victor's silvery new Cadillac, he asked, with a look of disappointment, "Where's Rosette?"

"She's at a friend's house for the night," I said.

"I made it clear I wanted her to come." The voice of a man accustomed to getting his own way.

"I'll get her," I said quickly. "She's not far away." And raced after Rosette.

He took us to an expensive seafood restaurant, then to a movie. Every Saturday night from then on he asked us out for dinner. Sometimes he brought his brother and sister-in-law, who had no children and enjoyed Rosette. Her slim figure was just starting to show curves; she was interested in everything we talked about.

Victor treated her like the daughter he never had. He invited us to his cabana club for Saturday night parties, arranged for Rosette to dance with boys her age. He gave me money to take her to *The Diary of Anne Frank, Carmen Jones,* and other Broadway shows. She seemed fond of him. He was the first father figure in her life since her real one, whose image was long forgotten.

Each Saturday early in the morning Rosette would set out for the beauty shop and even though Victor would not pick us up until six, she would be dressed and waiting three hours in advance. She sat in the car between us as we drove all over Long Island and Manhattan in search of new restaurants. For the first time in her life she knew the feeling of going out with a mother and a man who, like a real father, was able to pay for food and small pleasures.

I fantasized that Victor might be a husband for me and a father for Rosette. I thought of how, with his fortune, he could send her to the best schools and colleges, buy her luxurious clothes, add stability to her life as head of the family. He was a parsimonious man, believed all his money should be put in stocks except what he spent to dress himself fashionably. He rarely gave me money except for theater tickets and twice handed me fifty dollars to buy clothes for Rosette. He did bring us all the lingerie we wanted—but how much lingerie can you wear?

Several times Victor spoke of marrying me in that half-jesting tone which tells something of the truth. I know I had only to push a little—women are usually the ones who force marriage. I was very fond of him but I did not feel that overpowering yearning that supposedly is love.

Whatever—I did not seize the moment and it vanished. With it disappeared my only chance to be a wealthy woman.

But Victor remained a close friend and occasional lover for four years. I made sure that when we did have sex it took place in his apartment, not mine, so Rosette would have no more traumatic experiences due to my love life. Victor gave Rosette and me steady comfort, understanding, and companionship. In my peculiar snobbishness, I disliked him for calling blacks "niggers" and voting for Eisenhower. Also, he never shared a word about his personal life and it is hard to relate to someone who keeps such emotional distance.

Perhaps I have never been able to feel real passion for a man. There may be something too frightened in me to permit myself to express that feeling of wild abandon necessary for sensual love. I have felt deep affection for a man but never thought I could not exist without him. Maybe it is difficult for me to trust a man, since I could never trust my father.

In spite of all Victor and I did for Rosette, she continued to be lazy around the house. Then she started to act withdrawn, at times even did not hear what I said. For her thirteenth birthday I bought her a bicycle but though she had wanted one for years showed no interest in riding it.

She also refused to do homework. I wrote her English compositions, not wanting her to fail. When Blanche learned this, she scolded, "You're not helping your daughter." To earn extra money, I tutored two pupils in Spanish, doing their homework too, so I thought it natural to help my daughter.

One day I received a note from the assistant principal asking me to come to the school. He told me what I already knew: Rosette's marks were slipping.

That night I said to her, anger in my voice, "What's happening to you? You're not only lazy around the house but failing at school. You, with your 142 I.Q.!"

"The teacher doesn't like me," she said. "She makes fun of me in front of the class."

"What do you mean?" I felt indignant.

"She praises the others when they get good marks but when I get a poor mark she says with a sneer, 'Rosette only got 60 percent.' When I get 95 percent she says nothing."

Why this insensitive teacher held my daughter up to ridicule I did not know. But I felt she was destroying Rosette's confidence instead of helping her. And that she failed to take into account Rosette was two years younger than most of her classmates.

I tried to raise her self-esteem by holding a party for her class, a party at which she sat silent. But in another way I made it harder for her. I could not stop blaming her for failing in school. I did not try to understand what troubled her. Or assure her she was not a failure as a human being because she could not concentrate on work too difficult for her.

I took it out on her in other ways. Up to then, we did not own a television set. My second cousin, Sophie, and her husband Morris, a young couple with no children, lived in the adjacent building and sometimes we went to their apartment to watch programs. Now I decided to buy a television set, thinking this would cheer Rosette. She liked *The Hit Parade* but I would often switch to *Victory at Sea,* with its dramatic scenes of bloodshed that appealed to me more than the anemic popular tunes of the moment.

She started to become anxious over tests, saying she could not concentrate enough to study for them. And, for the first time in her life, she refused to go to classes. She protested against getting dressed in the morning.

"I can't face school, mom," she would say.

"You're going to school!" I was enraged. I would have given anything at her age for the privilege of an education. When I was thirteen, I had to sew by hand all day for months to own a winter coat and a pair of shoes. I thought of the many times I had gone hungry in Rio, no money for food, my education still a dream. Rosette's education was being handed to her on a silver platter. She was gifted in dancing, acting, painting, musically. And she was throwing it all away. She was an ungrateful, spoiled, selfish child.

"Get dressed at once!" I screamed.

She did not move.

"Don't you understand how much a good education means?" I shouted. "You *have* to get good marks so you can qualify for a scholarship to college."

She stared at me with those large, expressive dark eyes that pleaded with me to understand she felt incapable of competing with the children in her class.

But I could feel only rage at her obstinacy. I lost control and struck her hard, struck her with fury.

"Is this my thanks for all I've done for you?" I said in contempt.

She did not lift a hand to defend herself. Or utter a word in retaliation. She just sat in silence.

Then I felt guilty, tears came to my eyes. "I'm sorry I lost my temper," I said. "Please get dressed, precious. I'll take you to school. Try. For me."

That day she gave in. But sometimes she would get off at Avenue U and I would watch her walk away from the train, ostensibly headed for school. When I reached Manhattan I would call the school and be told she had not shown up. After my train pulled out of the station, she would cross to the other side, take the subway home. To prevent this, I got off with her at Avenue U, walked her to school, then went to my office. But this did not work either. As soon as I turned the corner, she would hurry away from school, return home.

It became harder and harder to persuade her to leave the house in the morning. When I was dressing, she would run out of the apartment, either race down the boardwalk as I chased her, or to the roof where I would find her staring at the ocean.

One day the principal called me to the school to complain of Rosette's truancy. He warned, "If she does not attend regularly, we will send a truant officer after her and she will be committed to a reform school."

That evening I really let her have it. I called her a parasite, irresponsible, thankless. I struck her, shouted, "You're an ungrateful child!" I accused her, "You're ruining your life and you're ruining mine."

Victor tried to reason with her but she seemed miles away. Nothing could change her mind. Day after day she refused to go to school. I left home in the morning not knowing what to do next, wondering where I had gone wrong.

She made one effort to pull herself out of the depression. A few of her friends were planning the following fall to go to the High School of Music and Art or the High School of Performing Arts, both in Manhattan. She wanted to audition for the latter, a special public school for students who want to become actors, singers, musicians, or ballet dancers. She had decided to study acting.

"Do you know the hard work and frustrations that go into the life of an actor?" I said.

"I don't care, I want to try it," she insisted.

For her first audition, she went with Blanche to the school on West 46th Street. Rosette was given a scene in which a young girl breaks off with her boyfriend. The teacher told her she passed the first audition and scheduled a second the following week.

I took her to that one. Unfortunately we got lost, arrived late. She felt anxious and angry, refused to try out, but I managed to convince her to go through with it. She was so nervous she did not pass. She became even more depressed after the rejection by this special school.

One afternoon as I arrived home from work I found Sophie and Morris in our apartment. They had walked over to make sure Rosette was all right. The Venetian blinds were drawn, the living room was in darkness. Rosette sat in a chair holding her head in her hands, staring at the floor, as though she had not moved all day.

Sophie said, "You have to do something about that child, Jenny. She does not feel well in the mind."

"She's just lazy and defying me," I said.

But I thought over Sophie's suggestion. I went to the Jewish Family Service, which had a branch in Brooklyn. I had taken two courses in psychology at Brooklyn College and knew the value of trying to understand troubled behavior. I was assigned a thoughtful woman in her forties, Mrs. Frances Julian. I saw her once a week to discuss my problems with Rosette. She asked to meet Rosette, interviewed her.

At my next session Mrs. Julian said, "You have a lot of anger at your daughter."

"I am furious at her for not going to school," I admitted. "I don't understand how she can do this to me."

But in spite of her absences and poor marks, Rosette was notified in the spring she would be graduated from Cunningham Junior High. Her teachers evidently though she was gifted enough to take a chance on her, considered the fact she was two years younger than most of the class. She had completed the seventh and eighth grades in one year, then the ninth, and was now entitled to be a sophomore in any city high school.

For her graduation I bought a long white chiffon dress at Macy's on my lunch hour. She looked at it only long enough to say, "I don't like it." I returned the dress, brought home another. She refused to go to the ceremonies, spent the day sitting alone in the apartment.

There was now the question to which high school she would go. I enrolled her at Lincoln High on Ocean Parkway. It was a large, overcrowded school for children from many neighborhoods but it was the nearest, ten blocks away.

Mrs. Julian arranged for Rosette to spend six weeks that summer at

Camp Bronx House in Copake, New York, for deprived children from poor sections of the city. Rosette wrote me she had fallen in love with a fourteen-year-old boy named Daniel. She described how the rest of the girls and boys had gone on a hayride as she stayed behind with Daniel. They went into his cabin where he threw her down on a bed and kissed her passionately.

Horrified, I showed the letter to Mrs. Julian. I was afraid my daughter might lose her virginity at the age of thirteen. Parents were not allowed to visit the camp but Mrs. Julian generously offered to take the three-hour trip to see if Rosette were all right. On her return she assured me my daughter was not sexually involved with Daniel. I felt ashamed of Rosette's behavior. I did not want her to disgrace herself or me, though I realized at her age natural sexual feelings were growing strong.

A neighbor once told me her daughter spent evenings on the boardwalk necking and kissing one boy with whom she went steady. I said, "How terrible!"

"No—how beautiful," she answered. "My daughter is discovering she is a girl and what love is."

I could not understand her attitude, thought it harmful to her daughter. Perhaps because I had never been a "teenager" in today's terms. I had been concerned chiefly with survival, I had not known the joy of romantic love or courtship. I thought it more important Rosette learn of the world's art and culture than become a promiscuous adolescent.

When she returned from camp, she started at Lincoln High as a sophomore. Classes were crowded, noisy, and confusing. She did not know anyone, all her friends were at the special schools in Manhattan. Her female classmates, who were older since they had not skipped two grades, wore very tight skirts and heavy makeup. Rosette imitated them in what I thought whorish dress. Having been brought up in a small town in Romania half a century in time behind New York, where in 1930 there was no electricity, I did not understand these were different times, a different world, and Rosette wanted to be like the rest of the girls in her class so they would accept her.

I went to see her home-room teacher, who told me Rosette was quiet and withdrawn, refused to take part in any activity, threw away the sandwich I made her each day, ate no lunch. She often remained in the cafeteria after the other students left for class, sitting alone until the last bell rang.

She attended school for a few weeks, then flatly refused to leave the house in the morning. Day after day I screamed, "You *must* go to your classes."

"I can't," she said quietly.

That was to be her answer all through life when she did not want to do something: *"I can't."*

Again I became so upset I hurled anger at her like a hurricane. "You spoiled kid!" I screamed. "Why are you so mean to me?"

And again she just sat and looked as though I would never understand her, she would never understand me.

I was at my wits' end. It seemed an impasse between mother and daughter. Mrs. Julian warned that if a truant officer from Lincoln came after Rosette, she might be sent to a state reform school where, because of her beauty, she would inevitably be raped by older, more hardened girls and exposed to unimaginable hardships and cruelties.

"What am I going to do?" I asked Mrs. Julian in panic.

She suggested Rosette be placed in a private boarding school that helped adolescents who could not be controlled by parents. I will call it the Forest School.

"Who will pay?" I asked.

"The city and a Jewish philanthropic organization," she said. "Your daughter will receive both education and psychological help."

The school was located in Westchester County, about twenty-five miles north of the city. I would be allowed to visit Rosette on weekends. Victor said he would drive me out every Saturday. On Sundays I would have to take the subway, then the train, a trip of three and a half hours.

Against my better judgment, I agreed that Rosette should go to this special school. Reluctantly she said she would try it. This was the first time we were to be parted since the days of the nursery school in Chicago, except for the few weeks of summer camp. Victor did not believe she should be sent away, saying he did foolish things as a boy and she would lose her desire to rebel against school. But I had to make my own decision.

A social worker from the school arrived in a taxi. I carried Rosette's suitcase, filled with the expensive skirts and sweaters Victor had bought her, to the taxi. Then I hugged and kissed my daughter many times to reassure her of my love.

"Be good, precious," I said.

I stood on the sidewalk, tears in my eyes, watching the taxi swing out of sight carrying Rosette to a place I hoped would rescue her from her school phobia.

I believed blindly in the professional advice given me. What did I know of the causes of truancy?

I only knew my brilliant, gifted daughter, at the age of thirteen, was throwing away her intelligence and talents for reasons neither she nor I understood.

III

The Separation

The apartment seemed deathly silent with Rosette gone. I ached for her in many ways. The other half of the bed was empty at night. I ate alone, except for Saturday nights when Victor took me out, or when I cooked for friends.

No other voice sounded at home from the time I woke at dawn until I fell asleep at night. I often cried in sorrow and loneliness. I could not believe Rosette was in an institution. Call it Forest School, or what you may, it was still an institution.

The first Saturday after she left, Victor drove me to the school. A social worker, Mary Simmons, who was to be my contact there, told me Rosette had not made a good adjustment because she was so homesick. Rosette begged me to take her home at once. Victor and I pleaded with her to stay, to give the school a chance.

Her therapist was a woman in her late fifties, Dr. Margaret Blau, who came from Vienna. Rosette was to see her once a week. Dr. Blau encouraged Rosette to paint, told her she was extremely gifted and a "fine human being," called her "Rosette dear." Their relationship seemed friendly and I was happy Rosette had finally found someone to whom she might freely talk.

But after she had been at the school three weeks, Rosette ran away.

Not having enough money for the train, she walked along the highway toward New York. One of her teachers, driving to the school, recognized her on the road and insisted she return.

The next day Rosette made another attempt to run away. She called me from the railroad station, sobbing, said, "Mommie, I'm running away. Please let me come home."

It was like the Chicago nursery all over again. I told her I wanted her home but the social worker had warned against this and she had to return to the school.

Over the next months I noticed a change in her. She started to make friends, took an interest in art and in her school classes. Her teachers praised her ability to draw and paint. She wrote that she missed me, still disliked the school and would give anything to be home, but would try for high marks.

On Mrs. Julian's advice I sought a therapist for myself. I consulted a mental health referral service and found a psychologist, also a native of Vienna. He spoke with such a strong accent I could hardly understand him. He tortured me twice a week for an hour, at a cost of seven dollars each time, pointing his finger at me and announcing, "It's all your fault. Children are born without problems. It's the parents who make them sick."

I stayed with him for two years even though I resented his punitive attitude. Finally I discovered he had never even studied psychology, he had been a music student in Vienna. I had lost valuable time and money listening to an unemployed musician who knew no more than I about my problems.

Rosette remained at the school for almost two years. Then all at once she was told she would be sent to another boarding school nearby where there was "a more controlled environment." Both she and I were very surprised at this decision by the school authorities.

I believed it occurred because of two things that involved her. She was the victim of a near-rape by three town boys who took her into the woods. Both she and I wanted the boys arrested so they would not try to rape other girls. But Dr. Blau and Miss Simmons strongly advised us not to sue. Dr. Blau said she could not allow the incident to reach the courts in order to protect Rosette. If she admitted that she had allowed one of the boys to kiss her, which she had, the judge would conclude she had tried to seduce him. Miss Simmons told me a suit would harm the school's relation to the townspeople, a precarious one at best.

The second experience to involve Rosette was her telling Dr. Blau she had looked at a bottle of iodine and thought of drinking it. When Rosette mentioned this to me, I was in a panic, for this was the way my mother had killed herself. I was now afraid of what might happen to my headstrong daughter if someone did not exert more control.

So I did not argue against her transfer to a school I will call Riverview, where she would receive stricter supervision. But first she was sent for a temporary stay, because Riverview had no vacancies, to a private mental hospital in the vicinity. She was placed with emotionally disturbed women of all ages. Some were mute, others talked only to themselves or jabbered to the air. Rosette told me she started to doubt her own sanity, wondered if *she* were psychotic, else why had they sent her to such a crazy place? Her asthma attacks started again and she coughed almost constantly.

I spoke to the social worker there, complained that my daughter was shut up with severely disturbed adults. I asked, "Wouldn't it be better for me to take her home?"

"That would be harmful to your daughter," the social worker said. "She is too self-destructive. You have no way of controlling her."

After two months Rosette was taken to Riverview. I was asked not to see her for six weeks. Double punishment, I thought, in the nursery it had been three weeks.

Meanwhile, Amy Hess, a spinster in her fifties, was assigned by Riverview to be my social worker. She too blamed me for all of Rosette's problems, accused me of lowering my daughter's "self-esteem." I cried bitterly all through the half-hour sessions, feeling like a monster-mother. After six weeks, I was allowed a brief visit with Rosette and when I complained I wanted more time, Miss Hess said, "Your presence only upsets her more."

Rosette begged me to take her home. She said, "I don't like what's happening to me here."

I asked for a special session with Miss Hess, told her, "I'm taking Rosette out of this place."

Miss Hess said angrily, "You can't sabotage your daughter. What

you want to do indicates your need to destroy her. She isn't ready to
go home."
Then she added, "The psychiatrist says you're psychotic."
I was furious. "How dare he call me that! He's never even talked to
me. Much less seen me."
"Well, he says you are," she said lamely.
What right does this doctor have to pin a stigmatic label on me
without even interviewing me? I thought. Is this science? He was undoubtedly judging me by what Miss Hess had told him. I gave up, returned to the city. I was damned by Rosette if I left her there, damned
by the authorities if I didn't.
I called the school at six each evening to find out how Rosette was.
One night the telephone operator said, "Mrs. Spinoza, Rosette and her
friend Christina have been missing since early morning. But don't
worry. The police have put out a four-state alarm. They can't get far."
The week before, two college girls had been found murdered in a
field in New Jersey and I had visions of Rosette kidnapped, raped, and
murdered. In a panic, I called Victor, who said he would be right
over. I phoned all the police districts in New York—there was no 911
then—describing the two girls, especially Rosette's red winter coat.
The police said they had no news of the two missing girls.
Victor suggested I also try New Jersey. I contacted the police in
several cities there, then sat waiting by the phone hour after hour in
case there was a report from one of the many police stations I had
called.
The night passed and the following day, which I spent at home
nearly going out of my mind. I sobbed for hours. I had always known
exactly where Rosette was, almost to the minute. Now I was out of
contact with her, fearing for her life.
About five the next morning, the police from Hoboken called. They
had picked up the day before two girls hitchhiking to New York but
neither had given the name Spinoza. I asked for a description. There
was no mistaking Rosette—in her red coat—and Christina, with her
long blond hair and brown coat.
I thanked the police, said I would call the school at once. I reached
a social worker, told her what I had learned. She assured me someone
would be sent immediately for the girls.
When I saw Rosette two days later, she said she and Christina had

decided to run away. They picked up a ride from two strange young men who took them to their apartment in Hoboken, where they spent the night. Rosette said she had sex with one of the boys. I was stunned. I thought this outrageous, indecent behavior.

Feeling in a state of collapse from shock and fatigue, I signed myself in at Kings County Hospital in Brooklyn—my first and only experience in a mental hospital. I had to get away from everything and everyone—Victor, my job, thoughts of Rosette. During the week I was supposed to be "observed," I never saw a psychiatrist. I lived—existed—in a ward with about fifty other women, some young, some old, some sobbing in despair, some screaming in terror. A number slept on cots in the hall because there was no room in the ward. The food was tasteless, I was not required to take a bath for the whole week, there was no television, no radio.

Finally I was interviewed by a young resident who asked, "Why are you here?"

"I told a lie," I confessed. "I said I was suicidal. But I just wanted a rest."

He laughed, said, "We have enough patients. Go home."

But I was thankful I had gone to the hospital. It prepared me for the next shock. Riverview reported it could not deal with Rosette and was sending her to Grasslands, a hospital for the mentally ill in Westchester County. After two days she was transferred, ironically, to Kings County, as though following in my footsteps.

I had to confess I felt relieved that she was locked up so she could not run away, perhaps next time to be raped and murdered. But I was grief-stricken to realize that at the age of fifteen she was in her fifth institution. Counting the eight months in the Chicago nursery, she had spent four years and eight months in institutions—more than one-quarter of her young life.

Kings County kept her for three months. I visited her as often as they allowed though something had happened to our relationship. It seemed strained after her sexual escapade. She never spoke of it nor did I ask—as though it were a dead, ugly thing to be buried forever. When I told Victor about the night she spent in a strange man's apartment and my indignation, he said it probably would never happen again, just part of growing up.

One day the psychiatrist at Kings County called and said in a very serious voice, "Will you please come to see me, Mrs. Spinoza?"

"What is it?" I was alarmed.

"I don't want to talk on the telephone," he said. "You'll have to come in."

All the way to the hospital I wondered what Rosette had done now—had she made another suicide attempt? She could not be dead, he did not sound funereal, just didactic.

When I sat across the desk from what, to me, was a fat Jewish boy with a mustache and pompous manner, he announced, "Rosette is pregnant. She must have an abortion. She is not well enough mentally to bring a baby into the world."

"I don't believe it!" I gasped.

"Her period is three weeks late. We gave her the rabbit test. It was positive."

Then he said, "She refuses to sign a paper agreeing to the abortion. Will you try to get her to change her mind?"

"Of course," I said. "I don't want her to have a baby."

I faced Rosette in the ward, said quietly, "Sweetheart, they say you're pregnant. Is it true?"

"I could be, mom," she said. "Because of that night I spent at Jim's apartment."

"But you couldn't be pregnant from that," I said. "You've had your period since."

I had kept track of the date of her menstrual periods, and mine, ever since her first and my first—I call it my bookkeeping work at home. I have always been very methodical—I kept records of what she ate and when she ate when she was a baby.

"I did have a period, didn't I?" she said. "I forgot that."

"Have you had sex with any boy since?"

"No."

I believed her, for she usually told the truth, painful though it might be. I said, "Then you couldn't possibly be pregnant."

"How do you explain the rabbit test?"

"I don't know," I said.

"Suppose I *am* pregnant by some fluke?"

"Then you must have an abortion, Rosette." I was adamant.

"Don't be angry, mom, but I want a baby."

"Over my dead body," I said. "Without a father? Who do you suppose will wind up supporting it? I've had enough trouble bringing you up without taking on your baby out of wedlock."

That night I discussed the problem with Victor. He said in his direct way, "If she's telling the truth that she hasn't slept with anyone since her period, then she is not pregnant."

"How do you explain the rabbit test?" I was puzzled.

"Maybe a mistake," he said.

He was right. Two weeks later the fat, mustached psychiatrist again called me to his office. He said, "Mrs. Spinoza, we were wrong. The results of two tests got mixed up. It's another girl who's pregnant. Rosette just got her period. I guess her delay was caused by anxiety at being in the hospital."

I was so furious I could hardly speak. Finally I said, "Do you realize the worry you have put Rosette and me through? And that she could have undergone the torture of an unnecessary abortion because you were wrong?"

He spread each arm sideways like an eagle about to fly and shrugging his shoulders said, "So we made a mistake."

I was stunned by his lack of feeling, his refusal to accept responsibility for what could have been a very damaging experience, physically and psychologically, for my daughter, a young woman already depressed enough to think of taking her life. Nor did he understand the hell I had gone through for two weeks, thinking I might have to take care of an illegitimate baby, the result of my daughter's one-night stand.

I said, "I want to take Rosette home. I'm capable of caring for her. I'll quit my job. Babysit at night to earn money or go back to sewing at home for a living."

"She needs a hospital," he insisted. "We're having her appear in court before a judge next week. We want to commit her to Rockland State Hospital."

"May I go with her to court?" I asked.

"We'll see," he said.

He never notified me of the hearing. Rosette was taken before the judge, who heard only the hospital's side. He committed her to Rockland State Hospital, thirty miles upstate across the Hudson River in

Rockland County. There she spent her sixteenth birthday, one week after she entered. She was assigned to a ward of women from sixteen to ninety years of age. Many were out of their minds, alcoholic, or senile or all three. Some were suicidal, others violently dangerous at times. At the end of a year Rosette was released. Her diagnosis: "Early childhood behavior conduct disorder. Primary behavior conduct disorder, reaction to childhood experiences. Repressing, holding back."

I took her home on a cold February day. As she passed through the hospital gates, I prayed this would be her last institution. She said, "Mommie, I'm almost afraid to go home. I've forgotten how to get along in the real world."

Victor took us to dinner, gave Rosette money to buy new dresses. She had left home as a child of thirteen and returned a young woman of seventeen after four dark years.

Because of a book on stenography I brought Rosette at Rockland, she became interested in a secretarial career. She registered at a business school to learn shorthand and typing from nine until noon.

After a week she also found an afternoon job, her very first, in an office in Manhattan, putting labels on diamond rings. Then Victor offered her work in his office and she and I sat side by side every day.

Rosette started seeing Vicky again; all the other girls Rosette had known were now at college. Vicky had dropped out of high school, bleached her hair, plastered heavy makeup on her face, lived in too-tight skirts. During the day while her mother worked, Vicky watched television. In the evening she would walk the mile to Coney Island, pick up black-leather-jacketed boys on motorcycles. This was the James Dean era.

Jeanette asked me, "What should I do with this daughter of mine?"

"Take her to a psychiatrist," I said.

"I don't have the money. Besides, all she needs is a good beating," Jeanette retorted.

Vicky asked Rosette to go with her on the Coney Island jaunts. I told Rosette, "Don't have such a low opinion of yourself. Give Vicky up as a friend."

"I don't have anyone else," she said.

She talked for hours on the phone with Vicky, went out with her evenings and picked up boys, I am sure. Sometimes she did not get home until after midnight. When I asked what she did, she said, "Nothing much, mother. Had a few Cokes with Vicky."

"How can you waste your time like this?" I fumed.

"I need friends and a social life," she said. "I've gone long enough without them."

She spoke of moving away from me, of sharing an apartment with Vicky. I felt alarmed but in a weak moment even offered to help pay the rent though I wholeheartedly disapproved of the idea. I wrote to Berta, enlisting her support, telling her I was worried about the company Rosette was keeping. Berta had been married to Kurt for ten years but had no children.

She wrote back and asked me to send Rosette to live with her. She said Brazilian families were very strict with young women and she would look after Rosette carefully.

I asked Rosette, "Would you like to live for a while with Aunt Berta and Uncle Kurt in Rio?"

She said as though surprised, "You'd let me go there?"

"If you'd like," I said. "The change might be good for you."

"I'd love it," she said. "I'd feel so at home in South America."

"Do you remember it?" Now I was surprised.

"A few scenes," she said. "And the feel of it."

She wrote Berta that she would be overjoyed to visit her. Berta replied at once, saying the day Rosette arrived would be the happiest one of her life. She also said she knew all the institutionalizations were not Rosette's fault or mine, that "your mother could not look after you as mothers usually do in normal families. She had to be your father and mother, brother, sister and friend, and perform all the duties a lot of people perform in a normal family, where there is security and discipline and roots." She added she hoped that in Rio Rosette would make new friends, study, and "marry a good boy," and she could stay as long as she wished.

Rosette and I were pleased by Berta's graciousness, but put off making any decision about the visit. Four months later, one evening in June, 1959, I received a call from Kurt. He was in Mexico City attending a convention of anthropologists and urged me to fly to Miami the next day with Rosette, saying he would meet us at the airport and take off with Rosette to Rio. He promised that Rosette, after studying Portuguese for six months, could enroll at the university where he was now a professor.

She agreed to go providing she could take Twinkle, her cat, as far as Miami, where she would turn Twinkle over to me to bring home. She would not trust his care to a neighbor. So the three of us— Rosette, Twinkle, and I—set out for Miami. Kurt met us at the airport. It was the first time I had seen my sister's husband, other than a photograph which showed him as startlingly good-looking. I was prepared for his handsome face but not his dynamic intelligence and charm. He was short and slender with dark hair that sometimes fell provocatively over his forehead. His brown eyes, full of fun, sparkled with zest. He also enjoyed pranks, seemed somewhat of a child at heart in spite of his brilliance.

I felt sharp pain at the thought of separating from Rosette, the way I have always felt when we part. As at the Chicago nursery, and again at the Forest School, in a sense I was sending her away. She told me later she thought she would never see me again but, as throughout her life, she remained silent at the moment of deepest fear. If she had spoken of how she felt, I might not have let her go. But she seemed bored with typing for a living and I believed she was headed for a life of wantonness if she followed her friend Vicky many more times down the boardwalk. So we kissed goodbye with sorrow in our hearts.

She left behind for me to mail, and obviously to read, a postcard for Vicky. She said she had found out the reason why I was "shipping" her so far away—because she had told me she intended to move out of our apartment to live with Vicky.

She wrote from Rio that Berta at first did not recognize her, not having seen her since she was five, then hugged and kissed her joyously. Berta's apartment took up the entire ninth floor of a modern building in Copacabana. Its ten rooms were elegantly furnished. Rosette had her own bedroom and bath, and radio.

Though I knew Berta would take fine care of my daughter, I longed for Rosette. I wrote every morning, waited for the mailman to bring letters from them. Berta wanted me to come to Brazil to live but I thought twice about leaving my job and Victor. Then one day, after Rosette had been gone a month, I received a telegram from Berta. She wrote that a chartered plane carrying missionaries on a visit to Rio would leave Miami within a few days and suggested I accompany them. I called the missionary headquarters in New York and they welcomed me as part of the tour because I knew Spanish and Portuguese and could translate for them along the way. They offered a reduced rate. I accepted.

I arrived at Berta's apartment late at night to find that she and Kurt were at a party. Rosette was sound asleep in her room. I tried to wake her but she would not stir. I sat on the bed, hugged and kissed her inert body. After a few moments, she opened her eyes, said drowsily, "Mom, I'm so glad you're here," and promptly fell asleep again. I went to bed in a room one of the maids said was mine, spacious like Rosette's, with private bath and radio.

Early the next morning I had breakfast with my sister, caught up on news of Rosette. At noon, when she was still sleeping, I became suspicious. I went into her room, tried to wake her, but she still wanted to stay in bed. Finally, in the late afternoon I forced her to sit up.

"What's the matter, Rosette?" I said. "This isn't like you."

She said groggily, "Mommie, I took an overdose of sleeping pills I found in Aunt Berta's medicine chest."

This time she had actually tried suicide. I was in a panic. I ran for Berta, who called two doctors. They came at once and gave Rosette an injection. She slept the rest of that day and night, but got up the next morning feeling more herself.

She explained she had taken the overdose because a young man with whom she had fallen in love failed to show up for a date. His name was Alfredo Diaz; he was a captain in the Brazilian navy and a cousin of Kurt's. Rosette and he had met the week before as she and Berta were walking on Avenida Atlantica. Alfredo, eighteen years older than Rosette, had invited her to a ball at the Naval Academy, seemed to have fallen in love with her, but had forgotten his date for the next evening.

Berta was furious. She wanted to forbid Alfredo to come to the house again. But I insisted he probably had a good reason for not showing up and would explain to Rosette when he next saw her. He called a few days later and they went out several times. She never told me what he said nor did I ask.

Every day Rosette and I took long walks along the boulevards bordering the ocean. In the evening, prominent scientists and educators visited Kurt. Berta gave parties in honor of Rosette, who appeared in fancy evening gowns looking like a fashion model. I could not believe this was the same girl who six months before was shut up in a violent ward at Rockland.

Not wanting to take advantage of Berta's hospitality for too long, Rosette and I rented a one-bedroom apartment on Avenida Atlantica on the eleventh floor of a modern building with a view of the same ocean that bordered our Brighton Beach apartment. Our lease ran six months, at which time I would decide whether to stay in South America or return to New York.

Rosette wanted to help pay the rent and found a job at the American Insurance Company, where she typed correspondence in English. Her salary was only forty dollars a month, which did not even cover lunches, but she took pride in earning money. I discovered an old friend from Rishcon who owned a large children's apparel store that had made her a millionaire. She paid me forty dollars a month as a saleswoman. I thought perhaps after some experience I could open my own shop.

Rosette and I had lived together only a few weeks when Berta asked if she could take Rosette back into her home, saying she missed her. Rosette admired and loved her aunt very much—Berta had become Rosette's alter ego. Besides being an anthropologist and a very cosmopolitan woman, Berta was also to me the acme of femininity, a superb housekeeper and hostess. In the elegance of Berta's home, Rosette was forming a new image of herself as she mixed with highly educated, sophisticated men and women.

I did not begrudge my daughter her new pleasures. At the same time I realized it was far easier for an aunt to give wholehearted love to a niece than for a mother. The aunt did not undergo the daily frustrations and angers inherent in bringing up a child.

But I could not live apart from Rosette and she obviously could not live apart from me. I was appalled at the thought she had tried to take her life. She had never been this self-destructive when she lived with me and I would not risk it happening again. She insisted she was in love with Alfredo. I thought him a nice young man, admired him for working to put two sisters through college and a brother through medical school. But Rosette was scarcely ready to be a wife. Not if she wanted to kill herself just because a man she hardly knew failed to show up for a second date.

I could not work for the pitiful wages they paid in Brazil. And the idea of starting my own store was an illusion for I did not have the money. The trip had cost five thousand dollars, my complete savings.

I said to Rosette, after six months, "Let's go home."

She did not argue. We kissed Berta and Kurt goodbye, thanked them for all their kindnesses, and boarded the plane for Miami. Rosette would not speak to me the entire flight and even refused to drink champagne, which she loved. I knew she was furious but unable to express it. At the same time, she accepted the fact I could not let her live on a different continent, thousands of miles between us, exposed to heartbreaking situations that might result in her taking her life.

We returned home in a snowstorm. One neighbor had placed the sign "Welcome" on our refrigerator, another had cleaned the apartment. I felt relieved to be in my own house amid familiar possessions. I find it uncomfortable to live in strange places.

Several months before I left for Rio, I wondered if I should end the relationship with Victor. It was going nowhere. While away, I wrote him only one letter, telling him we were staying in Brazil. I thought he had suffered enough with Rosette and me and was ashamed to return with even greater problems—her attempted suicide. It was difficult to give him up after almost five years but I did. I never even called to say we were home.

Not wanting to work any longer for his firm, I assumed my leave of absence would be permanent if I did not notify them otherwise. I found a job as bookkeeper at an import-export company on Madison Avenue at 34th Street.

Ten years before I had put a deposit on a cooperative apartment in a development on the lower East Side. Now I was notified our building had been completed and I was to select an apartment. Rosette and I chose one on the sixteenth floor, consisting of four and a half rooms, and moved from Brighton Beach to our spacious new home. If we looked to the left we could see the *Jewish Daily Forward* building in the distance. To our right, far north, rose the silver spires of the Empire State and Chrysler buildings.

We were delighted to be nearer to the opera house, theaters, and museums. We explored the neighborhood, tasted the delicious foods for which the lower East Side is famous—herring, corned beef, pastrami, lox and bagels, pickles, knishes. We bought dresses and coats for one-third the uptown price.

We found prints of our favorite paintings for the many walls of the new apartment. My favorite was Millet's "The Gleaners," reminding me of the Russian peasants in the wheat fields across the Dniester. Rosette's was "Echo and Narcissus" by Waterhouse. She said the image of the Greek myth in which a woman's body disappears and all that is left is an echo appealed to her.

Now eighteen, she informed me one night she wanted to be a stewardess so she could fly all over the world, perhaps wishing to return to Rio. I thought it might be difficult for her to hold such a job but the next morning we went to an agency specializing in airline careers. To my surprise Eastern Airlines offered her office work at $85 a week on shifts that changed every two weeks from seven in the morning until three in the afternoon to three in the afternoon until midnight.

On her early shift we would get up in the dark at five and I would take her to her office, not wanting her to go out in the city alone at so dangerous an hour. As my job did not start until nine, I would sit in a cafeteria for two hours and read the *New York Times,* as I do every morning. When she worked the later shift, she would sleep until noon, then go to the office by herself. At midnight I would walk to the subway stop three blocks from our home to be there when she got off. That area was unsafe at night for lone girls.

For the first time in our lives, we were earning two respectable salaries. I allowed her to be as extravagant as she wished and she bought a new wardrobe. Sometimes the girls in her department worked ten days in a row then took a four-day weekend on which they could fly free anywhere in the world. We took advantage of those weekends, once flying to Miami to see Aunt Fanny, who had lost Uncle Sam through cancer, another time to Boston to visit a male cousin of Rosette's whom she liked.

Her social life, if not her academic, was improving. During her vacation in July, we traveled to a country club in the Adirondacks for a week. There she met a young Scandinavian actor, a handsome blond, who spoke with an English accent. He took her out several times. She also became friends with a few girls at her office and went with them to Washington, D.C. to visit the National Gallery of Art and tour government buildings. At my insistence, she joined a Zionist organization, where she met young men.

One Saturday afternoon a man I thought likeable and mature phoned to invite her that evening to the play *Milk and Honey*. She would not speak to him, said, "I don't want to go."

I told him she was out shopping, asked him to call later. I begged her to answer the phone when it rang again and say she would go to the play.

He called back in half an hour. She signaled she would not speak to him. I told him, "I'm sorry, she isn't home yet. Why don't you call again?" hoping in the meanwhile I could change her mind.

"What's the matter with you?" I stormed.

"I don't feel like going out with him," she said.

"You're impossible!" I shouted. "What are you going to do— become a social cripple?"

Instead of answering, she walked to the living room window. She stood there a moment, then crashed her fist through it. Luckily, she did not hurt herself—her knuckles just bled a little. Neighbors, hearing the tinkle of glass, came to their windows, called out to ask what had happened. Embarrassed and ashamed, I said there had been a slight accident.

This was Rosette's first show of violence. It was indirect but, I knew, aimed at me. When the young man phoned a third time, I told him Rosette was too tired to go out. From then on, she refused to have anything to do with the Zionist group.

Before leaving for Brazil I had decided to write Manuel, after fifteen years of silence, inviting him to visit us. I had not been in touch with him since the divorce, then one day thought, What am I doing to Rosette? I did not have his address so I wrote the Venezuelan government. It took them two years to locate him.

He wrote at once after my letter reached him. He thanked me for a photograph I had sent of Rosette, saying, "She is how I imagined her always, *beautiful.*" He ended the letter, "In regard to our separation, there were mistakes on both sides but the most important ones were 'the dreams' which Fanny's letters awoke in you," referring to her promise to take care of Rosette and me, a promise she had been unable to fulfill.

Rosette had called Dr. Blau after she left Rockland and arranged to see her once a week at her New York office on Park Avenue and 39th Street, where she worked part time. This had been interrupted by our trip to Rio. Now once again I took Rosette to Dr. Blau's office, waited in the reception room, wondered what they were talking about.

One day Rosette told me she wanted to move into an apartment of her own. She argued that most of the girls in her office lived alone. I tried to persuade her we had a large enough home where she had a room to herself and all the freedom she wanted. I told her I thought she was too young, as yet, to live alone.

I wrote Berta of this latest problem and she promptly sent a letter to Rosette asking her not to move. She pointed out that Rosette was not ready to live by herself, would feel lonely and unprotected, and there would be no one to wake her in the morning to make sure she went to work or keep her company when she came home.

Rosette paid no attention to Berta's letter or my pleas so reluctantly I helped her search for an apartment. One night, after looking at some uninhabitable rooms, we planned to attend the play *All the Way Home,* based on the book by James Agee. Half an hour before curtain time we stood on East Eighty-sixth Street, almost an hour's ride by bus to the theater at that time of night.

I was so tired and exasperated I started to sob. Rosette understood the anguish I felt at her leaving. She gave up the idea.

I had not heard from Victor in two years. He must have seen my name in the telephone directory and realized I had returned to the United States, for one day he called.

"Jenny, how are you?" He sounded pleased to reach me.

"Fine, thank you." I wondered why he was calling, did he want me to return to work for him?

He said, "I'm getting married to a very rich woman and I wanted to know how you felt about it." Implying he was giving me a second chance if I wanted it.

The Separation

I was jealous of course but at the same time knew I did not love him
enough to marry him. I said philosophically, "You always wanted a
rich woman, Victor. So be happy."

"I'm glad you approve, Jenny," he said. "You always meant a lot
to me. I don't understand why you didn't call when you got back from
Brazil."

"I think of you often, Victor," I said. "But it's better this way."
Then I added, meaning it, "Thank you for all you did for Rosette and
me. I don't know what I would have done without you."

"Send my love to Rosette," he said. "I miss her."

Each year for the next twelve, Rosette mailed him and his wife a
Jewish New Year's card and received one in return. Then his wife
wrote Rosette that Victor had died of cancer after a prolonged illness.
I heard he left her a fortune that, I thought wistfully, might have been
mine—as my father may have thought many times about the money
his father would have left him had he not been such a rebel.

After Rosette had worked for Eastern Airlines two years, she was
offered a trip to Europe at 75 percent discount on both our fares. We
made plans to achieve one of our dreams—fly to Amsterdam, Paris,
London, Rome. Six weeks before we were to leave, Rosette fell into
such a depression she could hardly speak, or drag herself to work each
morning. On weekends, she did not leave her bed.

I became frightened and wrote Berta, asking her to come to New
York, thinking she might help Rosette over the depression. Berta flew
up, stayed a month. She accompanied Rosette to work every day, met
her for lunch and supper, then traveled home with her on the subway.
On weekends they went to museums and plays.

One night after Berta left, when Rosette was working the late shift,
we met for supper. She refused to eat. I thought her lack of appetite
due to the Dexedrene a doctor had prescribed because she wanted to
lose weight.

"Please eat a few bites, precious," I begged, recalling her hunger
strike when she was four months old.

"Mom, I hate the job. I want to quit," she said.

"Why don't you want to stay?" I asked.

She paused, as if deciding whether to confide in me. Then she said,
"I have the feeling all the girls in the office know what I'm thinking.

And there's one man who keeps staring at me and I know he is reading my mind too. I try to control my thoughts, especially the bad ones. But I'm afraid of the people in the office."

"How long has this been going on?"

"For several months. I didn't want to scare you. But now I'm terrified."

"Did you tell Dr. Blau?"

"She assured me nobody could read my mind. That my own fears were creating what she called my illusions."

Then she added, "I also told Dr. Blau I felt a stabbing pain in my breasts, as though someone were biting them."

She showed me a note her supervisor had written that said, "Stop scratching your head, take a shower." The Dexedrene caused her head to itch and she would occasionally scratch it. The doctor had also given her a tranquilizer so she could sleep, pepped up as she was from the Dexedrine. She was caught in a vicious circle of drugs but I could not stop her from taking them.

She left her job, would not look for another. She stayed home all day, listening to music, smoking, reading magazines. She imagined now that she was plagued by the Rosicrucians, a secret society of the seventeenth and eighteenth centuries supposed to have occult power. Its symbol was a cross with a red rose in the center. She told me the society had written asking for money but she did not want to join because she was afraid its members could read her mind, just as her co-workers had done.

While I understood the mental torture she was enduring, at the same time I could not stop blaming her for her indolence, which angered me. I called her "stubborn" and "spoiled," as I had done when she played truant. She listened in silence, stared into emptiness.

One time I warned, "If you don't snap out of it, I'll put you back in the hospital," the worst threat I could have made, though I did not mean it. Even if it were a marginal life, I wanted her to make it on the outside. I believed she would have what the psychiatrists called a "spontaneous remission," get well on her own. I also believed she was young enough so some miracle drug might yet be discovered to help her.

But I started to dread the weekends when she refused to get dressed and go out. She was afraid of crowds, "pushing, loud, noisy, vulgar people." Our apartment became her refuge. She wanted only to be left alone. She wore me down with silence, the polite smile that faked serenity. I was afraid to leave her alone when I went to work, obsessed by the fear our world would collapse.

Her friends were marrying, having babies. We were always buying gifts, sending congratulations. Everyone seemed to be enjoying life except poor Rosette, at whom I snarled, "Snap out of it!" or "For God's sake, use your willpower." Demeaning words, meaningless words, to her.

Then magically came the period of remission. All at once she felt a desire to become an artist and registered at the Art Students League of New York. Berta sent one hundred dollars for a month's tuition and art supplies. Rosette entered a class with eight other young men and women to learn how to draw the human body from nude models. She also got a job typing for an insurance company.

But within a few months she was again complaining she felt persecuted by the Rosicrucians. She also believed everyone in the insurance office could read her mind. I wondered what on earth to do next, where I could go for help. Dr. Blau did not seem to be solving any of my daughter's problems.

That New Year's Eve, 1960, Rosette and I sat home watching the festivities at Times Square on television. Guy Lombardo's orchestra welcomed in the year. On one program that followed, a comedian made ribald remarks about celebrities.

"He's really talking about me," Rosette said.

"Don't be stupid, Rosette." I was upset. "You're imagining things again."

She sat chain-smoking, as she had been doing for years, and insisted, "He *is* making fun of me."

I had been awake since five A.M., worked all day, was exhausted at this hour of one A.M. Rosette's refusal to be rational was more than I could bear. I screamed, "How much more can I take from you? Why are you bleeding me?" Words my mother had once hurled at me.

She put out her cigarette, stood up, and disappeared into the bathroom. When she did not return after fifteen minutes, I went to the bathroom door and called, "Sweetheart, are you all right?"

There was no answer. I tried the knob. The door was locked. I shouted, "Rosette! Answer me!"

Still no sound. I ran to the living room window, which projected a few feet beyond the frame of the building, and looked back at the bathroom window. I saw Rosette sitting on the ledge, nothing between her and the street sixteen stories below. She had taken off her black silk jersey dress, wore only a black lace slip in the freezing weather.

She was saying to herself, "Jump! Jump!"

I called out in a low voice, trying not to sound hysterical, "Come in, precious. Please come in."

She gave no sign she heard me. She sat as though deliberating when to hurl herself to the ground. I thought, even at that tragic moment, how beautiful she looked, her hair carefully styled for New Year's Eve.

I kept pleading, "Come inside, please, darling."

Finally she drew back from the ledge, edged her way indoors. I thought, Thank God. I walked to the bathroom, said quietly, "Rosette, open the door."

After a few moments she unlocked it. She looked at me blankly as she walked out.

There were thin red lines around her throat and her wrists. She told me she had tried to commit suicide with a razor blade, decided she could not do it in such a bloody way, then thought of throwing herself out the window.

I did not know what to do. There was no one to call on this night when everyone was out celebrating. I thought of the police but dreaded what neighbors would think. All my life I have had a deep fear of neighbors finding out things were different at my house. This probably goes back to the day—or night—my mother killed herself and neighbors swarmed all over our garden treating us with pity and contempt.

I stayed awake the rest of the night watching Rosette lying in bed to make sure she would not make another suicide attempt. I knew I had to do something the next day. In the morning, in freezing temperature, I spent hours in the corner telephone booth, not wanting to call from home where she could hear. I phoned every hospital in the city, looking up constantly at our windows to make sure she was not trying to jump again. It was New Year's Day and the hospitals seemed reluctant to accept a mental patient. Except St. Vincent's psychiatric clinic, which told me to bring Rosette in the next morning if she would come voluntarily.

But when she woke, she insisted she felt well enough to go to work. We went out to buy her a sweater with a high neck so the red line could not be seen. I took her to the door of the insurance company. On my lunch hour I called St. Vincent's, spoke to the psychiatrist, and told him Rosette now felt well enough to go to her office. He insisted I bring her to the hospital right away. He urged me not to take chances with her life, saying, "If she tried suicide once, she is likely to try it again."

I called Rosette, explained that she could not jeopardize her life, and I was coming for her at once. She agreed to sign herself into St. Vincent's. She stayed three weeks, highly dosed with tranquilizers, slept most of the day, ate little, and lost twelve pounds, about which she felt happy.

She did not want to go back to her job so I called the insurance office, told them she had to resign because of illness. The "remission," a short one, had ended. Again she spent the days listening to music, smoking, reading.

I had not wanted any of my family to know about Rosette's troubles. But now I was frightened enough to call one of my cousins who was an official of a large mental health organization. I described Rosette's condition, asked what I should do.

"Rosette will get better only in a hospital," he said. "You cannot handle so severe a depression at home. She needs long treatment."

Deep in my heart I disagreed, remembering the year at Rockland. I postponed a decision as she spent day after day in her pajamas, hair uncombed, refusing to do even the small chores like dusting or washing dishes.

My cousin called several times to find out if I had taken his advice. One night, during a lengthy conversation, he strongly urged me to send Rosette to a hospital. He said it was not fair to her to allow her condition to continue. I promised him I would call a hospital the next day.

After I hung up, Rosette seemed unusually withdrawn, no doubt aware, since she had heard my part of the conversation, of what I intended to do. I feared she would make another suicide attempt at the thought of separating from me.

I became so desperate that, for the first time in my life, I did not care what the neighbors would say. It was more important to save my daughter's life. When she left the room for a moment, I dialed the police, gave my name and address.

I said, "I think my daughter may try to kill herself again. Can you come here and take her to a hospital?"

"We'll send an ambulance right away." The man's voice was sympathetic.

When the doorbell rang, I let in two tall policemen. Rosette was wearing slacks and a blouse—she had at least made that concession to dressing. When she saw the police she realized they had come for her and started to cry.

"Mommie, mommie, don't let them take me away," she begged, as she had always begged when about to be pried out of my arms.

"It's for your own sake, dearest," I said. "I'm afraid to leave you alone during the day. I can't be with you every minute."

Then I had an idea. "We'll call Dr. Blau, see if she agrees you should go to a hospital."

The police obligingly waited as I dialed Dr. Blau's home number in the country, which she had given us in case of emergency. When she answered, I explained what I had done and asked her to speak to Rosette. Dr. Blau told Rosette that for her safety she should go with the police.

When Rosette hung up, she said not a word but stalked off to the bathroom. I followed. I saw her take a bottle of Chlorox bleach and start to rub some of the liquid in her eyes as though to blind herself. I seized the bottle, washed her hands before she could do any damage.

Finally she agreed to let the police take her to Bellevue provided I did not ride with her in the ambulance but followed in a taxi. I cried all that night, awake until dawn. Early the next morning, when I went back to Bellevue, I found her in an enormous room filled to capacity with women of all ages who had one thing in common—the same ugly robe, white with black stripes, tied with a string around their waists, and cloth slippers in which to shuffle around. Iron bars blocked the windows. The babble grated on my ears. Rosette said she heard mice run around all night and saw them crossing the table on which the patients ate. She would not touch the food, not even the coffee.

I would not leave her there another night, no matter what the risk. I looked for the psychiatrist on the floor, an agreeable young resident who listened sympathetically as I told him how I had persuaded Rosette to go to the hospital but now wanted to take her home. I begged him to release her in my care, assured him she was usually amenable. He spoke to her, was convinced she would not harm herself, and allowed me to take her home.

I called my cousin, told him I had removed Rosette from Bellevue. He said angrily, "How could you do such a destructive thing? I have told you over and over if she is depressed enough to have tried to kill herself once, she will try again. And this time she may succeed. Her blood will be on your hands."

He so terrified me that I called Bellevue, they sent an ambulance for Rosette and, crying and pleading, she was again taken there. But they kept her only one night, then committed her to Central Islip. This is a fortress of a mental hospital rising out of the forests in central Long Island, a virtual city of the emotionally disturbed.

The following Saturday, though it was snowing hard, reminding me of Khotin winters, I brought her books, magazines, fruit, her chess set. She accepted them lifelessly, not even thanking me. She looked defeated, as though I had sentenced her to death.

I walked through the snow to the Central Islip station to catch the last train home, a two-hour trip on the Long Island Railroad. It was past midnight as I sat alone on a bench. I waited over two hours in the icy cold, the snow having caused a delay. I kept thinking of the new hurt I was inflicting on my child—another institution where she would be shackled, psychically speaking, day and night.

A middle-aged psychiatrist, a Polish refugee, took an interest in Rosette. He suggested she join a selected group of patients undergoing insulin shock. He assured me there was a good chance the insulin would "cure" her depression. She agreed and they started treatment. But every visiting day she complained, "I can't take this much longer. Please don't force me to suffer."

Though aware of her fear, I told her over and over, "You *must* finish the treatments. They will help you get well."

All at once she did improve. She was given the responsibility of typing case histories in the main office. Her depression seemed to disappear. After six months, sixty-two insulin shock and eight electroshock treatments, she was discharged. She had gained twenty-five pounds, which infuriated her. She insisted she had to lose them quickly, that she was far too fat for a twenty-year-old.

The Monday after she arrived home, I saw a novel ad in the *New York Times,* one that seemed to fit Rosette: "Needed, a typist with artistic ability." The firm was Asiatic Petroleum, a subsidiary of Shell Oil Company, with offices at Rockefeller Center. Rosette took a four-hour series of tests, passed easily, was hired, and trained for a month at the company's expense. She learned how to operate a Varityper and construct difficult charts and graphs.

She resumed her once-a-week sessions with Dr. Blau. She also said she wanted to go to evening classes at Hunter College and work for a B.A. degree in Fine Arts, something I had urged her to do for years. It appeared as though the insulin treatments had worked.

For eight months Rosette coped with both her job and night classes. Then she started to complain that she was losing her ability to concentrate enough to type the complicated charts. She began to feel depressed again and decided to resign from Asiatic Petroleum. She stayed home, refusing to continue at Hunter.

Six months passed before I did anything about her and then it was another hospital, not far from our home, with a psychiatric unit for twenty voluntary patients. She shared an attractive bedroom with one other young woman, was given nourishing food and a sympathetic therapist.

But when I visited her one evening, I found her very agitated. She told me she had been resting on her bed in the late afternoon when a black attendant walked into her room. He sat down next to her, began to talk to her in a low voice, all the while slowly caressing her body, running his fingers up her thighs and touching her vagina. She was paralyzed with fear, afraid to call out and create a scandal. She was saved by her roommate's approaching footsteps as the man jumped up and raced out of the room.

I dared ask, "Are you sure you didn't imagine this, sweetheart?"

With tears in her eyes she said, "Mother, it was real."

I looked for the social worker, a mature Jewish woman, but the nurses told me she had left for the day. I stayed awake that night thinking, Is there no peace for the emotionally troubled, even in a luxury hospital? Is there always someone taking advantage of the mentally ill?

The next morning I telephoned my boss I would be late, heard him sputter in wrath. I set off for the hospital, found the social worker, told her Rosette's story. She said, "Mrs. Spinoza, I believe your daughter. We've had other complaints about this man. I'll talk to the psychiatrist in charge."

That evening when I returned, the nurse told me the doctor had left instructions for Rosette to be discharged the following day. Rather than punish the black attendant, or perhaps fearing a malpractice suit, the officials decided to get rid of Rosette, I thought.

I was enraged. When I went back to the hospital the next day instead of going to my office—I had difficulty over the years explaining to various employers why I missed so many hours—I asked to speak to the chief psychiatrist. He was not there—they never are when you need them, they are usually in conference or you are told, "The doctor cannot be disturbed."

Finally I was granted an interview with a resident. He appeared irritated at my bothering him. I explained the situation, then said, "What am I to do? Rosette is not well enough to go home. And she is covered by one more week of hospital insurance. Why shouldn't she use it?"

He said impatiently, "There is nothing to talk about, Mrs. Spinoza. Your daughter has been discharged and her bed given to another patient. She *has* to leave. I suggest you send her back to Central Islip, as we have recommended."

I thought, How cold, how inhuman, this young psychiatrist, he has absolutely no feeling for my daughter as a suffering human being. She reports a sexual indignity suffered at the hands of a member of the staff and instead of correcting the abuse, he and the other administrators merely perpetuate the uncaring attitude we have so often found in these places.

I persuaded Rosette to sign herself in again at Central Islip, telling her, "My darling, you are not well. I cannot care for you at home."

This time she received medication instead of shock. When I visited, she seemed calm, was again typing case histories. I wrote her every day, as I had done since she first left home, starting each letter, "My dearly beloved daughter."

After three months she seemed improved and had even started to play the piano again, something she had not done in years. I asked the psychiatrist if I could take her home for the weekend. Back in our apartment I said casually, "Sweetheart, do you think you'd like to stay home and get a job? If you can type at the hospital, why can't you type in an office here?"

"That would be great, Mommie," she said, her eyes sparkling.

Monday morning we went to an agency and agreed to pay a fee of two hundred dollars for the first three weeks of employment. The agent sent Rosette to the Merchandising Corporation, which owned a chain of department stores. She was hired instantly in the reproduction department, which took care of paste-ups and mechanicals for advertising.

I called the psychiatrist at Central Islip, told him Rosette had found a job. He seemed pleased and said she could remain home for one month. Then I was to report her progress.

Her new supervisor was a cultured young Spaniard, Henri Rodriquez, a rather bohemian soul who seemed to understand her. He praised her work, put little pressure on her to produce. She liked him and respected him, felt comfortable in the office. The employees received twenty percent discount in the stores owned by the company and Rosette shopped for dresses and accessories for both of us.

At the end of the first month I called the psychiatrist at Central Islip and told him how well Rosette was doing. He gave permission for her to stay away another month. At the end of the second month I took her back to the hospital for an interview and she was discharged. The psychiatrist urged her to see a therapist several times a week in an outpatient clinic. For a while we gave up on Dr. Blau and I registered Rosette at Beth Israel's mental health clinic. I also decided to get help there myself.

For the next two years we attended this clinic. But Rosette's psychiatrist took little interest in her beyond prescribing Mellaril and Tofranil, the tranquilizers she had received at Central Islip. She said he never asked her to tell him any of her fantasies or feelings. It cost each of us eight dollars a visit and I thought it a total waste.

We lived on my salary as, for a year, Rosette saved her $135 a week. She then decided to spend most of her savings. She replaced our old, worn furniture, buying a golden velvet sofa, striped in rose, with two matching chairs and a new bedroom set for each of us. She also carpeted the apartment in soft green. And bought herself a new piano on the installment plan.

"It's not realistic to spend all your savings," I objected. Never in my wildest dreams would I have been so profligate.

"We needed new furniture, I thought you'd be pleased," she said in that set, stubborn way of hers against which I cannot argue, perhaps because it is so like my own.

"You're spoiled," I said. But part of me was pleased she had been able to earn enough money for a few luxuries including a mink coat for me costing $600 wholesale and a zebra-stencilled calfskin coat for herself costing $400.

She told her psychiatrist proudly, "I spent on new furniture and fur coats what it would cost for years of therapy."

She said his reply was an amused expression as he turned to look at the clock.

Rosette also erupted in a burst of creative energy. She registered for evening classes two nights a week at the Beaux Arts School for a course in fashion illustration, spending hours in front of an easel drawing from a live model. She arrived home late at night, got up early to go to work. On Monday evenings we went to the mental health clinic, waited an hour for her busy psychiatrist who said nothing to her, she reported. She subscribed to the opera and ballet, became a member of the Museum of Modern Art. On Sundays she went to the Metropolitan Museum of Art to study the paintings there; it became her second home.

One day her supervisor, who knew she was studying fashion illustration, offered to transfer her to the art department, a promotion that meant more money. She thanked him but refused, saying she needed further schooling. A few months later he repeated the offer, again she declined. She told me she did not think her work professional enough.

On Rosette's twenty-fourth birthday Berta sent her a $100 check and wrote: "I'm very proud of you, couldn't have dreamed of a better niece. People can be very near physically but miles away psychologically. We are close through empathy. That's why we three are sisters and relatives not only by blood but affinity.''

On my fiftieth birthday Rosette invited my then-closest friend, Regina, and me to meet her after work at a French restaurant on West 55th Street. She arrived late, breathless from running, handed me a bouquet of pink roses and a bottle of champagne. After supper we went to the Harkness Ballet, for which she had bought tickets a month in advance. I thought, tears in my eyes, What a blessing you are, my little sweetheart.

She held this job for three years, the longest she had ever worked. Most of the personnel in her department had been promoted and she acquired seniority. I was optimistic about the future, thought, Maybe at long last something has worked.

One evening at supper she said, ''Mom, I talked back to Mr. Rodriquez today. He wanted me to stay late to finish some work. I said I couldn't.''

''He's your boss, you must obey him, Rosette.'' I was worried at her attitude.

''He's reading my mind and I don't like that,'' she said defiantly.

In despair I realized she was again gripped by feelings of persecution. The medication did not guard against illusions of the mind.

Every six months the company reviewed each employee's record, recommended a raise if deserved. Rosette now asked for a raise. But Mr. Rodriquez refused to give it, perhaps because of her defiant behavior. And she walked out—after one thousand days with never an absence. We later learned Mr. Rodriquez could not give her the raise because business was poor, the company was even planning to close one of its largest stores.

Rosette quit on May 23rd. One week later we were on our way to Europe, having decided this was the time to take the long-postponed trip. Since childhood she had heard me speak of the treasures in European museums, the beauty of the ancient churches and the old cities.

She slept most of the way to Amsterdam. We stopped there long enough for lunch and to browse in airport shops. Then on to Italy, flying over the snow-capped Swiss Alps, as I thought with a smile of the first time Berta and I had seen them, the day we greedily devoured the basket of bread. In Rome, Rosette and I marveled at the Coliseum and the Sistine Chapel, in Florence, the fabled museums. Then back to Amsterdam, where we walked through the small house where Anne Frank hid until the Nazis found her, as I felt the deep hatred for Hitler surge again through my body. I enjoyed most our stay in Paris, where I found a few of my old friends who had returned after the war. They gave me a party one night as Rosette went alone to *Carmen*.

On our return to New York, she slept late each morning, met me for lunch several times a week. In the afternoons she went to a movie, shopped for clothes, or read at home. I let her take a long rest, believing she would look for a job when she was ready. After six months she found work as Varitypist at the General Telephone and Electronics Company.

Manuel and I occasionally wrote each other, though I had given up hope he would visit us. One day I received a letter which made me very sad. He had never been completely well after his prison experience and now, he said, his hands shook so from Parkinson's disease that he had to hold his right hand with his left in order to write, and he could no longer work. He was only forty-eight. He reported that he went to the university clinic twice a year where the doctor prescribed trihexyphenidyl and Tofranil for depression, and that he also had attacks of asthma. He concluded the letter:

"As for my life, I feel I have been swirled around like a pebble in a very turbulent river. I never remarried and have no intention of doing so."

After three months at the General Telephone and Electronics Company, Rosette again felt so depressed that she left. The trip to Europe had whet my appetite for further traveling; I yearned to see whatever relatives were alive in the Soviet Union. I also wanted to visit my mother's grave in Khotin. So on June 1, 1970, as our summer vacation, Rosette and I joined a special tour of the U.S.S.R. First stop, Moscow.

I called my Uncle Mune, the youngest of my grandmother's sixteen children and his father's favorite. He had broken his father's heart by refusing to be a rabbi and had gone to the Soviet Union to write and teach, as my father had done. Uncle Mune had told his father, "You have soaked the blood out of the people of Rishcon and I will have none of it."

I had not seen him in forty years and we hugged each other warmly when he walked into my hotel room. We spent the first night talking nonstop. He described how my grandmother, as the Nazis approached, fled her home with her daughter, son-in-law, and grandchildren, and how the Nazis had captured her, marched her to the banks of the Dniester, and drowned her. I imagined my grandmother's beautiful blue-gray eyes filled with tears of shame as she faced death at the hands of the savages of the twentieth century. Her mansion was now Rishcon's city hall, Uncle Mune said.

I told him, "I want more than anything to return to Khotin to see my mother's grave."

He said, "Don't go back. You will only grieve. The Nazis destroyed the cemetery."

"I guess you're right." I gave up the idea.

Rosette and I flew to Sochi, a resort city in the snow-covered Caucasus mountains bordering the Black Sea, in which we swam. The Russians seemed the friendliest people in the world, asking endless questions about the United States, telling us of their lives.

Because she could not understand the language, Rosette was exceedingly quiet. She said, "Mom, I feel strange. As if I had stepped into another world." At Leningrad we stayed a week in the ultramodern Sovietskaya. The first night, we waited for darkness but at midnight the sky was still light. It was the time of the "white nights of Leningrad" when the sun does not set.

We visited the Hermitage Museum, the converted Winter Palace of Catherine the Great, consisting of over a thousand rooms, saw its many Rembrandts and other masterpieces. The next day the tour scheduled us for Petrodvorets, the summer palace of Catherine the Great, with its fantastic fountains and gardens, restored after the Nazis burned its priceless collections.

In spite of the beauty around us, Rosette became more and more withdrawn. When I spoke to her, she seemed not to hear, I had to repeat every question ten times. I also had to force her to go on the morning tours and to the opera or ballet in the evening. She wanted only to stay by herself in the hotel room. I was worried she might become suicidal again, wondered what I would do so far from home. I asked the clerk if a doctor were available in case of emergency. He said it took only three minutes for an ambulance to arrive, manned by a doctor, and that medical service was free.

I spent the next nights standing by the window, looking out into "whiteness." We were due back in Moscow, where my relatives were gathering from all over, summoned by Uncle Mune to give Rosette and me a royal welcome. I had waited forty years for this chance to meet the survivors of my family, knew I never again would be able to afford such a trip.

But I could not risk the chance of Rosette's getting more deeply depressed and perhaps trying to kill herself. At the end of the week in Leningrad, instead of heading for Moscow, I paid an additional $400 for our fares home via Finland. I called Uncle Mune and explained we had an emergency which forced us to return to the United States.

Everything possible had failed to help Rosette. The insulin shock and electroshock at Central Islip. The weekly visits to a psychiatrist. The daily tranquilizers and pep-up pills. What was left to try?

One last hope remained. Another cousin, a social worker at a private mental hospital, told us of this hospital's special ninety-day treatment program for young men and women. I called, arranged an appointment, and Rosette was accepted by the hospital, located on Long Island not far from Manhattan.

This hospital had a comforting intimacy not found in the massive state hospitals. It was made up of cottages, like the Forest School. Rosette was assigned her own psychiatrist and to group therapy classes. I was asked to attend a group therapy class with other parents twice a week, led by a social worker. When I asked her what Rosette's diagnosis had been, she said Rosette suffered from "anxiety."

I had heard this word before from psychiatrists but never understood exactly what it meant. One book defined it as a "persistent feeling of dread or of impending disaster." This was exactly how Rosette described what she felt. She said psychiatrists would tell her, "You have a lot of anxiety and must *will* yourself to get rid of it and we'll help with the medication." When I screamed at her to use willpower, I was only agreeing with the experts.

At the end of six weeks, the social worker told me the psychiatrists had decided Rosette needed a more prolonged treatment than the ninety days allowed and would keep her there, if necessary, up to a year. They wanted to try a new drug called Prolixin, which they said showed promising results. Rosette was asked to sign a form giving the hospital permission to use the new drug on her but not holding it responsible for any traumatic results.

The Sunday after she signed, when I visited, she told me she was afraid to take the experimental drug. I insisted she give it a chance, remembering her suicide attempts. The next day she ran away from the hospital, turned up at our apartment.

I telephoned Dr. Blau, once again asked for her help. With her usual kindness and concern, she explained to Rosette the importance of giving the psychiatrists a chance. I spent the weekend urging Rosette to return and on Monday morning, as I was about to leave for work, she agreed to go back.

Thanksgiving day she and I monopolized one of the hospital television sets watching *Swan Lake*. The ballet ended after the sun went down. I kissed and hugged her goodbye, walked the few blocks in the snow to the bus stop, thinking how depressed Rosette had seemed, wondering what good this hospital was doing after all. I waited half an hour in the bitter cold, happy to have my $600 mink to keep me warm.

All of a sudden I sensed I was not alone. I turned, saw Rosette. She was wearing only her short-sleeved brown wool dress. Her face was blue from the chill, her eyes held terror.

I asked, "Precious, how long have you been here?" Afraid she might catch pneumonia, I took off my coat to wrap it around her. She refused to put it on.

She said in a low voice, "I followed you when you left. Please take me with you. I'm afraid of this place."

I pleaded, "Please go back, sweetheart. Let me take you back."

"Never!" She seemed determined.

"What shall I do? Oh dear God, what shall I do?" I kept repeating.

The bus came and went as we stood on the deserted street arguing. I said in desperation, "If you'll go back and get your coat, I'll take you home. It's too cold to travel without it."

"I don't trust you," she said. "You'll make them keep me there."

But she followed me as we trudged the few blocks in silence. She insisted on waiting outside the cottage, saying, "You get my coat." She was right, she could not trust me, I had no intention of taking her home.

We argued again and a nurse heard us. She came out of the cottage, said to Rosette, "You must go inside."

"I can't," said Rosette.

The nurse summoned a six-foot male aide. Both of them grabbed Rosette. She fought back. They dragged her along the snow-covered ground by the arms, then into the cottage, as she screamed, "Mama! Mama!"

I stood against a tree and sobbed. I felt like a criminal, rejecting my child when she needed me so desperately. I wanted to follow her, hold her to my heart, tell her how much I loved her. But instead I stood silent in the snow watching the lights in the cottage go out one by one. Then slowly I walked through the gate, away from the hospital, to start the long journey home in the deserted subway, having missed the last bus.

Once in the apartment, I took two sleeping pills but could not fall asleep, still hearing the cry "Mama! Mama!" The cry I heard in Caracas as I left for work every morning, and again in Chicago when I walked away from the nursery.

The next morning exactly at nine as I sat down in my office, the phone rang. It was Rosette. In a low, sad voice she said, "Mother, I think they fractured my arms last night. I'm in terrible pain. Please come and take me to a doctor so I can get them x-rayed."

I looked up to see my boss, a rather severe man, standing near my desk, giving me an angry stare because I engaged in personal matters so early in the day.

I said to him in apology, "This will take only a minute."

When he walked away, I told Rosette, "Sweetheart, please forgive me but I can't talk right now. I'll call you from a public phone at lunchtime and talk with you the whole hour."

I hung up without waiting for her answer. When I called at noon, she said her arms felt better, they were only bruised, but that she intended to run away. I convinced her to stay. I promised she would not have to take Prolixin, knowing the threat of the drug had been terrifying her.

On Christmas day the hospital chef prepared a banquet of turkey and trimmings. The patients all seemed pleased except Rosette, who would not touch her plate, would scarcely talk to me. The next morning she called, insisted, "I must see you today, mother. I'm desperate."

"I'm not allowed to visit during the week, precious," I reminded her.

She burst into tears, hung up. She called back a few minutes later with the same request. Upset and exhausted, I gave in.

"If you are in such agony, Rosette, come home," I said.

That night at nine, she stood at the door. This time no amount of persuasion by Dr. Blau or me could convince her to return. She was certain the psychiatrists were going to use her as a guinea pig and she would die from an overdose of Prolixin.

We spent New Year's Eve together. This time she made no attempt at suicide. But I could tell she was severely depressed. Coming home had solved no problem. The next night, after seeing on television *The Children's Hour,* a film based on Lillian Hellman's famous play about two women teachers accused of lesbianism, Rosette suddenly ran out of the house and into the snow.

I followed but could not find her. Frightened, I called the police. By the time they arrived, she had returned. They took her by ambulance to Beth Israel Hospital. She stayed two weeks, then was discharged.

I asked her to return voluntarily to the hospital where the black attendant had tried to seduce her, figuring by now he had been fired.

The hospital accepted her for two weeks. Then a psychiatrist told me, "We are sending your daughter to Bellevue. We can't help her here."

Nobody had been able to help her anywhere. Something inside me finally fell into place, a peaceful place.

I said calmly, "No more hospitals. Ever. My daughter has taken enough punishment."

Starting at the age of thirteen, she had spent eight years in ten institutions over a span of fourteen years. That was enough. The psychiatrists had their chance.

Now I wanted mine.

IV

The Compromise

Nine years have passed since my moment of decision, years in which I have had much chance to think of what has happened to Rosette's life and to mine.

I gave up my full-time job to devote most of my day to caring for her. I cook for her and stay with her as much as I can. I hold a part-time job two days a week, helping senior citizens. I also work a full day typing and doing research for Rosette's present psychiatrist, Dr. Aylin Radomisli, whom Rosette and I both like very much. Rosette receives a monthly disability payment from social security because she worked seven years. We live very frugally.

Three days a week Rosette and I go to classes at Hunter College, where we are both on scholarships, expecting to get degrees in June, 1980. Rosette is working for her B.A. in Fine Arts and I am working for my M.A. in gerontology, minoring in psychology. For four years I took Rosette to her classes, waited for her in the hallway, then one day thought, As long as I am here, why don't I study for my M.A.?

Most of my money has gone for Rosette's therapy. There have been so many psychiatrists, psychologists, and social workers I have lost track. In order to function, Rosette has had to live on Thorazine. She is supposed to take 100 milligrams a day but sometimes it reached 400 or 500 when she felt very depressed. Since Dr. Blau would not give prescriptions for medication, I took Rosette to a series of psychiatrists, the best I could afford, paying from $35 to $55 a session. They prescribed tranquilizers and handed out advice and diagnoses.

I asked each psychiatrist after ten weeks for an evaluation of Rosette. I took down the exact words in shorthand. Here are some of the opinions:

Dr. A: "Your daughter has suffered from an early childhood trauma and fear of abandonment, maybe an intolerable environment."

Dr. B: "Your daughter has a schizoid personality but she can and should go to work. She does not do things because you do them for her. Why should she give up a good thing that is going for her? She should work and pay for her therapy, so she is motivated."

Dr. C: "I see only neurotics, I do not know how to treat psychotics."

Dr. D: "You and your daughter are locked in a destructive, mutual dependency pattern. You seem unable to break out of it. The heart of your problem is your unwillingness to let her live a life independent of you. Her survival depends on trying to get her to fight for herself, for her right to live. Your daughter gets an unconscious message from you not to be independent."

Dr. E: "Rosette will never get better."

Dr. F: "Rosette is *not* psychotic, not delusional. She is very angry and frightened, fearful of going out by herself. She will not lose control, will not hurt anyone. She has low self-esteem, thinks little of herself. She must learn to trust herself. She gets a lot out of acting like a little girl, unable to cope without mother. She lives through you, she does not have her own motivation."

Dr. G: "You two have a symbiotic relation. You tell her what to do, what to wear, what to eat, what to listen to. She can't do anything by herself. When you die, she won't be able to take care of herself and will have to be committed to a hospital."

One psychiatrist told Rosette he did not wish to see her because she lacked the "motivation" to get well. I thought, If a patient lacks "motivation," should not the psychiatrist try to find out why and help the patient become motivated?

A question haunts me. Could it have been different if Rosette had never been sent away from home but given help in the community by someone who would have reached her deeper conflicts as, at the same time, I also received help? Did I let the wrong people tell me what to do?

When you have little money, your choice is limited in many things. When you are both poor and mentally troubled, you do not get the best kind of help. I don't want to use this as an excuse for what happened to Rosette, but it is a fact that both private psychiatric hospitals and the psychoanalyst's couch were beyond my reach. Rosette had to endure the indignities of the state mental hospital system once she got caught up in the institutional world. I will never understand why the richest country on earth inflicts such pain, such humiliation, such death blows to pride through its mental hospitals.

One question I ask out of torment: Should an adolescent be sent to an adult mental hospital? When I asked a resident at Rockland State, "How could they have sent my child here?" he said, "She needs hospitalization for her own protection. She has to learn right from wrong. She seems to form the wrong kind of friendships." What kind of answer is that?

I shall never recover from the grief I felt on her sixteenth birthday, spent at Rockland. I had dreamed for years how we would celebrate the start of her "sweet sixteen" year. Instead of a joyous party in her home, Victor and I took ice cream, cake, cookies, wine, and a tablecloth to the state hospital, set up a table on the grounds, and invited some of the other patients and nurses as guests. It was a travesty of what should have been a memorable day in the life of my daughter who, a few years before, had been voted by her classmates as "the most likely to succeed."

Four years later, as I left her at Central Islip, that forbidding institution for the mentally damned, her words rang in my ears like a Greek chorus, words that resound even louder today: "Mother, I don't belong here. I'm not crazy. Why are you forcing me into this hideous place? Will you *ever* understand me?"

And then, staring at me: "I wish I had tears to cry."

At that moment I had no tears either. I looked into her flowerlike face, saw the stricken look in those luminous black eyes, and wondered, Does she really need *another* hospitalization? Wouldn't it be wiser to take her home, give her all my love as cure? But the authorities said no. And I trusted them.

There were many things against me besides lack of money and ignorance. There was no one close to whom I could turn for guidance. I felt alone, as I have always felt alone since the day my mother killed herself and I had to begin surviving by my wits. This feeling of aloneness has never left me and I do not expect it will.

I had to trust the authorities even as I raged at myself for my fear of psychiatrists and social workers. It was a fear that kept me from putting up a fight for Rosette's freedom. I felt more and more helpless, more and more guilty, as I blindly obeyed the orders and rules set by the experts. I felt like the prisoner in Kafka's *The Trial* who did not know the crime of which he was accused.

I often wondered whether the psychiatrists in charge were too young and inexperienced, whether their diagnoses and decisions might not occasionally be wrong. I realize we cannot expect psychiatrists to be God but at the very least we should expect them to show some compassion for tormented human beings, as well as some knowledge of the causes of emotional suffering.

There is no greater fear than losing the mind. I know. I have lived for many years with that fear because of my daughter's condition. As I look back at my life I even wonder, Was I psychotic at times? What *was* my state of mind? What would *I* have been labeled?

I loathe labels. Maybe they help the psychiatrists but they are very destructive to patients, who carry with them forever the stigma of the label even if they recover or, as has happened, the psychiatrist is wrong in his diagnosis. When psychiatrists call a person "psychotic" or "schizophrenic" he is apt to believe he will always be "crazy," that there is no hope for sanity.

And of course I have been deeply tormented by the question of my responsibility in my child's illness. So many of the social workers and psychiatrists have blamed me. Miss Hess told me, "You are the cause of your child's sickness, your presence brings on her depression, rebellion, withdrawal, and acting out."

When I grew up in Khotin, the people spoke of living in fear of the "evil eye" and at times I wonder if I might have turned the "evil eye" on Rosette and somehow caused her illness.

Can you give someone *too much* love? I love Rosette more than anyone else in the world. I believe I love her more than any parent ever loved a child. I could not live one single day without her. She is my best and only friend. I must know at all times of the day and night what she is doing. Even what she is thinking.

I have a terrible fear of losing her. Like the fear that seized me when I took Berta to Rio, holding her hand to make sure she would not fall over the side of the ship, sleeping close to her in the tiny bunk so she would not wander off. When Rosette and I left Caracas by plane, we could have traveled by ship for much less money but I was afraid she might somehow leave me and fall into the ocean.

Rosette and I have lived through despair, fear, and helplessness, neither of us knowing what to do, in which direction to turn. But we also have enjoyed many peaceful, companionate hours. Months go by as we live in harmony. We visit museums, attend the theater, opera, and ballet if she feels up to it. She still suffers occasional delusions but most of the time is reasonable, affable, quiet, affectionate. She becomes withdrawn if she feels anxious, if something upsets her or just before her menstrual period.

Our relationship is a warm, loving one. Sometimes we hug and kiss each other twenty times a day. Or lie close on the couch for a few moments of tenderness as a deep love for her envelops me.

I am convinced she belongs with me. When she was first taken from me and sent to Forest School, she went through a dramatic change of personality, became wild and abandoned. Most of the time she has lived with me, she has been meek and kind, not self-destructive or destructive to others. She was always an obedient, compliant little girl, a quiet, shy child, according to her teachers and camp counselors. In the classroom she rarely volunteered her thoughts.

There are times I feel the net of fear draw more tightly around her. I cry for her pain, her sadness, her suffering, the years of misery in institutions. But I too suffered during those agonizing years. The sleepless nights, running to the door every time I heard a noise, thinking it might be her once more desperately fleeing an institution. Not knowing whether she was dead or alive when the school reported her missing. Wondering if she would ever speak to me again after I forced her to remain in a place she hated.

Once I wrote her after an argument: "How I love you, my poor darling. What can I do to make you well? I would give a thousand times my life to see you happy, my dearest. I shall never give up and as long as there is a breath in me, I shall be at your side and love you and try to be of some help to you."

Sometimes as she listens to a symphony, her face softens in pleasure and I think how much her father missed, not knowing her. He was never aware of her suffering, for I wrote only what a lovable child, then young woman, she was. Many times I have regretted leaving Manuel, realize I did not act wisely in taking a small child to a strange country, expecting to rebuild my life.

I had been irresponsible and unrealistic in removing Rosette from her father, from the country where she was born, to travel thousands of miles to the home of a neurotic aunt who did not keep her promise to help us. I was a dreamer like my father. If I had known what was going to happen to Rosette, if I had only stayed with Manuel—if, if. But you cannot build your life on "ifs." You must eventually face what you have done.

I was impractical about many things. When the Chicago judge, granting me a divorce, asked whether I wanted alimony or child support, I said, "I don't need it." I am sure, if I had insisted, Manuel would somehow have managed to send something regularly for Rosette's care—a matter of pride with him. But I was naïve. Nor was I wise about my American relatives. When I arrived in the United States, I could have asked my father's two millionaire brothers for help but I was too proud.

If I stood before a judge, I would put myself in jail for the many mistakes I made along the way. I cannot forgive myself, as I have said, for blindly listening to psychiatrists, psychologists, and social workers who made me feel so guilty I allowed them to do as they wished, even though I sensed it was not best for Rosette or me. When I realize what my child went through at the hands of authorities in command of children's lives, authorities who sometimes act in their own selfish interest, if I were a judge I would convict them too.

For they abused her. Are not sixty-two insulin shock treatments and six electroshock treatments like sixty-eight beatings? I wrote her at Central Islip that I knew how much she suffered during the ordeal of the shocks and wished I could make it up to her but it was not in my power to design a happy world for her, parents were often powerless, there was a limit to how much they could protect their children. I said it was up to her to make her life a creative and constructive one.

And what of the pounds and pounds of drugs that have poured into her frail body? Are they not also beatings of the mind and physical system? She has added forty pounds, is no longer petite, and her face has lost its fragility.

I wish our story had a happy ending, though it could have been far unhappier. At least Rosette and I are alive and still hope she may be helped. I doubt either of us will ever marry. I could have thought only of my future, allowed my once-spirited, brilliant child to turn into a depressed, aging woman who would spend her life in institutions, given up as hopeless. But I decided this would not be her fate even if I could do no better with her.

Dr. Blau had faith in Rosette, told her she was gifted, that if she could separate from me emotionally she could more fully use her creative gifts. The sessions with Dr. Blau were the only real therapy Rosette received. She told me she was afraid to reveal her feelings to the overworked psychiatrists in hospitals who rushed from one patient to the next, whom she saw perhaps a few minutes a week or every other week. Her psychiatrists changed from month to month except for Dr. Blau, who remained in the picture on and off for twenty-one years.

I know what courage it has taken Rosette to study for her B.A. and to function at times without help from me. A young girl at Rockland, when I asked, "How are you?" had replied, "I feel as if I am in purgatory," and I realize this is how Rosette sometimes feels.

She can go to the store by herself for groceries but she cannot travel long distances alone. She is dependent on me for her very being. She cannot exist by herself for long. She is nervous on her own, wants me with her most of the time. Even now there are nights she crawls into bed with me, saying, "If you don't sleep with me, I'll die." Or insists I sleep in her bed.

One night when she was sleeping with me she woke from a nightmare screaming, "The Martians are after me!" Sometimes she insists I sleep with her for a week at a time until she loses her fear of whatever is frightening her, real or unreal. If, in the middle of the night, I slip away to my room, she is apt to call out, sensing I have left, "Mom, come here," and I return.

One night I woke to find her standing at the foot of my bed shrieking as if wounded. "What's the matter, Rosette?" I said in alarm.

"For a minute I thought your bed was empty and I felt blinded," she said.

There are times she feels either complete attachment like a helpless baby, or wishes to be utterly isolated—either feels merged with me or orders, "Leave me alone." Dr. Blau said one of the goals of Rosette's therapy was to enable her to separate emotionally from me. Once I asked why Rosette did not achieve this independence over the years. Dr. Blau said critically, "It is the duty of parents to help their children grow up and become independent."

But how can I do this? No therapist as yet has helped me solve this problem. I evidently tie Rosette to me without meaning to. If I have hurt her, it is not willfully but because I do not know what I do.

Victor would say, "Let Rosette talk for herself. Don't answer for her." Sometimes I did not let her finish a sentence, cut in, and spoke for her as though we were one mind. Often it seems there *is* mental telepathy between us. If my fingers ache, she will ask, "Mother, does your arthritis hurt?" before I have had the chance to mention it. Is there anything wrong in such empathy?

Our closeness has led to freedom in conversation. Rosette has always felt she can talk to me about sex, for instance. I have very strict morals but I am for love, the love described by Shakespeare and Tolstoy, a far cry from today's obscene pornography in art, movies, and books. I believe in decent, true love—the motherly love I feel for Rosette, the pure love and friendship I had for my husband, the admiration and respect I felt for Victor. There have been only those two men in my life. Rosette loved one man, Alfredo, perhaps in part because he looked like her father.

She tells me she has sexual difficulties, that she is afraid of men. I say, "I also had difficulties when I was young. I have always been particular who I would consider letting into my bed."

"I feel the same way," she says. "There was a time I wasn't so particular but now I am."

I point out to her a woman must know how to stay young and beau-

tiful because men are funny animals. They forget the love they once
held for a woman and turn to younger ones, as my father did.

I know I have been strict with Rosette as I have tried to give her
values and goals, telling her not to be a parasite like so many others
are, that she must learn responsibility for herself, the way I have. I
told her, "My grandmother was never in a bar. My mother was never
in a bar. I have never been in a bar. And you are not to go to a bar." I
did not want her to be wild, like some of her friends. I was proud of
her because she did not haunt the bars or become involved with married men.

Once she told me she did not want to continue with a particular psychiatrist and when I asked why, she said, "Because he does not listen
when I talk about sex."

"I thought psychiatrists were especially interested in sex problems," I said.

"Not this one," she said. "He seems embarrassed."

What torments me the most are my sudden flashes of anger. They
do not happen often but when they occur, Rosette is the one to be
hurt. She has only me to depend on for love and she cannot—dare
not—fight me for fear of losing that love. The times I go out of control
she seems to sink into a state of catatonia, deadening all feelings. I
would rather hurt myself a thousand times than hurt her once but
sometimes I am unable to stop losing my temper. It is a sickness and I
hope in my lifetime to be able to conquer it. I have told every therapist
I must learn to control my temper.

There have been times I screamed at her like a madwoman as something within flamed up when she opposed me or acted as though I
were not there. I felt assaulted and reacted with rage, as if she had
struck me. The rage blinded me, cut off all control, and words of fury
flew at her.

Why? Why? Why do I hurt the one I love most? I wish I had an
even temperament, calm, understanding, and gentle. One psychiatrist
asked what I expected of him and I said, "I want to be helped to
reach a stage where I will *never* get angry at Rosette. I want to know
what causes my anger. I even want Rosette to help me by telling me,
when I get angry at her, not to let my feelings go, that I will only
be sorry."

Always, after the anger, I feel guilty and apologize. I draw her close in love, tell her she is my angel, my precious, my sweetheart, my dearest. The woman psychologist I now see once a week warns, "As long as you feel guilty, Mrs. Spinoza, Rosette cannot become independent. Because she knows you do things for her out of guilt, not love."

In the past twenty-five years, but particularly in the last nine when we have been together, I have made hundreds of resolutions to hold my tongue no matter what she says or does. I keep the resolution a few months, then utter a criticism, or a shout, or an accusation that she has ruined my life, which to a certain degree is true. I have accused her of being cruel to her hard-working mother. I *have* been hard-working ever since I was eleven—over fifty years without a stop, six days a week, sometimes eighteen hours a day. But I do not regret working so hard, it made me responsible and mature. I am only sorry I never found work that allowed me to express myself creatively.

But I wonder whether any psychiatrist, even Freud, could understand what it is like to live with an emotionally ill person who, as though physically paralyzed, sometimes refuses to move. I ask Rosette to help around the house or return a book to the library, and she will say, "I *can't*." And there is no way to change her mind. Maybe she really can't, maybe she does not have the inner strength to empty an ashtray or lift a hanger and put it in the closet with her dress on it.

It is hard for me to live with her occasional apathy, her aloofness. Her flatness, her lack of joy. Her distorted perceptions and poor motivation except as I provide it.

My day is very disciplined. Each morning I wake at four, my mind most active at this hour. I read or study for my classes. Then, as they come on I listen to the news programs on the television set in the kitchen, whose picture tube has been long broken, as I clean house or sew. Three days a week I leave at eight with Rosette for Hunter, an hour and a half each way by bus.

Often I switch on the radio at 5:30 A.M. to listen to WQXR and the words "Every day is a fresh beginning. Every morn is the world made new." I hope this day I will start anew and be patient with my beloved daughter. I repeat to myself the thought of General Kutusov in *War and Peace:* "Time and patience, patience and time."

Sometimes Rosette moves very slowly or refuses to move. Even as a child, she ate and dressed more lethargically than other children. I do not know whether she is naturally slow, or acts in rebellion against my pushing her, or has a calm disposition like her father's, or is slowed down by the medication, or her fantasies. But her inertia drives me crazy. I think, Let's go! Let's go! and she pulls me to a dead stop.

I *need* an orderly house. I must have method and neatness. I get furious if she leaves her clothes strewn around. There are always ashes for she has smoked three packs of cigarettes a day since she was fourteen. She drinks four or more cups of coffee, double strength, and several Cokes daily. I worry because, what with the Thorazine, I fear she will not be able to do her homework.

The four days we do not go to Hunter, Rosette wakes at eight or nine and we eat breakfast, plan the day's activities. She is thirty-seven and every night I thank God we are together, that she is not confined in some archaic mental hospital. I know she is a battered child—person now—battered by life and sometimes verbally by me. I cannot shield her from a reality that includes pain as well as pleasure, some of the pain inevitably inflicted by the mother who must discipline her child into being civilized.

Often I give in to her. One night after I begged her, she agreed to go to *The Sleeping Beauty,* danced by Fonteyn and Nureyev. But as soon as we arrived at the Metropolitan Opera House, she demanded I take her home by taxi. I did not plead with her to stay, fearing a scene in front of hundreds of elegantly dressed men and woman, so I hailed a taxi.

But another time I was not so understanding. We spent the morning at the Metropolitan Museum of Art, then went to the restaurant by the indoor pool. Rosette refused to eat. Then I saw her slip a chocolate cookie she had brought with her into her mouth. I was enraged because she had been complaining of fainting spells from diabetes, from which she suffers.

I screamed, "I'd rather have died in a concentration camp than endure what I am living through with you!" At that moment I felt, as in Genesis 4:13, "My punishment is greater than I can bear."

She looked at me startled, as if she were going to cry. And I felt guilty, remembered Dr. Blau once called me "venomous."

Another day as we sat in this restaurant, she nagged me to buy a print of *Portrait of a Young Princess, Margaret of Austria,* by an unknown Austrian artist of the late 15th century, part of the new Robert Lehman Collection. It cost sixteen dollars and I reminded her, "Rosette, we have several prints of that painting at home. Don't waste money on another."

I left her for a moment to refill my cup of coffee. When I returned, I discovered she had disappeared and my purse lay open on the table. She had taken money from it. She came back in a few minutes with a print of *The Little Princess* purchased in the museum shop.

I said in quiet fury, "Why didn't you listen to me?"

She looked at me with a shamed smile, said nothing.

I hissed, anger beyond control, "Why don't you just die? I haven't had a good day since you were born. Why don't you swallow that whole bottle of Thorazine tonight?" As a small voice inside reminded me my mother had once hurled the words at me, "I wish you were dead!"

I stood up, took the print to the shop, explained we had several at home, got back my money, which we needed for necessities. When I returned, Rosette said calmly, "You were right, mom, you were right."

But she was silent for a week, sat on the sofa smoking continuously, listening to music. She refused to eat until she became starved late at night. When I saw her psychiatrist and told her of the incident, she said, "Rosette feels very guilty." I thought, *I make her feel guilty, I use her guilt to force her to obey,* and did not like myself for doing this to my child.

Another day I asked her for the twentieth time to vacuum the living room while I went shopping. When I returned laden with groceries, I found her chain-smoking on the sofa, playing with her cat. I flew into a rage, screamed, "You are killing me, you parasite!"

Tears came to her eyes. Then she laughed, a soft, cacklelike laugh that she emits when she is anxious. I saw in her eyes she could not handle any more anger from me and kept quiet. For days after, she said not a word, smoked constantly, did not want to or *could not* do anything around the house.

When I told one psychologist that my mother would sometimes scream at me, "May your children do to you what you are doing to me!''—a typical Jewish expression in Bessarabia—he said, ''You provoke Rosette into being bad so that your mother's words will come true because you felt guilty as a child and must inflict this on your self as punishment.''

It is not easy for either of us. For instance, the weekend of July 4, 1972, we spent in the apartment. I knew Rosette was temporarily in a world of fantasy because she was writing notes to imaginary people. She told me that until she felt well, I was not allowed to touch her or to kiss her. On the fourth of July at 6 P.M. she became angry at me and locked herself in my room. I watched the news on television, then ate. When I opened the door to my room at 8 P.M. she was asleep.

The next morning she woke me at 7 A.M. to tell me a dream in which she won a box of animal toys. She became angry because I looked out the kitchen window. She again locked herself in my room and when I opened the door she screamed, ''Leave the room!'' I went shopping and when I came back she was in the kitchen. She put away the groceries and we ate and listened to records.

A few days later she told me she would go to Dr. Blau's office only if I called a taxi, took her, and came home by taxi. I begged her to take the bus at least one way because we needed the money for necessities. She refused to leave the house. I became so nervous I yelled, ''Murderer! What do you want from me? I cannot take it anymore. I will swallow the whole bottle of Thorazine while you are asleep and when you wake up, you will shake me and shake me but I will be dead!'' She still refused to go except by taxi both ways. I gave in and we caught a taxi uptown, then she agreed to come home by bus. The therapy helped her feel more reasonable.

The next day she said, ''I didn't believe you yesterday when you called me a murderer, because you were not yourself.'' Tears came to my eyes and I apologized. I assured her she was a gifted, beautiful person, that every day I was more amazed at her intelligence and clarity of mind when we talked about politics and life in general. But for several days she would not let me hug her, kiss her, or touch her.

Once I screamed at her when she refused to help around the house, ''You are garbage!''

She said quietly, ''I am not garbage.''

I thought, Oh God, why do I say such things, I am destroying her.

What comes over me? Why do I explode against my will? Why isn't "will" a stronger thing?

I wrote her after my first visit to a psychologist. I said: "Whether he will be able to help loosen up this state of complete amnesia I get when I am angry at you and sometimes other people, I don't know, but we will both try to see what causes this anger. I love you so much, I hate myself for hurting you, but I cannot help myself. It is a sickness within me. I know just how much harm I have caused you, my poor darling, how scared you were of me when you were very young and how much I would upset you. Even Berta suffered from my anger when she was a child, when she visited us the first time in Chicago and when I was in Brazil. In this I am like Fanny."

After my outbursts Rosette usually sits quietly, does not move, looks at me with those beautiful, black eyes, smokes nervously, one cigarette after another. Slowly I get hold of myself, start to cry, and apologize, "Rosette, please forgive me, sweetheart. I know I am destroying you. I make you nervous, guilty, sick. I create a terrible anxiety in which you have to live." All the words I heard over the years from psychologists, psychiatrists and social workers.

One time we discussed the Nazi atrocities. She recalled a photograph of a little Jewish boy who held his arms high, waving a courageous goodbye as he was marched off to a concentration camp. She started to cry. She sobbed as if she would never stop. I had never seen her cry so heartbreakingly.

The following week she spent either in her bedroom with the Venetian blinds lowered or in the kitchen. She imagined that in nine days she would get an electroshock treatment and the "monsters" would leave her body. She said she did not want to tell such a fantasy to Dr. Blau because "she will think I am crazy and commit me." I assured her Dr. Blau would never do this.

So at her next session she told Dr. Blau that for a long time she had felt there were monsters inside her, strange people who tormented her. Dr. Blau said this meant she felt she was "bad" but attributed the badness to monsters within. Rosette also told Dr. Blau she read that compulsive personalities had deep fear of an impending evil, which was really death, and added, "I have a fear of impending catastrophe." Then she came home and told me she remembered from childhood that I would sometimes say to her, "Why were you born?" or "I wish I were dead" or "I wish you were dead."

At her next session, which I attended, as I sometimes now did, she told Dr. Blau, "I have to find out why I am sick, why I am afraid of certain things." Then she said, "I feel guilty that I never repaid my mother for all she has done for me, even though she tells me it was a pleasure." She also recalled that when she was fifteen and pubic hair started to grow, she was terribly upset and ever since had thought she was ugly.

The next day she remained in her room, telling me she wanted to be by herself. Later I assured her I loved her and she said, "I don't feel it. Don't say it, prove it. Actions speak louder than words." She would not let me kiss her.

One winter we flew to Florida for a short vacation, arriving in a driving rain at the condominium of a friend who offered us her home for two weeks. It was a large apartment on the twelfth floor. The sixth day Rosette said, "Mother, I have a compulsion to jump off the balcony. I feel someone just died in this room."

"Let's go home." I did not want to risk another suicide attempt.

"I won't fly," she insisted. "I'll only take the train." She had a deep fear of going up in the air.

After we arrived home exhausted from the long train ride, Rosette called Dr. Blau long distance twice, talking about how depressed she felt. Dr. Blau had closed her New York office but accepted calls at her home from Rosette. When Rosette hung up, she was still depressed.

She said, "I just heard the voice of a girl, someone like me, who said, 'I wish I had someone else for a mother.' "

"It is you who wants another mother," I said.

That night she was very angry. In one of her rare outbursts she said, "You are a bitch. A horrible person! A hypocrite!"

I wondered what set off the rage. The next morning she apologized, "I didn't mean it, mom."

Later, as we sat in the living room she said, "I wish you were an alcoholic, then I could be an alcoholic too." She was telling me, like mother, like daughter.

I went shopping, when I returned she said she had thought of calling Berta to tell her I had turned into an alcoholic.

"You must not do that!" I was furious. "How can you tell such a lie? What are you trying to do to me?"

A few nights after, she left the house hurriedly and before I could find her had spent $180 at a travel agency for two tickets to Miami. When she told me, I shouted, "How can you bleed me this way?"

Another evening she was playing a record of *Anitra's Dance* by Grieg, her favorite composer, so loudly that I turned the hi-fi lower. She screamed, "I'll kill you!" And once when I asked her to clean up her room, she muttered, "Why are you such a curse?"

She has shouted at me, "You hate me and want me to die!" She showed her death wishes toward her cat, Twinkle III (we have had three Twinkles and a kitten, Violet). Late one night she suddenly put on her coat. I asked, "Where are you going?"

"To buy the TV Guide," she said.

"The store's been closed for hours." I knew she was lying.

I noticed she was carrying a shoebox with Twinkle in it. I asked, "What are you going to do with the cat?"

"I have to get rid of him," she said. "I have a feeling I might cut off his head and set him on fire."

"Give him to me."

I took Twinkle to the laundry room in the basement, left him there in the box. When I got back to the apartment, Rosette had swallowed 400 milligrams of Thorazine and fallen asleep. In the morning she asked, "Where is Twinkle?"

"I left him in the basement last night," I said.

"Thank you for being so understanding, mom," she said. "When I went into the bathroom, his litter box upset me."

It was snowing and as I looked out the window I thought of Twinkle perhaps frozen to death in the snow. I went to look for him. When I returned I found Rosette also had been out. She said she scoured the neighborhood, adding, "I was crying inside for him." After the evening guard came on duty, I asked if he had seen Twinkle. He said the night porter had taken the cat home but brought him back in the morning because his wife refused to keep him. I ran to the storage room and there was Twinkle. I picked him up, hugged him, though he looked very dirty, as though he had been playing in ashes, and brought him back home.

There are moments I wish I had never left Khotin. When the Nazis marched in I would have fled to Siberia along with some of my relatives, returning when the Russians freed Romania.

I wish, too, since I am wishing, that I had been born a boy. Early in life I realized it was a man's world and I would have it easier if I were a boy. Women suffer far more than men, as I have seen in my own family. I have often thought what a different life I would have led if I had been a man.

There are also times I wish I were dead. When a ship of immigrants sank off the shores of South America not far from where they were to disembark, I imagined I were on it, all burdens finally lifted. No more anguish, no more anger.

All the books and articles today about psychology say it is important to express anger when you feel it, or at least be aware of the anger. Especially anger at the person who originally caused it—your mother. But the Jewish culture in which I grew up believed the mother was the soul of the family. I thought my mother a saint. The memory of her goodness and patience has given me strength throughout life. Her love has been my greatest inspiration. I do not blame her for my unhappiness. I feel I am master of my fate. The emotional damage my mother did to me by killing herself is long gone. I could not honor my daughter more than naming her after my mother.

I understand the tragedy in my mother's life. Even as I wish she had not left Berta and me homeless, I know she could no longer face life. I could never desert *my* daughter in such a drastic way. My dedicated life has proved just the opposite.

If there is anyone at whom I am furious it is Aunt Fanny, who died several years ago of cancer. When Rosette and I first came to this country at Aunt Fanny's urging, after all my family did for her in Khotin she could have temporarily provided a home and security for my child while I worked and saved us both deep suffering. But Aunt Fanny was too selfish to give us a thought.

My dream in life was to carry out my mother's dying wish and get an education, to be like her in that respect, as well as like my intellectual father. Maybe I have stressed too much the importance of an education. But I believe no person can be complete without a formal education, no matter how intelligent. Also that education does not end with a Ph.D. Every evening before I lie down to sleep I ask, "Did I learn anything today?" A day in which I learn nothing is a day wasted. This philosophy caused me to push Rosette and she responded with a school phobia, as though telling me, "Stop, I can bear no more!" I struck and humiliated her in front of her friends when she refused to go to school. I did not allow her to make mistakes. I expected her to be the perfect little creature I never was. She felt she had to be a success to be loved and accepted by me.

I cry when I think how I handled the crucial early years of my daughter's life. She thought she failed herself but I failed her. So did her teachers and the social workers who tried to help. She did not get the encouragement that would have given her the strength to continue school, to accept her mixed feelings about the relationship between Victor and me, and Victor and herself, as he tried to become the father she never had.

Now I do not have Victor or anyone else. I do not think I have one friend in the world. Not even Berta. She wrote recently, with her customary honesty: "You really don't like me and Rosette despises us because we are failures. As both of us have so many problems, we could never live together. I'll live in Brazil and you don't like it here so you live in the USA and we'll see each other occasionally. We'll go on being very close sisters but at a distance."

When I first moved to our apartment in Brighton Beach, I decided to make lasting friendships, for I have always enjoyed many friends. I met several young women at work, school, and lectures and invited them to our home for Saturday night dinners. They seemed to like visiting us, after eating we would go to the boardwalk, sit, and talk as we gazed out at the ocean. I had two close friendships that lasted many years—until Rosette started her trips to institutions.

Then my two friends, who had no children, grew distant. When they called, they asked the inevitable question, "How is Rosette?" I always told the truth. I sensed they were getting impatient at asking and listening.

When we moved to Manhattan, the two women still came for dinner. I would cook and bake all day, happy to entertain them. But after a while they started to make excuses for turning down my invitations. These were women who had done well for themselves. European like myself—one was Viennese—they also finished their education. One became a social worker, the other a college professor. As their status went up, so did their financial position. We were no longer in the same economic class. Our very moods seemed different—they were successes, I was a failure.

One day I asked my professorial friend, "Why do you never call me? Why is it I always call you?"

She said, "It's too depressing to hear about your life."

I never phoned her again, nor did she get in touch with me.

Today I have a few superficial friends, the only thing in common that our children are mentally ill. We call each other and talk only about the children and the inadequacies of the therapeutic profession and discuss the possible psychiatric treatment of the future. All of these friends, whether rich or poor, are very unhappy. People in all walks of life suffer when a child is mentally ill.

My thoughts are all of Rosette. In the quiet of night, as I lie in the dark, I ask, Child, can you forgive me? I have pushed you, shamed you, accused you, called you parasite, lazy, bad, spoiled, garbage. I have never been able to understand you, know what was going on inside you, though I have tried desperately.

I let them take you away from me at a time you were so very vulnerable. There was no one to come to your defense, to say there were other, better ways to help us both.

I cannot forgive myself for what I have done. One of the lessons I have learned is that when something goes wrong with a child it is the fault of the parent. Not enough love, not enough compassion, not enough wisdom. I believe parents who cannot give love, who are not mature enough to guide their children, should not have children.

If I had to sum up in one phrase how I have felt all these tormented years I would say, "I suffer an indescribable guilt." Every day of my life has held dreadful guilt, especially since Rosette became ill.

I feel guilty because I have hurt all those I loved most. The guilt started when my mother committed suicide. I have thought all these years that if only I had been sympathetic to her the night before she took poison, when she sat on my bed and tried to hug and kiss me, perhaps she would not have swallowed it.

When my father died at the hands of the Nazis, gassed at

Auschwitz, I felt guilty. Not only did I leave Paris without saying goodbye but I neglected somehow to have borrowed money, as other daughters did, to give to the Nazis to save his life. I have lived with this corroding guilt over the haunted years.

I also felt guilty about never writing to my grandmother after I left Rishcon for Brazil. I promised faithfully to let her know what happened to me. But I was so overwhelmed by the hardship of earning a living I did not write anyone in the family. Not a single letter. When I heard my grandmother had been drowned in the Dniester, I could hardly bear the guilt at not having written her after all she did for me.

I feel I destroy everything I touch. My own life, that of my husband who loved me, and Rosette's. She is my deepest guilt.

I wish more than anything else I could relieve her suffering. There is a saying in Portuguese, "O gosto de sofrer que tanto me diverte"— the pleasure of suffering which amuses me so much—that implies we take pleasure in our suffering. But I grieve over Rosette's suffering, her struggles, her lonely anguish. As I have always grieved for every suffering human being. Troubled by the injustices of the world I cannot bear the injustices to which Rosette has been subjected—by both society and me.

I want her to be happy, not just drag through the days. If God himself were to put before me all the children of the universe and tell me to choose a daughter or a son, I would still choose Rosette because even though I do not know exactly what a *soul* is, I am convinced she has a beautiful one.

I am not religious but I pray every night to God for Rosette's sake, hoping He will somehow help her get better, as well as help me understand her more.

I cry inside much of the time, though tears do not flow. Tears that seem copious enough to fill the Dniester as it sweeps toward the Black Sea.

II

Rosette

I

Life with Mother

I have a recurring, terrifying nightmare.

I dream it is a cold, rainy day in a small town and the radio announces a savage tiger has escaped from the zoo and is loose on the streets. Everyone is warned to keep doors and windows locked, stay inside.

But one cruel woman orders her young daughter to go to the bakery and buy bread. The little girl cries and says she is afraid to leave the house. The mother insists. She pushes the little girl out of the house.

When the little girl arrives at the store, the baker says in surprise, "Haven't you heard there's a ferocious tiger on the loose? What are you doing here? Run home as fast as you can."

The little girl runs home and knocks at the door. Without opening it, the mother calls, "Have you brought the bread?"

"No, mommie, the baker told me to run home as fast as I could because it's dangerous to be out," the little girl says, tears coming to her eyes.

"Go back and buy the bread!" the mother orders from behind the closed door.

Suddenly the mother hears the snarls of a wild animal and the shrieks of a child. Then the mother sees a stream of blood flow under the door from the spot where the little girl stood.

Who is the tiger? Is it my mother or myself?

When I was nine years old I saw a movie thriller in which a black panther escaped from the zoo. Several bodies were then found mauled to death, including that of a girl on her way to meet a lover in a cemetery. There was a shot of her looking up at a tree. The next shot showed her murdered, mangled body.

After I took a Rorschach test, the psychologist asked, "If you had to murder someone, who would you murder?"

My mind went blank. I did not know what to say.

My trouble is that I have never been able to please my mother. I have tried very hard to become what she wanted—an educated, artistic person. I made a good start but then something—I don't know what—interfered.

I became a truant, what they called a "bad" girl. I was sent away to institutions to be "straightened out." But instead of becoming like other people, I felt more threatened, more anxious. I imagined terrors that were not real and heard voices that had no bodies speak to me.

My first memory, at the age of three, is of lying in a large crib in Caracas where it is warm all year. The room around my crib is dark. I hear strange sounds floating in from the next room and I am afraid.

The door opens and light streams into the blackness. I see my father. He is tall and dark. He comes over to the crib, picks me up, holds me to him. Then he puts me down, walks out of the room, and closes the door.

Now lying in the darkness I do not feel threatened. The sounds from the other room seem like laughter.

My mother told me she never looked at traffic lights before crossing a Caracas thoroughfare, not caring what happened to her, until she learned she was pregnant. After that she looked up at the traffic light very carefully.

Two weeks before I was born, my mother went to the hospital on the advice of her doctor because she was suffering internal difficulties connected to her bladder. A pregnant woman who had just recovered from the measles entered the hospital. This alarmed my mother. She insisted my father buy a bassinet to be kept by her bed so I would not be put in the nursery with the other babies and exposed to a contagious disease.

The obstetrician told my mother I was the most beautiful baby he had ever seen. He dubbed me "little Jenny" and took me from room to room to show me off.

My mother tells me I was four months old when I lifted my head at the sound of my name and only eight months when I said mama and papa. When I was twelve months I held a crayon in my fingers like an adult. This, she believed, was indicative of the artist I was to become. It prompted her to proclaim me a child prodigy.

But by thirteen months I had made no effort to walk. Then one evening my father brought home a pink rocking chair he had built for me. As I saw him at one end of our patio, holding the pink chair, I stood up and ran to him. From then on I had trouble sitting still, mother said.

I vaguely remember, when I was three, a torrential rainstorm. Our little house, near a river, was the first to be flooded. Mother wrapped me in a blanket and with Maria, our Indian nurse, set out for higher ground. Leaving Maria and me high on a hill, she returned to the house, then almost inundated, and piled everything not nailed down, on top of tables and bookcases. Hours later the swollen waters receded. My mother had managed to save almost all our possessions.

One day, not long after, I sat on my father's lap in a limousine that took us to the Caracas airport. That was the last time I saw my father. He wrote mother that after the memory of our leaving had become a blur, he still missed us painfully.

I found myself in a strange, cold country, boarded out in a nursery where no one spoke my language, Spanish. My mother vanished during the week. I had never been separated from her for such a long time and felt completely alone in the world. I thought I had lost her love, wondered what bad thing I had done to deserve such cruel punishment.

I fell ill with chickenpox and was quarantined in a room all by myself, taken out of the dormitory where I slept with eight other children. This isolation made me feel I was going to die, that everyone had forsaken me. I felt better when a few of the other children caught chickenpox because then I had company.

On weekends mother came for me and took me to her porch room. It was so cold in winter she used the parlor rug as a second blanket. I hated leaving her Monday mornings and would cry when she carried me back to the nursery.

One weekday evening as I lay in bed, I felt a kiss on my cheek. It was my mother. A few seconds later I saw her framed in the light of the doorway, sitting hunched over a sewing machine as it made a gentle hum. She had persuaded the nursery to allow her to mend the children's torn clothes at night just to be near me.

My mother thought I was a docile little girl but there were times I became very angry, though never at her. Once another girl at the nursery named Nell tried to get in my bed. From our first encounter we repelled each other like two positive charges of energy and I wondered why she was now invading my territory. As she started to climb on the bed, I poked her in the eye with my index finger. She let out a bellow. A nurse appeared, grim-faced, and rescued the screaming Nell.

A few moments later the nurse threatened me, "You've made Nell cross-eyed and the police are coming to punish you." In later years the police *did* come and punish me—by taking me off to Bellevue.

Though Nell's eye returned to normal by the next day, I lived in fear the police were after me. When my mother visited that weekend, I begged her to take me away, not daring to tell her why I was afraid.

After eight months, each day of which seemed endless, she rescued me from that intolerable nursery. Before long we were on our way to New York. Our new home was an hour's ride by subway from Manhattan. The apartment was clean and spacious compared to our bedbug hovel in Chicago. Mornings I woke to the chirping of a robin in a tall tree outside our window.

Mother enrolled me in first grade at the Rambam Yeshiva, a religious school. There I met Vicky, my best friend for many years; life without her would have been grim. One teacher, a man, demanded that once a week we bring a dime for charity. I forgot the dime one morning and he threatened, "You will be bathing in tears when I get through with you." He made me place my fingers, outstretched, on the desk. Then he cracked down on them with a ruler. Some teachers like to torment little children.

We were taught the first Testament, arithmetic, geography, writing, and spelling. The class bully was a girl named Ellen, who teased the younger children. One day Ellen shouted at a small girl for using the slide without her permission. I found myself eye to eye with Ellen and, trembling with anger, warned, "Don't yell at a smaller child." She backed away, a coward at heart. I had absorbed my mother's courage in the face of tyranny.

Vicky and I went into second grade together. The first weeks she kept talking to me in class but the teacher caught only me and punished me by taking away my play period. After this happened three times I was furious. I wrote a note, which I intended to destroy, describing the teacher as the worst tyrant I had ever known because she punished me but never Vicky. I was about to tear up the note when a girl who was class monitor, trying to show her authority, grabbed it out of my hand and deposited it with a malicious flourish on the teacher's desk. The teacher read my note without a trace of emotion, coolly placed it in her desk's top drawer, and continued correcting papers.

An hour later we were given a special test, which proved very important in my life. I finished it ahead of the rest of the class. The teacher noticed I was through, collected my paper, marked it.

The next morning as I was about to hang up my coat, she said, "Don't sit down. Take your coat and books and go to the principal's office."

I was petrified. I thought she was angry because I had called her a tyrant and was about to be expelled. Walking down the corridor to the principal's office, I wondered how I would ever explain the expulsion to my mother and whether I would be treated as an outcast the rest of my life. As I entered the principal's office, I saw with surprise he was smiling. He motioned me to an empty chair opposite him, then embarked on a long monologue which I was too frightened to understand though his voice sounded neither angry nor reproving.

Suddenly I heard him say, "Because of your high marks on the test, we have decided to let you skip second grade and go right to third."

He even escorted me to my new classroom. There the teacher told me to hang up my coat and pointed to an empty desk. Then she said, "Start taking the test on the blackboard, as the other children are doing."

I looked at the blackboard, to me it was like hieroglyphics. I thought in sorrow, I really will be expelled now.

After twenty minutes the teacher clapped her hands, signaling that the papers were to be handed in. She looked at the blank sheet bearing only my printed name. She asked, "What is the meaning of this?"

"I don't know how to read script," I explained. "I was told to skip second grade and come in here."

"Tomorrow I will teach you script," she said.

I discovered I liked to write short stories. When I was eight I wrote: "Once upon a time ago there lived a little girl and her mother. . . . The little girl's name was Jane . . . she didn't love her mother but she loved herself very much. Then her mother grew very sick and the little girl began to grow worried that something worse would happen to her mother and for the first time in her life she was in love with someone other than herself . . . this made her mother grow stronger and finally she became well and they lived happily ever after."

This showed my deep attachment to my mother—after all, a girl is supposed to think of living "happily ever after" with Prince Charming.

That winter I caught one cold after another and when I coughed up a minuscule amount of blood, the doctor told my mother I had a touch of tuberculosis. He suggested she take me south for the winter. We flew to Miami, where Aunt Fanny now lived. I was enrolled in a public school where I met two girls, Jill and Crystal, who I thought were my friends. But when we went to a ballet school and the instructor praised my dancing, they evidently were consumed by a jealousy that erupted one afternoon as we walked down the street. Both girls picked up wooden boards studded with nails. Jill said to me, "You'd better run because we're going to kill you!" At first I thought this just an ugly joke, then realized they meant it.

I walked away slowly, trying not to seem afraid, then broke into a run. In panic, I raced across the front lawn of the nearest house and rang the bell. I hoped someone would answer before the girls attacked me. Luckily a woman in a red apron appeared at once at the door.

"What do you want?" she said impatiently.

I begged, tears in my eyes, "Please help me. Those girls," motioning to the two crouched at the edge of her front lawn, holding their planks aloft, "are after me."

The woman called out to Jill and Crystal, "Go away or I'll phone the police."

They threw down the planks, giggled like embarrassed children, and ran off. I said to the woman, "Thank you. They would have beat me up if you hadn't opened the door."

"Stay away from those two," she warned.

I arrived home late and when my mother asked why, I did not tell her, afraid of what she might do to the girls. When I saw them in class the next day, they acted as if nothing had happened. I was relieved when mother announced we were going home since I was now tanned and healthy.

I had trouble with another girl that summer when mother sent me to Camp Crestwood, on a Connecticut estate, where Lauren Bacall was supposed to have gone. There was a very aggressive, snobbish twelve-year-old girl in my cabin named Susan, who continually criticized my manners and clothes. One night she came over to me and put her arms around my neck in a stranglehold, as if she meant to choke me. To make her let go I bit her on the flesh of her arm below the elbow.

She screamed, as did the other girls in the cabin and the camp director came running. He called me on the carpet and when I told him I was only defending myself, he said, "You should have hit her—not bit her."

When I was twelve, we moved into a larger apartment, one with a bedroom, in the same building. Up to then I shared a sofa-bed with my mother. Mother now gave me the bedroom. But most nights I watched television, which was in the living room, and fell asleep on mother's sofa. So it was as though we still shared the same room, the same double bed.

I skipped still another grade when I scored 142 on the Stanford-Binet I.Q. test and was selected for the Special Progress Program at Cunningham Junior High. This meant I would complete both seventh and eighth grades in one year. Which I did.

But in the ninth grade I met trouble. I could not concentrate and failed tests, at which the teacher ridiculed me in front of the class. She would say, "You 'special progress' pupils are supposed to be geniuses but some of you obviously do not belong here," glancing at me. I wanted to shrink into nothing, disappear under the desk.

So I stayed home from school, not wanting to face my classmates or the mean teacher. Mother fought bitterly with me. She struck me, screamed at me, called me lazy and irresponsible. She did not understand how miserable I felt.

Even though that year I was out of school sixty days, some of the time with asthma attacks, I graduated and was entitled to enter the sophomore year at any city high school. I was not a total cop-out.

But by now mother was afraid to leave me alone, fearing I would run away or suffer some horrible accident. Oddly enough, the only time I had a near-fatal accident she was with me. One summer both she and I went to Camp Unity House, a resort for families who did not have a lot of money. I had learned to swim at camp the previous year and was anxious to show her my new skill.

"Mommy, watch me dive into the lake," I called out as she sat on the sand, talking to a friend. Wherever she went, she made friends quickly.

I ran up to the dock and plunged into water seven feet deep. I started to show off my stroke, then noticed my mother was still talking to her friend, not even looking at me. I tired quickly and decided to stand, not realizing the water was over my head. I was shocked to find I was sinking below the surface. In a panic I started to claw my way up and managed to thrust my head above water for a moment before sinking again. I fought to the surface a second time, tried to get the attention of the lifeguard, absorbed in conversation with a guest. As my head broke through the water a third time, a voice inside me said, "If you drown, you will never see your mother again."

I called out, "Help!" Then swallowing water, I started to go down for the fourth time just as I saw a man suddenly dive into the water and swim toward me. I felt his arms around my waist as he propelled me above the surface and toward the dock. Then he pulled me out of the water. My mother came running, sputtering at the chattering lifeguard as I lay totally ignored, choking on water.

I was grateful to the unknown man who saved my life. I probably missed my father very much though I had few memories of him. One Father's Day, when all the children were asked to draw a special card for their father, I did not make one, thinking, There is no one to whom I can give it. I am proud of my Spanish blood. The famous Spanish philosopher Spinoza was distantly related to my father.

When I was twelve my mother started to go with Victor Lehrman, the millionaire owner of the lingerie company where she was a book-keeper. He was a tall man with white hair who liked a drink or two at night. Mother described him as "well preserved in bourbon and steak." One time he insisted I taste his bourbon, my first drink of liquor. Mother smiled, veiling her disgust, for she never drinks except for wine on rare occasions.

Every Saturday night Victor took us to dinner and a movie. He would often ask me, "What movie would you like to see?" I remember choosing one, *Lovers and Lollipops,* throughout which I felt very uncomfortable. It was about a divorced woman, her daughter, and the woman's lover. The situation was too close for comfort.

I felt Victor cared for me and was considerate of my feelings. Once he gave me a mother-of-pearl compact. I thought of him as a fixture in our lives. At first I was shocked to think mother and he might be having an affair. While I was outwardly gracious, I resented his taking mother's time and attention. It took a while before I could think of her not as someone who belonged totally to me but a woman with her own feelings and needs who was entitled to a man.

About this time, my friend Cynthia, my backup pal when Vicky was busy, and I were determined to find out about sex. We started by reading *True Confessions.* One day as we were playing with my doll-house, per my mother's suggestion, I said to Cynthia, "Enough of this. It's boring. Let's go out and meet boys."

We strolled along the boardwalk. We stared at all the boys. We did not dare stop to talk to one of them. But it was a first step.

That summer at a camp called Bronx House, in Copake, New York, a fourteen-year-old boy, Danny, developed a crush on me. One night when most of the campers went off on a hayride, he asked me to stay behind and then invited me to his cabin. I was happy to oblige, thinking that now at the ancient age of thirteen, I would probably find out what sex was all about. Like the women who wrote those true confessions, who reported that after vague intimacies with a man, such as kissing, they found themselves pregnant.

Danny and I stole like criminals to his cabin, my heart beating as if to jungle drums. We could not find the light so we stumbled in the dark to one of the beds.

Danny sat down and I timidly perched beside him. Suddenly he pushed me down on the bed and began kissing my neck, then my lips. It was the first time a boy had kissed me and the room whirled like a merry-go-round. I could not control my feelings as small animal moan sounds burst from me. Embarrassed, I tried to stifle them. I wondered if perhaps I were having an orgasm.

Danny lay his head on my chest and I softly stroked the soft blondness, the first time I touched a boy's hair in tenderness. I closed my eyes in ecstasy. Then he thought he heard a noise and jumped up. I felt as if one of my limbs had been torn off me.

He would not return to the warmth of my arms, convinced he heard the other boys and girls returning from the hayride. We walked out of the cabin without a word.

I was frightened and thought I might be pregnant from Danny's kisses because of the strange feelings they evoked in my body. When I told the girls in my cabin Danny had kissed me and I was afraid I might have a baby, they burst into derisive laughter.

One of them said, "You only got Danny hot."

" 'Hot?' What does that mean?" I asked.

"Oh, come off it, Rosette." She looked at me as though I could not possibly be that naïve.

There was only a week left of camp and, feeling embarrassed and ashamed, I avoided Danny by taking arts and crafts and working on the farm, activities I knew he disliked. Once back in Brighton Beach, feeling like a woman of the world, I told Cynthia of my affair.

She said, "That's nothing. I met a dozen boys in motorcycle jackets at Coney this summer and let most of them kiss me."

"We're not playing with that dollhouse any longer," I announced. "We're going to have fun."

One night, wearing fashionably tight skirts, we arranged to sneak out of our apartments—Cynthia lived only a few doors away. My mother allowed me to wear lipstick but Cynthia had to steal her mother's lipstick, then put it on under a streetlight. We walked the mile to Coney Island, the beacon that signaled pleasure.

When we reached the amusement park, I said, "Let's wiggle our hips and pretend to be sexy."

Within five minutes of strutting, we were approached by two

sailors, one very tall, one very short, like Mutt and Jeff. Cynthia, shorter than me, took Mutt. Jeff, with a distinct accent, hailed from the south. My attempts to be wry and amusing fell flat but once on the rides, there was no need for brilliant conversation. We held hands stiffly, like robots.

Shortly before midnight the swabbies informed us they were due back on the ship. Jeff asked, "May I kiss you goodnight?"

I thought it only fair in exchange for the rides, cotton candy, and ice cream cones. "Okay."

Standing in the middle of the boardwalk, he bent me over backwards like he was the Sheikh of Araby and gave me a wild, long kiss.

Cynthia was shocked. She said as we walked home, "How could you let a boy kiss you on the first date?"

It was almost one when I walked in the door. My mother was furious. "Where have you been?" she shouted.

"Having fun at Coney Island with a sailor who picked me up," I said. "His friend picked up Cynthia."

"You shouldn't have done that!" my mother screamed. "You can get venereal disease from a strange man."

"From a kiss?" I really wanted to know, but she did not answer.

Cynthia's father was not as understanding. He hit her, and we could hear her screaming from her apartment, "Save me, Rosette! Save me!"

I ran to her door and rang the bell. Her father threw the door open, snarled at me, "Don't ever set foot in this house again, you little tramp!" and slammed the door in my face.

Cynthia and I did not go back to Coney Island to pick up boys because we were afraid the next time my mother and her father would skin us alive. They seemed to have no sympathy for the strong feelings that stirred inside us. It was hard to imagine they had ever been young.

After I was graduated from Cunningham Junior High mother registered me as a sophomore at Lincoln High, ten blocks from our apartment. It was an overcrowded school yet I had not a friend. For days I sat by myself during lunch hour in the jammed cafeteria where everyone seemed to know everyone else except me. Then, after two months, I started to leave school before lunch. Then, not go at all.

Mother and I fought fiercely about my truancy. She screamed, taunted, struck me. But I didn't care what she did, a strange lassitude overpowered me. I could not drag myself each morning to a class where I would sit in fear and self-hatred, unable to think. I tried to concentrate on how to concentrate but this did not help.

My mother took me to a social worker, Mrs. Julian, to help resolve our battles. Mrs. Julian handed me two puppets from a collection on her desk. She said, "Let's play a game. One of the puppets will be you and the other, your mother. Make up a little scene between them."

I thought, She wants to believe my mother and I have fights all the time so I'll give her what she wants. I took the mother puppet and made her say to the daughter, "I hate you! I'm going to kill you. You're a bad girl!"

And then the daughter puppet cried and said, "You're always mad at me because I never do anything the way you want. Please don't hate me so."

And the mother puppet: "I'm sorry I got angry at you. It's because of my boss, he gives me a hard time on the job and I take it out on you because I don't dare take it out on him."

Which, I had to admit, was sometimes the way it happened.

One day Mrs. Julian asked, "How would you like to go to a school in the country?"

This was no surprise. My mother had threatened if I continued to play hookey she would send me to a boarding school where I would have to obey strict rules.

I asked my mother, "What do you think of my going away to school?"

She said, "I don't want you to leave home but I can't control you enough to keep you in school here."

I agreed to try the school in the country. A social worker came to the apartment house in a taxi. Mother pressed me to her, kissed me goodbye many times as though she might never see me again. She literally covered my face with kisses.

Before I stepped into the taxi, I took one last glimpse of the blue-gray Atlantic just outside our door. I would miss the peace it brought on sunny days, the excitement on windy or stormy ones.

As we drove away, I looked back. Mother stood on the sidewalk, tears streaming down her face.

I was too terrified to cry.

II

Death in Small Doses

Thus started my years in institutions, years somewhat blurred by now though certain memories haunt my daydreams and my nightmares.

The journey into horror started with the taxi ride to Grand Central Station, where seven years before mother and I had so joyfully arrived from Chicago. Then an hour's ride on the train, then another taxi to the school.

As we headed through the gate, the social worker, Mary Simmons, said, "There's a girl here named Rosa whom all the other children dislike. Maybe it would be a good idea to change your name slightly so you're not mistaken for her."

I was originally named Sylvia Rosa, a name I did not like. I was happy to give myself a new name. I asked, "Would Rosette be enough of a change?"

"Fine," she said.

The cottage where I was to live had on the first floor a small library, a room for the cottage mother, and a living room with sofa, easy chairs, television set, and baby grand piano. All the rooms had colorful curtains and scatter rugs. Upstairs were three rooms, each with three beds. An attic was used to store suitcases.

But in spite of the cheerful atmosphere, on that first night, miles separating me from my mother, I thought, This is what dying feels like. I had been away from her at summer camps but there I felt free and relaxed. Now I felt restricted and imprisoned.

The girls in my cottage, for the most part, were different from any I had known. There was a clique, or gang, who lived for a rough-housing that passed as camaraderie. They had their own peculiar code of honor and any infraction by a newcomer brought contempt and rejection. They treated the staff as mortal enemies, referred to them in obscene words.

A few girls did not fit into the clique, including one of my roommates, a tall girl with raven hair, a Dresden doll complexion, and almond-shaped hazel eyes. Her name, like the legendary heroine of Homer's *Iliad,* was Helen and she had an odyssey of her own. Born in Czechoslovakia, she was saved from the Nazis by a neighbor as her parents were dragged off to a concentration camp. Her friendship helped me bear my punishment when I innocently drew the fury of the gang, who informed me, after pawing through my clothes, they were entitled to borrow anything they wished, including my expensive green wool skirt, the color of jade, a gift from Victor.

They also insisted I find a "beau" so I would not steal their boyfriends. They took me for a walk to inspect the unattached boys. They asked, "Which one do you like?" In a panic, I pointed to the first boy I saw, hoping he was a safe choice. Word reached him via the grapevine that the "new girl" had chosen him as her steady. His name was Mike and he sent a messenger, a younger boy, to say he would like to take me to the Saturday night square dance. I had a heart-shaped face that vaguely resembled Elizabeth Taylor's, a gamin face like my mother as a young woman.

I was glad to get the invitation but resented the control by girls I thought dominating and threatening. I composed a letter to my mother describing their "tyrannical" attitude, calling them "uncouth" and "crude." I also referred to the "beau" I had been forced to choose as "a rude barbarian who belongs in a reformatory along with other juvenile delinquents." I put the letter in my box of stationery intending to mail it the next day and went out for a walk in the cool evening air.

An hour later as I approached the cottage, I found myself facing a belligerent Mike. He said angrily, "So you think I'm a juvenile delinquent and not good enough to take you to a square dance. Well, find someone else,'' and stalked away before I had a chance to apologize.

I knew the gang had opened my letter—nothing was sacred to them—and would be even more furious than Mike at what I said about them. No sooner had I put a foot through the door than several of the girls rushed at me and called me ''bitch'' and ''cunt.'' One of them struck me on the face. I offered no resistance. My pride hurt more than the smarting cheek.

Then, out of a wish to be accepted by the gang, I acted foolishly. One night I insisted on accompanying Helen and Fern, the third girl in our room, when they walked to town for ice cream. They had permission to leave the grounds until eleven but I, as a newcomer, did not.

At the ice cream parlor we met three of the local boys and started talking to them. When Helen and Fern said we had to leave, I asked the boys, ''Would you like to come back with us?''

This was against the school rules, for town boys were not allowed on the grounds; even the boys at the school were not permitted in the girls' cottages at night. I knew that to entice a town boy to the school after dark was something even the girls of the gang would not dare and hoped they would respect me for my courage.

The boys walked us back to the school, about half a mile. Fern and Helen were aghast at my temerity. Helen whispered, ''We'll all be in trouble.''

It was midnight as the six of us climbed the cottage fire escape that led into our room. We made such a commotion we woke up girls in the adjoining rooms. The boys fled down the fire escape and away to town. One stool pigeon of a girl ran to the house where the director, our official disciplinarian, lived.

He marched upstairs and into our room within five minutes, hair rumpled, trousers and shirt obviously thrown on, furious at having been waked.

He walked over to Helen, slapped her across the face, and said, ''You tramp!''

Then he slapped a girl who, with several others, had gathered in our room to watch the fireworks. She turned on him in shocked fury and said, ''What in hell did you do that for? I wasn't with them.''

''I'm sorry,'' he said.

He came over to me, slapped me across the face, and said, "You little tramp!"

He did the same to Fern. He stalked out of the room after announcing, "You will all be punished severely tomorrow."

Helen, Fern, and I climbed into our beds without a word, exhausted and ashamed. The next morning one of the leaders of the gang, a coarse, blond girl named Laura, said to me, "We don't want you in the cottage. You're a tramp and a whore. You're giving the rest of us a bad name." Then she threatened, "I'm going to beat you up and teach you a lesson."

The cottage mother told me, "You're a bad influence, Rosette."

"What do you mean?" I felt I had done nothing wrong, I had hurt no one.

"You necked with one of the town boys in your bed."

I was stunned. "There wasn't even time for a kiss."

"Well, you *were* the one who invited the boys to the school."

I wondered which roommate had told, knew it had to be Fern, Helen would never betray me.

As punishment for ignominiously sullying the reputation of the school, I was ordered to the infirmary for two weeks, which meant isolation. I had tried to act like the girls in the gang—rough and tough—figuring this was the way to win their approval. But instead, I had earned their enmity and the unwarranted reputation of a "tramp." I crept in shame to the infirmary, taking my old brown teddy bear of childhood days that I had packed under my dresses when I left Brighton Beach.

I felt relieved, though, to be safe from Laura and her threat to beat me up. But late that night, after the nurse fell asleep in her room downstairs, Laura appeared at the door of my room on the second floor. She walked over to me, her right fist raised. She said, "You thought you could escape but you can't." Gangland ethics.

She started to punch me angrily. I kicked her in the shin. She got in several more punches. I kicked her again. Hard. She moved to the door and sneered, "I'll be back. Next time with a knife."

I was terrified. How could I protect myself against a knife? My bedroom door had no lock but the bathroom did. So I put my pillow, blanket, and teddy bear in the tub, locked the door, and slept there until I was released from the infirmary. By then Laura seemed to have forgotten her grudge, as had the rest of the girls. Perhaps they thought I had suffered enough by the isolation.

I met a woman who helped me not only through these first terrifying days but the difficult years to come. Dr. Margaret Blau became my psychiatrist and my friend. She was not particularly striking in appearance but more than made up for it by the power of her emotional and intellectual capabilities.

She was soft-spoken, warm, and compassionate. She told me I should not have been punished so severely for the escapade with the town boys—which I dared not tell my mother about for months. Dr. Blau asked my version of the incident for which I alone had been punished. I said I thought of it as "initiation rites" that would have allowed me to become one of the gang. She said Fern and Helen, who had been at the school for over a year, had neglected their responsibility to stop the boys from coming to the school and should have been the ones punished.

She helped me realize how frightened I was not only at the separation from my mother but a separation that hurled me into a group of boys and girls different from any I had known. I never did make friends with the girls in the gang, most of whom seemed bent on smoking themselves to death behind Cottage 10, set in the woods, where no one could see them. They were as emotionally troubled as I, some even more so. But when you feel anxious, as both they and I did, it is hard to be tolerant of hostility in others.

For days I was so homesick I could force little food into my mouth. I drank liquids or ate the hardboiled eggs our cottage mother—who eventually revised her opinion of me—kept in the refrigerator in case we were hungry at night. Each evening at eight I trudged the quarter of a mile, through deep snow in winter, to the phone booth in the main house to call mother. I looked forward all day to this one act. Sometimes she was not home, out at a movie with a friend, and I would sit and wait for hours until she answered the ring.

I was allowed my first weekend home over Thanksgiving. There was a mixup as to which social worker had my train ticket and by the time I located it the taxi had left for the station. My friends, coming back from dinner in the main house, were surprised to see me still at the cottage. In tears, I explained how I had missed the taxi. They rushed me to the office of a Mr. Petinsky, who was busy with papers. But he listened to my sad story, phoned the social worker to verify it, then took me to his house where his wife was getting supper ready.

His two little girls hugged him, then seeing me, tear-stained and nervous, raced away. He told his wife he would be late for dinner, led me to his car, and we sped to the depot just in time to see the train pulling out. He raced it to the next town, four miles away. We had trouble parking and had to run a block to the station. My shoes kept slipping off but he grabbed my hand, kept me running and we made it on time. He even boarded the train and found me a seat, then stayed to wave goodbye. I will always cherish his sympathy and thoughtfulness at a time I desperately needed it.

On the weekends I spent home, though I liked Victor, I also resented the time he took away from my chance to be alone with my mother. As soon as I set foot in the house, she ordered me to help buy the groceries, help clean the apartment before he arrived, go to the beauty parlor, get dressed. After dinner we would see a movie and I would come home exhausted and feeling like an intruder. I would have preferred to sit home and talk, but Victor liked to keep on the move, as did my mother.

The one hour a week with Dr. Blau was not enough to get me through all the other lonely hours. After seven weeks, I decided to run away. I did not have enough money for the train so I walked along a highway leading to New York—the girls talked of hitching rides to the city. After covering only two miles I was picked up by my guidance counselor, who happened to be driving by, and returned to the school.

Mother gave me five dollars a week for extra food, stamps, phone calls, and magazines and I managed to save enough so I could pay for the train. Two weeks later I ran away with greater success, to arrive home in the evening. Mother greeted me with the news that the director of the school had phoned and advised that not to return me would be "a serious mistake." I saw in her eyes she would not defy him.

"I would be setting a bad example for you, sweetheart, if I let you stay," she said.

The next morning I took the train back, feeling even more helpless and defeated. But gradually, with Dr. Blau's support, I became interested once again in painting. I spent hours drawing and learning to use oils and watercolors. I even attended school classes regularly, which I had refused to do at first.

Mother and Victor came out every Saturday and mother came alone on Sundays, giving me the chance to talk to her of my feelings about the girls and boys. Mother was not a prude and as I grew up she occasionally spoke of sexual matters. Once in the dark, when we were in bed, sharing the split sofa, she asked, "Do you ever feel your clitoris tingling?"

"Sometimes," I admitted.

"Don't feel embarrassed," she said. "It's natural to have such sensations in your body."

I confessed, "I have those feelings all the time."

Then we both fell asleep.

I never masturbated until Forest School, where I did at night under the blankets. There was so much talk of sex it was impossible not to feel aroused.

My first romantic crush took place the second year at school, inspired by a boy named Benjy. I was attracted by his sturdy, confident walk and his blond hair that gleamed in the sun. He seemed to like me, though he never put it in words. Then one night he sent the message he was going to break the rule forbidding boys to visit girls in their cottage after dark, and come to my room. I took a shower and put perfume behind my ears, in my hair, and on the pillow.

As the lights were turned off, I reached out an arm to Helen, lying in the next bed, and said, "Good-night, sweet dreams."

She whispered, "Do you think he'll come?"

"I don't know. I hope so." I felt like an adolescent femme fatale.

I lay awake for hours, listening to the crickets chirp, suddenly thought, Benjy must have been teasing. Then just as the clock in the living room chimed three, I heard a creak, the screen door downstairs was opening. Then footsteps mounting the stairs. I wondered if anyone else heard but Helen and Fern seemed to be sleeping soundly.

He must have known my room for he headed straight to it. The moon was full and I clearly saw him at the door. He walked over to my bed and without a word lay down beside me. He started to kiss and fondle me. His hands were hot; they burned right through my chiffon sky-blue shortie.

I closed my eyes in unbelievable happiness. When I opened them, Benjy had a shocked look on his face. He was staring at my small naked right breast, unexpectedly exposed by my traitorous shortie. He seemed nervous and sat up, as though a spell had been broken. I put a hand on his shoulder as though to reassure him but he shook it off.

Then, without even a goodbye kiss or word, he walked out of the room. I heard him go down the stairs, then out the front door. I knew he had been frightened by the sight of my bare breast; he was not very sophisticated after all. My eyes filled with tears at the thought I had lost my first love before I had even found it.

The next day I flirted with some of the other boys, trying to make Benjy jealous, but he never again came near me. I was boy crazy at the time, as was every other girl at the school. We were at the age when girls naturally are attracted to the opposite sex, particularly precocious girls like we were, who had to be sent away because we were uncontrollable at home.

From then on, I had to adore Benjy from afar. As I did Elvis Presley and James Dean.

One night on a dare from Helen, I phoned James Dean. To my surprise, the operator put through my call, connecting me to his residence. A woman answered. I assumed she was his housekeeper.

I said, "Could I please speak to James Dean? I'm calling long distance from New York."

She said in a low voice, "I'm sorry but an hour ago we learned he had died."

I hung up, my face pale.

"What's the matter?" asked Helen.

"Some woman says he's dead. I don't believe it," I said.

"Let's listen to the news," she said.

We learned it was true. He had been killed that day when his motorcycle crashed. I had been one of the first to learn of my hero's death. It was eerie I had decided to call just at that moment.

My love affairs have been all mere romances. I have had only one orgasm in my life, when Danny kissed me on his bed at the Bronx

House camp. Years later I thought I was having an orgasm in the subway one evening coming home from work. I felt a tingling all over my body, also felt high as if I had smoked opium. I closed my eyes to enjoy the peaceful feeling, then opened them quickly, not wanting to miss my subway stop. As I stepped off the train, my senses felt sharper. Another time, one night in bed, I suddenly sensed the mattress twirl round and round, spinning like a top. I wanted to write about the sensations but it is difficult to be objective and to feel at the same time.

The months at Forest School now passed more swiftly. One day I found a wounded bluebird. I carried it to the cottage, placed it carefully in a box, then walked to a nearby lake and collected worms to feed it. For several days I spent most of my time caring for the bird so it would get well and fly. That weekend I was scheduled for a trip home. I could not take the bird and asked several of the girls to feed it while I was away. When I came back, the bird was dead. I asked what had happened but the girls only shrugged their shoulders and said they didn't know. I wondered if they had deliberately starved it.

I learned a lot at the school and it helped me grow up. I felt more secure, surer of myself, not quite so bitter, suspicious and frightened as when I arrived. Though I still felt like picking up boys, my studies and art work kept me out of trouble. "Sublimation," one of my teachers called it.

Mother and I seemed to be getting on much better. I wrote her: "I was so happy after our last visit. Don't you think we're improving, we don't scream at each other as we used to. Of course I'm not perfect and I never shall be but I can try to be near-perfect. It might take some time but I'll reach it." I so wanted to please her.

But the wish to be perfect seems to exact a toll. Even though I obeyed all the rules and no longer acted the rebel, I started to feel as if I were having a nervous breakdown. I was afraid to walk on the grass. I thought the grass had feelings and it was like trampling on people's heads. I told Fern and Helen, "Don't walk on the grass, you'll hurt it." They looked at me as though I had lost my mind.

I became obsessed with thoughts of religious redemption. I felt I had sinned against God and had to repent. I wandered into town, walked from one church to the next, seeking a few moments of serenity. I thought I heard God's voice telling me to become a nun. I decided that was what I wished to be.

One day I had what Dr. Blau called a screen memory—a memory that hides a deeper one which has been repressed because it is terrifying. I saw myself in a room where a fire burned in the fireplace. There was also a little child in the room who was suffering because it felt cold and unloved. I was seized by an overwhelming desire to throw the child into the flames so it could feel warmth and love.

Strange feelings were building up inside me. They were not helped by what happened next. One hot summer afternoon three other girls and I walked to town for ice cream malteds at the local drugstore. Afterwards we stood outside the store, hoping to get a ride back to school from one of the town boys.

A car with its top down stopped in front of us with three local boys inside. Two of them, Ed and Henry, sometimes dated girls at the school. The third, Tony, whose father owned a nearby bar and grill, was the driver.

"Want to go for a ride and cool off?" Henry asked.

Eagerly we crowded into the back seat. About a mile from town Tony pulled off the main road and headed for a wooded area. The side road led to a pond. Tony stopped the car, the three boys stepped out, and without a word stripped and plunged into the pond.

I had never seen a boy naked and turned my eyes to the trees. When the boys dressed after their swim, Henry got into the back seat with one of the girls. The two other girls paired with Ed and Tony and walked off into the woods. Left alone, I stood by the car, aware that Henry and his girl were kissing each other ardently.

Suddenly Henry called out to me, "Come here," and released the girl he was kissing. She stepped out of the car, looked angrily at me, and marched away. I took her place.

Henry put his arms around me, kissed me a few times. I tried to respond but felt nothing for this strange boy with whom I had exchanged hardly a word. Then he said, "Let's go for a walk."

We headed for a flat rock in the woods, out of sight of the car, and sat on it. Henry kissed me again and this time I felt my lips warming to his. We kept kissing and hugging, and I noticed he was breathing very fast.

Suddenly I became aware of a deathly quiet. I asked, "Where are the others?"

"They've gone for a ride," he said. "I heard the car take off."

Alarmed, I ran to where the car had stood. It and all the other boys and girls had vanished.

Henry had followed me and now he said eagerly, "We're all alone. Come on, let's do it."

I knew what he meant. I said, "I can't."

"Why not?" He looked sullen.

"I'm a virgin."

"I don't believe it," he sneered. "Not one of you girls!"

I wondered how I would convince him. At that moment I saw the car coming down the road and felt rescued. But only Ed and Tony were in it. They stepped out and walked toward me with menacing looks.

I shrank nearer Henry. He said, "If you give in to me, I won't let them touch you. Otherwise they'll rape you. Like they did to another girl from the school a few weeks ago."

My throat burned with fear. I sensed if I "gave in" to Henry, the others would want their turn. The three started to close in on me. Tony said hoarsely, "We're going to rape you, Rosette. The other three girls escaped but we've got you."

"Please don't," I begged. "I'm a virgin."

"All the better," Tony sneered.

I ran to the empty car, thinking I could defend myself more easily inside, slammed the doors shut. Tony pulled open one door, Henry, the other, and tried to force me out. I kicked, scratched, tried to bite.

"A wildcat," said Henry and grabbed at me.

The three tore my white blouse, ripped my blue dungarees, trying to get them off. It was then I screamed. At the top of my lungs, hoping someone, anyone, would hear.

I was lucky. A man stepped out of the woods into the small clearing. I thought he might be a hunter for he wore a red and white checked shirt and his trousers were tucked into boots. When the boys saw him, they stopped tearing off my clothes.

To my surprise the man called the boys by name. He said, "Ed, Tony, Henry. What are you doing to this girl?"

I cowered in a corner of the car, not wanting the man to see me so disheveled.

The boys tried to be casual. Henry said, "She's from the school. We took her for a ride. We were just having a little fun."

Knowing well what they were up to, the man said, "I know all your fathers. And if you don't return this girl at once, unharmed, to the school, I'll tell your fathers what you tried to do."

I could see the boys were frightened. They promised to take me back to the school immediately and the man walked away. Henry said to me threateningly, "You're lucky this time. And you'd better not tell anyone what happened or we'll fix you good."

Tony drove to the main road, where the three other girls, more successful than I at repulsing the boys' advances, were trying to hitch a ride to school. Tony stopped the car and ordered them to get in. The girls looked curiously at my torn blouse and dungarees.

After the boys left us off, the girls asked what had happened. I said grimly, "I was almost raped by the three of them."

I realize now the risk I took getting into the car with those particular boys. The town looked on us as wild and obsessed with sex. We four girls had asked for trouble. But we had meant only to flirt, not "make it." I was not ready for sex, brought up as I was by a mother who insisted I remain a virgin until I married, as she had done.

I felt so depressed I thought of swallowing poison, as mother told me her mother had done in the Khotin garden. When I saw a full bottle of iodine on Helen's bed, I stared at it, thinking, This may be the answer to all my problems. I picked up the bottle and broke the cap. I rested the tip of the bottle on my lower lip. Then I thought, I still have a spark of hope, there have been many happy times, and put the bottle down.

In my therapy session I told Dr. Blau what I had done. She looked at me in a concerned way but said nothing. I also insisted I wanted to sue the three boys to stop them from trying to rape the girls at school. She convinced me this would only harm me and the school.

Shortly after, she told me I was to be transferred to Riverview, a school that gave stricter supervision and more psychiatric help. One afternoon in August a member of the staff came to my cottage and ordered, "Pack your suitcase."

"Where am I going?" There was fear in my heart. Perhaps they were sending me to prison for enticing the three town boys.

"To a private mental hospital until there is a vacancy at Riverview."

"How long will that be?" The words "mental hospital" terrified me. Was I to live with "crazies" and "loonies"?

"I don't know." She snapped, "Better hurry. A car will pick you up in twenty minutes."

I dragged my suitcase down from the attic, packed my clothes, picked up my gray cat Twinkle, whom the school had allowed me to bring from home, carried him and the suitcase downstairs and waited in front of the cottage. I felt once again abandoned and in isolation. I had never felt comfortable at Forest School though in two years I had become somewhat accustomed to it. I would miss Helen and Fern. And Dr. Blau, who had so much faith in me.

In about half an hour a car drove up, one of the cottage fathers at the wheel. Beside him sat Dr. Blau. She smiled at me and said, "I'm going to take you to the new place."

I was grateful for her company, though she and the cottage father talked to each other all the way, saying not a word to me. I sat in the back seat, holding Twinkle close. When we arrived at the "new place" after an hour's drive, Dr. Blau said, "Rosette dear, one day you will thank me for bringing you here."

"I thank you now for all you've done for me." I meant it from the bottom of my mixed-up heart.

At the mental hospital, which they called a "private sanitarium," the psychiatrist who admitted me was a tall, thin, dour-faced man.

I asked, "Why am I here?"

"Because you're suicidal," he said.

Perhaps it was not true there was no vacancy at Riverview, and I had been sent to a lunatic asylum because they thought I might be crazy.

"I only put the bottle of iodine to my lips," I said. "I didn't swallow any."

"But you had the wish to die," he said. "Next time you might really act on it. We want to save you."

What looked like a three-hundred-pound nurse walked into the room. She ordered, "Take your suitcase and that cat and follow me."

I picked up Twinkle and the suitcase and walked behind her across a lawn to a large brown wooden house. She unlocked the front door, selecting a key from a large ring. She announced, looking at me with her small beady eyes lost in mounds of fat, "No animals allowed. You'll have to leave the cat outside."

"He's all I've got," I said sadly.

"No animals!" An order.

"I can't desert him," I protested. "He'll starve to death."

"I'll take the cat to my home until you're ready to leave," she said.

I put Twinkle down, believing her. I never saw Twinkle again. She told me he had wandered from the grounds.

Inside the brown house stood, sat, or lay on couches women of all ages, some talking to themselves in gibberish, others woefully silent. One frail, wizened woman showed no sign of animation until I came within touching distance when she suddenly burst into an Irish jig. I laughed, for hers was, in a way, not an unpleasant welcome. But then I thought, in sudden shock, I am really shut up in an asylum, I have always been deathly afraid of such a place, do they actually think I am insane?

The obese nurse assured me I was to stay only until there was an opening at Riverview School. At least here I finally had a room of my own. Though for the first time in my life I was terrified because of the locked door. If there were a fire, I would be unable to save myself unless someone first unlocked the door. I was literally imprisoned.

The nurse burrowed in my suitcase, searching for concealed weapons with which I might kill myself. She looked through my purse and took away my cigarettes. This, I thought, was the ultimate invasion of privacy. I had learned at the school to depend on cigarettes as a prop for self-confidence. While I held a cigarette, it was as if no one could touch me.

"Give me back my cigarettes," I said. "I can't kill myself with them."

"You aren't allowed to have them." She looked as though she enjoyed depriving me.

"Bitch!" A word I had learned to toss around casually at the school.

She slapped me hard across the face. Tears rolled down my cheeks. I felt she had taken away my last shred of dignity.

A small yard in the rear of the house was bordered by a barbed-wire fence seven feet high. After dinner the patients shuffled into the yard for a breath of cool night air. The temperature during the day had reached almost 100 degrees. One woman walked around and around a tree in a perfect circle as though never intending to stop. I planned to escape. I started to dig a hole under the barbed wire, as a dog might do. No one seemed to pay any attention, all wrapped up in their own fantasy worlds.

I had just squeezed my body halfway under the wire when a nurse looked out a window and saw me. She shouted, "Stop! Stop!" and disappeared, obviously on her way to give chase. Feeling defeated, I crawled back.

The next day they filled in the hole. I could have dug another but decided to wait a while. The third day it rained so hard we were kept indoors. To my surprise I was handed a large sketch pad and a box of pastels. A nurse explained it had been given to a patient by her parents but she was too upset to paint and the psychiatrist, noting in my file that I painted, suggested the pad and pastels be turned over to me. I spent many pleasant hours using them.

When mother was finally allowed to visit, she took me to a restaurant not far from the sanitarium. I pleaded with her to take me home, saying I felt scared because of the locked door. She begged, "Please stay, precious. It won't be for long."

I told her Dr. Blau had remarked, as she left me, that one day I would thank her for bringing me there.

"Do you agree?" I asked mother.

She looked at me helplessly, as though to say, What else can we do?

I had another run-in with the fat nurse, my bête noire. I was washing out a bedsheet, stained during my menstrual period, and an older woman patient who regularly spied on the rest of us ran to the nurse to report what I was doing.

The nurse plodded over and ordered, "Stop this at once. The laundry takes care of such things."

I felt angry to be reprimanded for cleaning up a mess I had made. My mother would have praised me. I said, "That old woman is a snoopy bitch."

Furious, perhaps because I had previously called her a bitch, the nurse grabbed me from behind, twisted my arm, and shoved me down the hall to a room used for solitary confinement. It held no furniture, just a mattress without sheets as a bed. She left, locking the door. I started to cry in rage and panic.

The next day she told me the psychiatrist said I could not go to Riverview because I was "bad." This was a lie but I did not know it. I was afraid I might never see the outside world again. When you are held prisoner behind locked doors, the fear is they will never let you out.

A man hung himself in the basement and I wondered if that would be my end. Most of the patients received electroshock treatments but I was spared, probably because of my age. When I was let out of solitary confinement after three days, I started to suffer the severe asthma attacks that had plagued me since childhood.

One day the woman who had danced the Irish jig said, "You've changed since you came here."

"What do you mean?"

"You seem detached. As if you don't want to talk to anyone."

I *was* feeling different. Remote and melancholy. My twilight world seesawed between romantic fantasies of meeting an elusive Prince Charming who would carry me off to the never-never land of happiness and painful guilt at the suffering I was causing mother.

Then came my reprieve. After a month I was sent to Riverview. No more locked doors. No more demented men and women. Instead, a country boarding school where forty teenage girls and boys with "severe emotional problems" were supervised by a chief psychiatrist, five social workers and six attendants.

This school, in contrast to the cottages of Forest, was one large building set in the woods. The dining room and kitchen were on the first floor, the second held the bedrooms. The boys were separated from the girls by a wide door at the end of a long corridor. Each of us had our own room. Mother brought flowered curtains and a matching bedspread to go with my pink walls. Besides regular meals, we could eat any time we wished from a refrigerator stocked with food.

I saw my therapist, a social worker, three times a week. She was a personable young woman but I did not feel nearly as close to her as I did to Dr. Blau. I made one friend, Christina, a rather plump blonde with blue eyes and a baby-doll face—the way I wished I looked. Yet she was no happier than I. One day she confided she was going to slash her wrists that night and made me promise not to tell any of the staff. I felt I had to tell my social worker, who then prevented Christina from committing suicide. Christina was not angry at me for breaking my promise. I thought she would not have told me unless she wanted me to save her. Christina was Catholic and talked for hours about her guilt over having sex with a number of boys, which she called "sinning."

I also was unhappy at this place. One social worker did not like me. As I was sitting in the living room reading one afternoon, she ordered, "Go and clean up your room."

"I don't feel like it," I said.

She nodded to a heavy-set attendant, a handyman of sorts. He pulled me out of the chair, dragged me by the hair to my room. As I burst into tears of pain, he sneered, "Now will you clean up your room?"

"Yes," I sobbed.

When Christina asked me to run away with her, saying the only chance we had for freedom was to find two boys who would love us and protect us from our families and the school, I agreed.

On a mild December afternoon when no one was watching, we slipped into our coats and walked slowly away from the school, bound for the nearest highway about half a mile south. For the first time in months I felt excited rather than anxious.

"We'll hitch a ride from two boys and get them to take us with them wherever they live," Christina said.

"Fine." I was willing to try anything other than an institution. For two and a half years I had been told when to eat, when to go to bed, when to study, when to dress, when to see visitors. I wanted to be on my own.

We walked along the highway for half an hour; not many cars passed at this time of year. Then a battered Chevrolet slowed up, stopped. There were two young men in it.

The driver, Jim, asked me to sit beside him. He waved Jerry, who, he said, was his younger brother, to the back seat with Christina. They were not particularly movie star handsome but they had pleasant manners.

"Where you girls going?" Jim asked.

"We're running away from boarding school," I said.

"Where are you heading?"

"Anywhere."

"Want to stay at our place for the night?"

"Sure." I fantasied a sumptuous penthouse in Manhattan.

He drove toward New York, then across the George Washington Bridge and on to Hoboken, New Jersey. He stopped the car in front of a gray, wooden three-story building that looked as if it had been put together before the Civil War. He led us into a dump of an apartment on the first floor where cockroaches scurried across the kitchen table.

We had ham sandwiches and Cokes for supper. Jerry and Christina went into the bedroom after we ate and closed the door. Jim and I put torn sheets on an old musty sofa in the living room.

He took off all his clothes. He was tall and painfully thin. I felt frightened but knew Christina expected me to go through with sex out of gratitude for his rescuing us from the hated school. I stepped out of my dark green wool skirt, light green jersey blouse, white panties and brassiere. Then I lay down on the creaky sofa beside him.

He took me in his arms. I recoiled from a strong distasteful odor from his armpits. He kissed me on the lips in a flat, unromantic way, not warmly like Benjy had kissed. Before I knew what he was up to, he tried to put his penis inside me. Since I was a virgin, it was difficult and painful. I wriggled around to make it easier. I did not want him to know it hurt or to seem like a baby. So I choked back my gasps. It was soon over anyhow. He turned his back and fell asleep at once. I lay for hours thinking, Is this what sex is all about? Will I ever enjoy it?

In spite of the pain, I hoped Jim would ask me to be his girl, stay with him, and that Christina would live with Jerry. She and I could cook for and take care of the boys, who would come home each evening from their jobs in a nearby factory where they told us they worked.

But in the morning over coffee Jim said, "I forgot to tell you, I'm engaged to someone else. I hope you don't mind."

What could I say? I had no claim on him. I murmured, "No, of course not." It all seemed part of a pattern in which I was destined never to have anyone for myself.

On his way to work he dropped Christina and me at the highway so we could hitchhike to New York. I planned to go home and invited Christina to stay with me until she could find a suitable boy, trusting my mother would understand. But then the police picked us up. We gave false names, not wanting to be returned to Riverview. They took us to a youth detention center.

Meanwhile my mother the detective had called every police precinct in New York and Jersey, giving our descriptions as missing persons. The police identified me from my red coat. We were hauled back to Riverview. There I faced the psychiatrist in charge as he unleashed his anger. He blamed me for leading Christina astray since I was one year older. I accepted the blame, feeling guilty because I had not stopped her from running away, though also remembering I had probably saved her life by telling of her contemplated suicide.

He suddenly asked in a nasty tone, "Do you play pool?"

I thought that an odd question under the circumstances but said, "I've seen men play it in movies."

"Well, you're sure sitting behind the eight ball," he said.

I did not understand what he meant. The next day a social worker drove me to Grasslands, the Westchester County mental hospital, in nearby Valhalla. After two days, they sent me to Kings County Hospital in Brooklyn. I thought, At least I am getting nearer and nearer to home.

But I felt a terror indefinable, a sense of what the psychiatrist meant when he said I was sitting behind the eight ball.

For Kings County was a huge city mental hospital that dealt only with the severely mentally ill. I had left behind the schools for troubled adolescents which permitted a good deal of freedom. I was on my way to a different world, one that would not be as comfortable or compassionate.

A young, plump psychiatrist with a mustache, after interviewing me at Kings County, said, "You don't seem to belong here. You appear quite normal."

I felt deep relief, maybe I would escape incarceration.

Then he added, almost in apology, "I have to ask one more question. Do you ever hear voices?"

I did not want to lie, he seemed trustworthy. I confessed, "Yes."

He looked startled. Then he asked, "What do the voices say?"

"It's just one voice," I explained. "I hear God's voice telling me I have made my mother suffer, that I have hurt her very much. It says I am bad and my mother is going to die if I don't keep washing my hands."

This compulsion had come on suddenly after the night with Jim. Every day I washed my hands over and over to prevent my mother from dying. "Wash your hands like a good little girl." Washing my hands was associated with goodness and the riddance of dirt from the early days of my life.

The psychiatrist knew, from my file, about the night in Hoboken. When my menstrual period was two weeks late, he ordered the rabbit test, then told me it proved I was pregnant. I was delighted at the thought I might have a baby. At last I would have something for myself. I could bring up the baby as my mother had brought me up. I did not mind there was no father, I had no father most of my life.

But when mother heard his report she insisted I sign a paper agreeing to an abortion. I refused.

I expected her to fly into a rage but she said calmly, "I don't think you can be pregnant, sweetheart. You had your period since spending the night with Jim. Unless you've slept with someone else since."

"I haven't." There had been no one.

"Then you *can't* be pregnant."

"So why do you want me to have an abortion?" I asked.

Then the hospital learned they had made a mistake, mixed up my test with that of another girl who *was* pregnant.

Kings County kept me under observation for three months. Then "they," that nebulous but powerful "they," took me before a judge who committed me to Rockland State Hospital. I guess because of my running away from Riverview and the sex experience with Jim, the hearing of God's voice, and what they considered my suicide attempt with the iodine bottle.

Rockland had an adolescent ward but since I would be sixteen in a week, I was admitted to the adult ward. My companions included a few other sixteen-year-olds but mostly senile, alcoholic, catatonic, or psychotic women, one ninety years old. We slept four in a bedroom.

The way of life in a state mental hospital can only add to the depression that causes you to be there. I was humiliated by the lack of privacy, not only in the sleeping quarters but in the toilets without doors and showers without partitions, supposedly for our protection.

But the worst indignities were inflicted by the staff. Not all of them, or most of them, but the few that could make it a hell for some of us, especially the patients who could not control their anger. One morning a very disturbed young white patient became furious when a black nurse's aide asked her to pick up a dirty gown she had thrown across the room. She screamed, ''I won't, nigger!''

''Don't you call me that,'' warned the black aide.

''Nigger! Nigger!'' the patient shouted.

The black aide told the rest of us to leave the room. She put the young woman in a straitjacket. Some of us went outside and peeked in the window. We saw the nurse's aide ask a two-hundred-pound black patient to beat up the young woman. We heard her screams. When the nurse's aide was through with her, she could hardly walk, she was clutching her stomach.

At Rockland I also became aware of the meaning of, to me, the frightening word ''homosexuality.'' One of my friends, another sixteen-year old, was seduced by a nurse's aide who threatened to put her in a straitjacket if she refused to submit. I thought my friend would never stop crying when she came back to her room after the attack in a toilet.

Most of the nurses were not vicious, some even baked cakes and cookies for patients or bought them candy. They treated us with more dignity than some of the psychiatrists did. Once I was interviewed by a group of psychiatrists who made me feel like an insect pinned to a board. They bombarded me so with questions that the answers flew out of my head.

Another time, I told a resident I had run away from Riverview, spent the night with a young man who had picked me up in his car, and had been kicked out of the school. He said scornfully, ''One rotten apple spoils the barrel.'' I felt worthless enough without being cut down by someone supposed to help me. Though I admit my occasional willfulness must have aroused resentment in the authorities.

A woman psychiatrist with a thick German accent was assigned as my therapist. She had short, cropped blond hair and pale blue eyes, wore horn-rimmed glasses. Her manner was dictatorial and, I thought, anti-Semitic. She was straight out of a horror movie. I could hardly believe my ears when one day she said, "Why is it when you come into the room you don't say 'Good morning, how are you, Doctor? I hope you're not too upset having to treat a boring patient like me, who will only give you a headache.' "

Then she ordered, "Every time you enter this office I want you to apologize because you are so boring."

I did so, afraid she would report me as disobedient and fractious. I tried to be less boring. Because of the painful experience with Jim, I told her, "I'm afraid of men."

"Do you think you're a lesbian?" It was a sneer.

"No," I said.

"You *are* a lesbian," she insisted.

She unbuttoned her blouse as though to tempt me. Then abruptly ordered, "Go. I have given you too much time already."

A sixteen-year-old girl on the ward was annoying me for hours on end, asking stupid questions, refusing to leave me alone. One day in desperation I took a pencil and poked her in the arm. The tip broke her skin and it started to bleed slightly. She went to the nurse for iodine and a Band-Aid, explaining I had hurt her accidentally.

This incident was reported to my German psychiatrist. She promptly transferred me to the violent ward, where all my privileges were taken away. When my mother asked why I was there, I told her the whole story, including the woman doctor's unbuttoning her blouse when I said I was afraid of men.

Mother appealed to Victor for help, saying I was placed unjustly on the violent ward. He interceded, for the first time, in my welfare. He asked a physician friend to visit Rockland, talk to the chief psychiatrist, and find out the facts. The chief psychiatrist asked both the woman doctor and me to his office. Victor had evidently relayed my account of how she had exposed herself after insisting I was a lesbian.

The chief psychiatrist asked her if she had done this. "Of course not," she said. "You can't believe this psychotic girl."

But I was given a more understanding psychiatrist and taken out of the violent ward. And at the end of a year I was released from Rockland. I was free to go home after four years in institutions. Years that had started with the crime of truancy.

I had spent almost all my adolescence under supervision or guard, from thirteen to seventeen. But now I was entitled to return to the freedom of my old life and my old friends. If I could find any.

The first one I looked up was Vicky. She had dropped out of high school to her mother's sorrow, though *her* mother had not sent her away. Vicky hung around the house all day and picked up boys at Coney Island in the evening.

The four years had drastically changed her appearance. She had always been pretty but rather mousy; now she looked stunning, like a movie star. She had bleached her pale brown hair blond and wore heavy eye makeup and white lipstick, the vogue of the day, to contrast with the tight black leather skirts of the Beatnik era.

She seemed very feminine and next to her I felt masculine. I wondered if I might be a latent lesbian, as the German woman doctor said. If I were feminine, wouldn't I have enjoyed the act of sex with Jim instead of finding it repulsive? Wouldn't I have responded with passion to the feel of his body instead of fearing it? Vicky welcomed boys making love to her, she was not afraid of them. She said, "Sex makes me feel good—like a woman." I too wanted to feel like a woman, it seemed about time.

Victor kept telling me I could confide in him, that he wanted to help as a father would. He had a way of drawing me out, persuading me to talk about how I felt—much more than any psychiatrist except Dr. Blau.

One Saturday night when mother was out at the store I said to him, "I think there's something wrong with me. I'm afraid to let a boy touch me. Ever since that night in Hoboken."

"Why was it so terrible?" he asked.

"It felt like rape. Jim was rough and it hurt. And now I'm afraid of all boys."

"Don't be," Victor said. "You feel a natural dislike for one young man who thought only of himself. Don't judge all men by him. Many men are gentle and thoughtful."

One afternoon Vicky and I were walking down De Kalb Street and it started to storm. We ran into a record store to keep dry. A boy I had known at the Forest School was working behind the counter. We started to reminisce and he asked for a date. I went out with him several times, chiefly interested in what happened to Benjy, but he did not know. He complained to my mother that I would not even let him kiss me and she said, "Don't give up. Rosette's just had a bad experience."

I could not feel the love for this boy that I had for Benjy. But thanks to Victor's reassurance that I was not a freak, and Vicky's urging me to meet boys, I went with her to Coney Island. We walked along the boardwalk, picked up boys, flirted with them, and I felt feminine.

Mother would ask where I had been when I wandered home after midnight and I would say, "With Vicky, drinking Cokes." I am sure she did not believe me.

I thought, What's good for the goose is good for the gander, knowing mother had a man. In a small way, we even shared that man. One time Victor became more than fatherly for just a moment. He and I were standing in the kitchen and he bent over—he was six feet and I was five feet, four inches—and gave me an ardent kiss. I felt electricity pulse through me. He never kissed me that way again.

One psychiatrist told me that looking for a boyfriend was imitation of my mother and Victor—she had a man of her own and I wanted mine. This psychiatrist said when girls searched for a husband they were copying their mothers.

Perhaps I was preparing for the one love of my life. A love I was destined to meet a few months later when I received a surprise invitation to visit Aunt Berta in Rio. I had not seen her since Chicago when I was five. I think that mother, worried because I wanted to share an apartment with Vicky, wanted to ship me off to Brazil. I flew to Miami and met Uncle Kurt, who escorted me the rest of the way. I have always hated flying, afraid the plane will crash.

In Rio I discovered a new luxury to life in Aunt Berta's ten-room apartment where I had my own bedroom and bath, something I never had at home. Aunt Berta gave elaborate parties in my honor, dressed me in glamorous gowns.

One day as she and I were walking along Avenida Atlantica, we were approached by what I thought the most handsome man I had ever seen. He had classic Greek features, a slightly aquiline nose, perfectly shaped lips. He was tall and light-skinned, with dark eyes and straight black, close-cropped hair.

Aunt Berta introduced him as Alfredo Diaz, a cousin of Uncle Kurt's and a captain in the Brazilian navy. I thought wistfully, I'd love a date with him but he could have any beautiful girl he wished, why would he look at ugly me?

Aunt Berta and he talked Portuguese, which I barely understood. He smiled as he walked away. Aunt Berta told me he was thirty-four, seventeen years older than I, but even so she had asked him to take me to a dance the following Saturday.

"Oh no, Aunt Berta!" I protested. "He'll only do it because he feels obligated to you. Not because he wants to take me out."

But my reluctance was overcome when two days later, on a Wednesday, he called Aunt Berta to ask if he could also take me out Friday. She refused, saying she would not allow him to see me twice in one week before he even knew me.

She was a stickler for South American customs. Just before Alfredo arrived on Saturday evening, she said, "I will chaperone you for the night."

"We don't need a chaperone," I said. "There are no chaperones in the United States."

"You don't speak much Portuguese and Alfredo doesn't speak English very well. How will you get along?"

"We'll find a way." I can be as stubborn as my mother.

She gave in with a smile. "Have a nice time."

Alfredo came for me in a taxi and we drove to the navy officers club. I had picked up quite a few words of Portuguese and he spoke English fairly well. We smiled a lot at each other. I tried to flirt by snuggling close but he drew away as if afraid to touch me.

At the dance we did not need words. I wore my most elegant dress, deep rose chiffon, and felt, for one of the few times in my life, that I was not ugly as he swirled me around the floor in the samba and tango. I pressed my body close to his, thought, This man, even though he is twice my age, is so very handsome and charming I must not let him get away.

During intermission we walked in the garden. Suddenly he drew me close, kissed me warmly, tenderly, my Brazilian Prince Charming. He asked, "Would you like to go to my apartment?"

"Yes," I said, even though knowing Aunt Berta would be furious at such an act.

We taxied to his home. I expected a lavish place and was dismayed when we walked into two rooms filled with rickety, worn furniture and strewn with papers and books. He poured us a drink from a small, battered bar. I did not wait for an invitation but started to undress, stripping to my brassiere and panties. I was determined to seduce him before he changed his mind, believing me too young.

He looked somewhat shocked but gulped down his drink. Then he picked me up—I weighed less than a hundred pounds—and carried me into the bedroom. For the first and only time in my life I enjoyed the body of a man. He was gentle, thoughtful, a true lover. When he poured himself into me I exulted in the moment even though I did not have an orgasm. It was enough for me to touch and admire his muscular arms and legs. I thought the naked masculine body ugly every time I drew it in art class. But Alfredo's was the exception, perhaps because of the way I felt about him.

After he had two more acts of sex, we dressed. As he combed his black hair in the bathroom, I poured myself another drink. Suddenly I felt frightened of a man. For a different reason than his hurting me, as Jim had done. I was afraid, now that I had enjoyed sex with Alfredo, that he had supernatural powers. I did not believe any ordinary man could be so seductive and appealing.

He invited me to spend the next day and evening with him. To sail in the morning and dance at night. Then he took me home in a taxi and kissed me goodnight with lips that were sweet.

I was too excited to sleep, dozed fitfully and woke at dawn. I spent hours dressing and putting on makeup. The morning passed but he did not appear, or call. There was no word from him in the afternoon. In the evening Aunt Berta and Uncle Kurt went to a party. I did not tell them I had been stood up by Alfredo.

That night I sat alone, hour after hour, waiting for the phone to ring. I resolved if Alfredo did not call by ten, I would take an overdose of the sleeping pills I found in Aunt Berta's medicine chest. I felt too hurt and rejected to want to live. I could not understand how Alfredo could break a promise made in love.

At ten o'clock sharp, I rose from Aunt Berta's turquoise sofa and went into her all-white bathroom. I took the bottle of sleeping pills and swallowed seven—there was a warning on the bottle not to take more than one every six hours. Then I undressed, put on my sheer black nightgown, slipped into bed, and lost consciousness.

Mother found me in a coma later that night on her arrival from New York. She did not realize what I had done until I told her the next day. Doctors gave me an injection and I slept for another day and night. When I woke I told mother and Aunt Berta why I had tried to kill myself.

Aunt Berta was furious and said she would forbid Alfredo ever to enter her home. But my mother begged her not to do this because, she said, for the first time I had found someone for whom I cared and who cared for me. Though I could not figure out why, if he cared so much, he did not appear or phone with some excuse for failing to show up.

A week passed and I never expected to see him again. Suddenly he called to ask if he could take me out. He explained he had fallen severely ill with dysentery the week before, on our scheduled second date. He apologized for not phoning. He asked if I had forgiven him.

"Of course," I said.

We had dinner in a charming restaurant, then went to his apartment for another exciting evening of sex. As we left the bedroom I asked, "Would you ever marry me?"

"Only if you were pregnant," he said.

I prayed I would get pregnant each time I saw him, about once a week for several months. Then mother made me return with her to New York, saying she could not make a living in Brazil. I did not want to leave, for Rio had been six months of heaven. But I understood why mother did not want to be separated from me—I was all she had in the world. It did not seem right that she be destined to a life of drudgery in New York while I went to parties and enjoyed a love affair in a far country.

Flying home I felt so depressed I could not speak to her and refused to touch champagne, my favorite drink. I could think only of the loss of Alfredo and the enchanting evenings in his bedroom. When I got home I wrote him a poem in free verse that I never mailed:

Death in Small Doses

> *What makes you so special?*
> *You speak a foreign tongue which is harsh and*
> *   ugly yet on you is befittingly masculine.*
> *Your hair is straight and the cut ludicrous*
> *   yet you wear it with confidence and poise.*
> *You are poor yet you are clean.*
> *Your apartment is sloppy as a pigs-pen.*
> *I will never forget you*
> *O dearest love.*

"Dearest love" eventually married, had four children, and left the navy to teach economics. Looking back at my suicide attempt, I realize I was in a state of panic because I missed my mother so much. I used Alfredo to try to forget how desperately I yearned for her. When he did not appear that night, I felt as if she had deserted me and I wanted to die.

On her birthday I handed her a card I had painted. The outside showed the face of a beautiful woman I thought looked like her, which I captioned "La Vierge Marie." I wrote inside in gold paint: "You know that (next to Alfredo) I love you most in the world, and you love me (in your own way) most in the world. . . . For whereas a sister will abandon a sister and a husband abandon a wife, a mother will never abandon her only child nor will a child ever put anyone above its mother. So forgive me mother when I drop a careless word, for without your sweet, patient, tender love, this world would be very cold and cheerless indeed."

The only other man I ever wished as a husband was my cousin Steven. He was also tall and slender but with blue eyes and sandy hair. He wore suits ten times too large in which he looked lost. He also talked in a whisper; you had to listen carefully. He married an Israeli girl and is now a professor of sociology. I was attracted to future professors.

Mother and I flew to Waltham, Massachusetts, when Steven received his M.A. from Brandeis University, as Senator Hubert Humphrey gave the commencement address. All the relatives then gathered in our hotel room, where they sat hour after hour chattering like magpies. I kept wishing Steven would ask me to go for a drive in his car. At long last, as if reading my thoughts, he said to his mother, "Do you mind if I ride Rosette around and show her the town?"

His mother said, "You can't leave the rest of your relatives."

When my mother and I finally got rid of everyone, I waited for her to fall asleep, then had a good cry. That was the extent of my romance with Steven because when he later asked for a date, arranging to meet me at the Museum of Modern Art, one of us confused the time. I sat on a bench in the lobby for several hours, waiting in vain for him to show up.

As I rose to leave, a tall, rather heavy man, with dark hair, who had been sitting next to me in silence for at least an hour, said, "I see you've been stood up. May I show you the museum?"

His name was Joel Smith and he was likable and intelligent, the owner of a firm of interior decorators. He was twelve years older than I, invited me to plays, concerts, and the opera, said he was falling in love. Mother approved of him but I did not love him as I did Alfredo, with a yearning that makes you feel faint.

When mother asked why I would not marry him after he proposed, I said, "Because I'm not in love. It wouldn't be fair to him."

I was more excited by the fact we were now living in Manhattan, nearer the museums, Broadway, and many superb restaurants. I also relished the privacy of a room totally mine. Though sometimes at night I felt frightened of the dark or woke from a nightmare and ran to mother to ask her to sleep with me, either in her bed or mine.

I found a job at Eastern Airlines, made friends with several of my feminine co-workers, even traveled with them to Washington, D.C., the only time in my life, except for camp and the visit to Aunt Berta, I went someplace without my mother. I wanted to share an apartment with one of the girls, now that I was earning money, but my mother said I was too young and, in view of what had happened when I lived away from her in Rio, I should stay with her.

So I gave up the idea of moving out.

I liked my new job which gave my mother and me the chance to take trips we could not have afforded without the discount. I had friends who respected me, work I enjoyed. But then, suddenly, I started to believe my co-workers at Eastern Airlines could read my thoughts.

I became so agitated I resigned. I sat home day after day, feeling depressed and unwanted. I wondered if there were any use trying to go on, perhaps it would be better to end the agony.

That New Year's Eve mother and I watched television as the crowds celebrated at Times Square and we heard Guy Lombardo play "Auld Lang Syne." Then a comedian made scornful remarks about some movie stars. I said to mother, "He's making fun of me. He's reading my mind."

"Don't be stupid, Rosette," mother said angrily. "You'll kill me if you don't stop this nonsense."

Stupid! Ugly! Not golden like the American dream girl. I felt furious, as though life had played a horrible joke on me. God and the world were unjust. I wanted to punish God, and the loveless world.

I went into the bathroom, stepped out of my black silk jersey dress. I took the razor that I used to remove the black hair curling under my arms. I pressed it in a curving line around my throat, then my wrists. I did not cut deep, afraid of the sight of blood gushing out. There must be a less gory way to die, I thought. I looked at myself in the mirror, slim in my black lace slip, my hair carefully styled at the beauty parlor in case a man called for a date at the last minute. I stared at a face I detested. Then I opened the bathroom window, sixteen floors above the street.

I pushed myself out so I sat on the ledge and dangled my feet in the freezing cold of the first night of the new year. It was icy but I felt elated at the thought of hurling myself to the ground. I would fly through the air in a moment of ecstasy. Then—crash! The end of all despair.

I ordered myself, "Jump! Jump!"

But some small shred of self-preservation kept me immobile. I heard mother call from the living room window, "Go back! Go back!" She did not sound angry but loving. I thought, She really cares and she will be all alone if I kill myself.

Slowly I lowered myself into the bathroom and opened the locked door.

When mother saw me, she did not scream in fury but hugged and kissed me. She said, "Thank God! Thank God!" There were tears in her eyes, not sparks of rage.

The next day she asked me to go voluntarily to the psychiatric clinic of St. Vincent's Hospital. I found the experience painful. I am very shy, with strong feelings about appearing naked in front of anyone. When the nurse asked me to strip, I refused. She called in another nurse and they pulled off my clothes. I cried at such an indignity. I think they might have managed to find out if I concealed any suicidal weapons on my body in a more thoughtful way.

When I left the hospital after twelve days, I decided to enroll at the Art Students League, but soon even painting became too much effort. I now felt persecuted by a strange group. I believed that there were one hundred people in the world who belonged to an organization called the Rosicrucians and that they possessed supernatural powers. They could change their appearance to look like anyone they pleased. They knew more about me than anyone else did. They could read my thoughts, they watched my every move on a supernatural television set. I felt as if a movie camera were following me day and night, as if I were the center of the universe, and this made me very self-conscious. I decided I could be happy only if the Rosicrucians would let me become a member. Then I too could change my physical appearance, which I detested, take on a new identity and live a different life. I wrote asking how to become a member but they never answered. I thought, They must not want me to join because the other members would be jealous.

My mother, afraid I might make another suicide attempt, on the advice of a cousin who is active in the mental health field, committed me to Bellevue for diagnosis. From there I was sent to Central Islip, miles out on Long Island. They ordered insulin shock and electroshock treatments.

I was very frightened the first time I received insulin. Nurses woke a group of us at four in the morning and led us to a large room lined with beds. I was told to lie down on one. A nurse gave me an injection of insulin. About ten or fifteen minutes later, I blanked out, went into a coma. I woke up feeling more depressed than when I lay down. The depression was so deep I wanted to kill myself but there seemed no way, for they removed all possible weapons and watched us carefully.

After fifteen of these treatments, I told the psychiatrist, "I can't take any more."

"It's either insulin or electroshock," he said.

"I'll try electroshock," I said. "It can't make me any more depressed."

For that I was also wakened at four in the morning, marched to a large room, asked to lie down. Two nurses held my body to the bed. A man standing behind me put a gag in my mouth. Then he placed electrodes on both sides of my head. At that point I blacked out, went into convulsions, I was told. When I woke, I did not feel depressed, as with the insulin.

But on the sixth treatment something went wrong. They must have failed to give me enough electricity. I became conscious midway through the shock. I felt as though I were being electrocuted—every nerve in my body flashed fire.

I was so frightened I refused to take any more electroshock and went back to the insulin. In all, I had sixty-two insulin shock treatments and six electroshock before I was discharged. I think they may have somewhat impaired my memory for I find at times I cannot think as clearly as before the shock.

I knew mother felt frightened about the idea of shock treatments. I wrote reassuring her "they can only help me get cured once and for all, so this will be my last stay at such an institution." I described the classes in group therapy where I was encouraged to talk of some of my sexual experiences, as did other patients without seeming embarrassment.

I also had private sessions with a psychologist. I mentioned my fear of drowning and he said this represented a subconscious fear of returning to the womb and becoming too dependent on my mother. He also interpreted my not wanting to eat peaches and cherries as meaning the fruits were symbols of growing things and fertility and, in some way, symbols of unconscious hostility to my mother. I wondered if he knew what he was talking about.

I told him I did not feel very mature because I was an only child and spoiled and always had relied on my mother. I asked if he thought I had any insight into my problems. He said I was still "very impressionable" and must become more secure, rely more on my own judgment. Somehow I felt better, my depression lifted, and I wanted to live.

One day in group therapy the psychologist said there were secret compulsions in many of us which we denied but that showed themselves in other forms. I thought he might mean the sadistic impulses that are masked in such ideas as cannibalism (for me, the eating of certain fruits) or stepping on grass (like when I thought the grass represented people's heads and hurt as I trampled it).

After we left the session, a friend of mine and I found a dead sparrow on the sidewalk. She picked it up and placed it in the grass, saying it was still warm. The next day I looked for it but it had disappeared. Someone said a cat ate it.

At another group therapy session I was asked to talk about a recent visit home. I told the truth. I said my mother seemed like a stranger to me. The psychologist asked why. I said she always invited some friend to the house when I was there, as if she did not want to be alone with me. I also thought her aloof and melancholic and this depressed me. The psychologist asked why her insecurity should affect me adversely. It was a good question and I thought, I would like to know the answer, life is not a simple thing, perhaps to believe it is, is to look at it with childish eyes.

I liked the therapy sessions but on the whole Central Islip seemed a Clockwork Orange of insulin shock, electroshock, barred windows, women screaming in their beds at night, unappetizing food. I wanted to go home so desperately that when the psychiatrist asked, "How do you feel?" I said, "Fine," though I felt anxious, hoping he would believe me and send me home.

Finally he said I could leave. As the day approached, I was fidgety and restless. Though the depressed feelings had lessened I was by no means completely well or I would not have felt so anxious. Was it because I was leaving this protective environment? I wondered. Somehow I still felt "bad," guilty of whatever crime they were charging me with. Didn't the punishment meted out—the insulin and electroshock—prove my guilt?

Did *anyone* really care? I thought.

But at least after Central Islip I was able to find a job at Asiatic Petroleum, an international oil company, with offices at Rockefeller Center. About this time, much to my surprise, mother wrote to my father, asking him to visit us. I also wrote, telling him how much I had missed him over the years.

He answered promptly, saying he was so happy to hear from me and approved of my wanting to study Spanish so we could "communicate with greater ease." I had written him about the coming election and he said that John F. Kennedy, then running for President, was very well liked in Venezuela because "he is against Nixon, who is the symbol of approval of all the tropical tyrannies." He added, "I am happy to know you have political awareness but be careful with those friends who do not agree with you. Do not make yourself difficulties, my dearest, you have nothing to gain by antagonizing your friends. You have to study the minds of the people with whom you deal." He ended the letter: "Receive a strong 'abrazo' [hug] from your father who loves you."

In a second letter he told me I could write him in English, which he understood perfectly, that he wanted to read all about me—what interested me, my likes and dislikes, my tastes, my "afflictions and aspirations." He said it was his greatest hope that "from now on our bonds will be very strong, very firm, that you'll allow me to be a true friend."

I had sent him recent photographs and he thanked me, saying he treasured the ones taken "when you used to sleep in my bed in the early morning, when you were little and woke up before me." Again he ended by saying, "My beloved Rosette, receive a strong 'abrazo' from your father who will never forget you, not with all the years that pass or the geographic distance."

In a third letter he wrote: "I am glad you love to study. However, don't ever feel satisfied that you have learned enough because the learning process never ends. We are always beginning to learn, under a new phase. What would you like to study as a profession?"

I wrote that I wanted to be an artist, adding, "It is very interesting that you should have painted once, as mother told me. I wonder why you gave it up. It *is* very hard to paint for an amateur, lots of trials and tribulations, but also a lot of satisfaction." I thought maybe my desire to paint was a way of keeping part of him with me, since I had lost him so early in life.

Writing to my father, and the thought of his coming to live with us, proved very upsetting. Mother and I fought more than ever, then took turns being depressed. I wrote to a psychiatrist I saw on television, though I never sent the letter, asking if I should move out of the apartment when my father arrived. I said, "My mother has always been closer to me than the average mother and I in turn have always tried to run away from her overpossessiveness." Yet I was afraid of being cast out of the house if my father arrived. But I did not have to worry for long, it soon became clear he never intended to come.

After eight months at Asiatic Petroleum, I started to hear voices in my head telling me, "Shut up! Shut up!" One day I called mother and asked her to meet me in Central Park in front of the Plaza Hotel at lunchtime. I was there early, sat on a bench near the small lake with ducks swimming around it. Mother found me in tears.

"What's the matter, dearest?" she asked.

"Mom, I hear voices telling me to shut up," I said. "It's been going on almost every day for the past month. I can't stand much more."

She persuaded me to sign myself in at a hospital near home. They sent me to Central Islip again. This time I received no shock, only medication. After a few months I was home, taking medication daily. I have never been off it since.

I found a job at the Merchandising Corporation and stayed there three years. I also studied fashion illustration, thinking I might become a commercial artist. But then once again I had the illusion my co-workers could read my mind and resigned.

Mother decided we should take a long-planned trip to Europe. I could not appreciate the art in museums which mother had so often described because I felt strangely detached from everything. But I was moved by a visit to the house where Anne Frank lived before she was murdered by the Nazis. I thought of the time when I was five and found a book mother hid in her closet showing photographs of Nazi atrocities. It made a lasting impression of unbelievable horror.

I came to life in Paris where the very air seemed to sing. At the Louvre I stood in awe before *The Winged Victory,* the *Mona Lisa* and other incredible works of art. I marveled at the mythological scenes on the ceiling of the Opera House, heard *Carmen* performed as only the

French could do it, with verve, electrifying brilliance, and fiery passion.

But when we returned to New York I again sank into a depression even the medication could not ease. It did not help my self-image to have put on forty pounds at Central Islip. I covered all the mirrors in our apartment with white sheets so I could not see my pudgy body and ugly face. I asked a doctor for a prescription for an appetite-killer. But he did not want me to take the drug for more than a month and the minute I stopped, the voracious hunger returned.

Mother suggested we fly to Russia, fulfilling a long-time dream of hers. She thought the trip might cheer me up. When we arrived, she was joyous at seeing relatives and reliving memories but I felt lethargic, I wanted to stay in the hotel room all day and sleep. Worried about my depression, she cancelled our return to Moscow, where her relatives were to give her a party, and we flew home.

A few nights later I woke up on the floor screaming. I had wakened from a nightmare in which a gang of Nazis chased me, wanted to mutilate and kill me. Mother thought my screams had aroused the whole building. For days I was gripped by the feeling there was no escape from my torturers.

A relative who worked there told us about a private hospital in Queens that offered a ninety-day psychiatric program for young men and women. I sought admission and was accepted. I believed I might at last have found a place that would cure me. It was an attractive modern, open hospital.

I was scheduled for my first appointment with a psychiatrist whom I will call Dr. John Harris. I went at the designated hour, eleven-thirty in the morning, and stood outside his office—there were no chairs—for half an hour. Then I went to lunch, not wanting to miss it.

When I returned I found Dr. Harris, a bearded young psychiatrist with curly dark hair, in his office. I told him who I was. He stared at me and asked in thinly disguised anger, "Where have you been?"

"I waited half an hour, then went to lunch," I said.

"You should have stayed until I arrived," he said.

I could not believe he expected me to give up eating because he was late. We got off to an unfortunate start, neither trusting the other.

My roommate played continuous rock and roll on her radio and constantly asked me to do favors such as making her bed and cleaning up—I might as well have stayed home carrying out mother's demands. I felt uncomfortable both in and out of my room. I started to hear voices again ordering me to "shut up."

When mother visited I told her I felt something ominous in the air. "I don't like it here," I said. "I'm afraid something terrible is going to happen, mom."

"It's just in your mind, sweetheart," she said. "This is supposed to be a very fine place. Give it a chance."

After she left, I went to another appointment with Dr. Harris. He seemed repelled by everything I said so I did not say much. That night, lying in bed, I suddenly felt terrified, not knowing why. The nurse gave me a tranquilizer. A few hours later I woke from a nightmare in which supernatural powers, outraged by my existence, threatened to kill me.

Not wanting to endure further nightmares for they seemed so real, I drank coffee all day and eight to ten cans of Coke so I would not sleep at night, though sometimes I dozed. When we were wakened at seven, I was so tired I was afraid I would not be able to control my muscles. I used a machine in occupational therapy for cutting wood and feared that in a weakened moment I might cut off my hand.

I felt both the patients and the psychiatrists had only contempt for me. When a psychiatrist came to our cottage to lead us in group therapy, I sensed in him a cold fury toward me. I wondered whether the psychiatrists were the supernatural powers in my nightmares.

One night, so exhausted I was unable to stay awake, I dreamed I was reincarnated into a tiger. The tiger again. I woke with a scream, walked to the lounge for a Coke, joining a few sleepless patients. When I told them my nightmare, they looked at me in scorn. It is difficult to sympathize with the fear in someone else's dream.

I went through the following day's many activities like a zombie. In the evening I decided I could no longer bear this hospital. I put on the calfskin coat I had bought in better days and walked toward the entrance gate about a city block from my cottage.

Suddenly I froze in terror. I was seized by the premonition if I took one more step in the direction of the gate, I would be struck dead by an invisible bolt of lightning. I stared at the gate in appalling anxiety. A gray squirrel, looking strangely ominous for so small a creature, ran across the road in front of me. I turned and went back to the cottage.

The next day I told Dr. Harris of my tiger nightmare, my attempt to run away, and my premonition. He looked at me with what I thought deeper revulsion than ever.

At the following session he announced he had scheduled an appointment the next day for two other psychiatrists to interview me and determine whether I should be given the experimental drug called Prolixin. I spent the night in the lounge drinking coffee to keep awake so I would not suffer through another nightmare—no mother near to reassure me it was only make-believe. In the morning, when it came time to see the two other psychiatrists, I was spinning with exhaustion.

A nurse led me to an office where two strange psychiatrists and Dr. Harris sat around a table. They asked about my premonition, then told me to wait in the hall. When I was again summoned, they handed me a form to sign. It stated that in case anything happened to me as a result of taking Prolixin, the hospital would not be held responsible.

I was terrified at the thought of taking a new drug that might damage me. But I desperately wished the approval of Dr. Harris and the two psychiatrists. I did not want them to think me "bad." So I signed. I handed the form to Dr. Harris and he said in what sounded like derision, "You call this a signature?" My hand had been trembling so that I could hardly write my name.

I was possessed by a new fear. Why wouldn't the hospital take responsibility for the results of the drug? What might those results be? A crippling of the brain? Of the legs and arms? Seizures like epilepsy? Slow death? Why didn't the psychiatrists tell me what I might expect, if the drug was not safe?

Was I to be a sacrificial guinea pig in the interests of mental health? They were asking me to risk harming mind and body. Where were my self-preservative instincts? I was a cringing coward. I had needed their approval more than I had been willing to protect myself. Now what was I to do?

On mother's next visit, I begged her to take me home. I ran after her in the snow to plead further. But she would not listen.

I was assigned a new psychiatrist, a woman from the Philippines with a thick Oriental accent. One of her first questions was, "Why do you hate your mother so much?"

"I don't hate her," I protested.

Looking at me skeptically, she said again, "Why do you hate your mother?"

I began to wonder if I *were* the heinous mother-hating criminal she and other psychiatrists wanted me to be.

One night as I lay in bed, my mind flashed to an early memory of the infirmary at the Chicago nursery where, when I had chickenpox, I slept in an immaculate white room, empty except for my cot and a little white wastebasket. I sensed that my feelings at the nursery and now at this hospital were the same. I felt completely alone in the world and wanted it to come to an explosive end.

The next day I phoned my mother and said, "Tomorrow a girl just like me will call you and tell you she is very tired and would like to die."

"Try to understand they want to help you, precious," she said.

I was ordered to move to a new building in preparation for the administration of Prolixin. As I walked in with my suitcase, I had the feeling of déjà vu, as though I had once been in that place and died there.

My room was on the ground floor, next to a back door that stood open some of the time to air out the cottage. I caught a cold and ran a high fever, but the nurse would give no medication because of the new drug about to be inflicted on me.

That night I made up my mind to defy the supernatural powers and save my life. When it was dark I put on my coat and slipped out the back door next to my room. I walked in the icy cold toward the gate. There was a guard but he did not stop me, thinking I was a visitor or a patient with privileges.

I stopped one foot from the gate. I was again possessed by the premonition that between the two trees on each side of the gate lay a field of electricity and if I took another step forward I would be electrocuted by omnipotent powers.

But in sudden blind fury, I took the step. I thought, I will defy the supernatural forces, I do not care if I *am* electrocuted, I will not stay in this hell to face certain death. I crossed the magnetic field between the two trees.

Nothing happened. I kept walking.

When I reached the bus stop, I felt exultant at my escape. On the bus I chose a window seat, looked out with pleasure at rows of houses, the trees decorated with Christmas bulbs. I thought, Maybe someday I will live in a lovely home with a husband and a son.

Half an hour later I was in Manhattan. Another half hour on the subway and I was home.

When mother opened the door she stared at me in sorrow. She said, "Sweetheart, you'll have to go back."

I started to cry. "I can't, Mommie," I said. "They're going to give me a dangerous drug tomorrow. It might kill me."

She looked into my terrorized eyes. Then she said, "You don't have to go back."

I was proud of myself. While Prolixin may have benefited many patients, I read in the *New York Times* of January 6, 1979, about the tragic case of Henry Tucker. He had been a convict in the Virginia State Penitentiary in Richmond since 1964, serving a forty-year sentence on conviction of "breaking and entering with intent to rape." The *Times* announced he was awarded $518,000 in damages by a federal district judge in Virginia because he had been permanently paralyzed after doctors prescribed Prolixin, described as "a powerful antipsychotic drug said to require careful monitoring of dosage."

Unsupervised prison inmates had been allowed to administer the medication. Tucker went into a severe neurological reaction, first developing tremors, then slipping into a stupor. Doctors failed to diagnose his condition or to administer other drugs that could have reversed it. Ultimately he developed *myositis ossificans,* in which calcium and bone deposits form around the joints of the body. His hip joints became so badly affected that his legs were permanently drawn up to his chest, making it impossible for him to lie flat or sit in a chair. The hip joints were surgically removed and though he could not use his legs, he could sit in a wheelchair. His arms were also paralyzed. The prison planned to release him in the next few weeks, the article said.

His lawyers stated that their evidence included medical records showing he had been given "excessive doses" of Prolixin by other prisoners assigned as aides in the prison hospital and that for six months he lay in the hospital essentially without medical treatment while his immobilized body became covered with maggot-infested bedsores.

A reaction this drastic could not have occurred at a place like the hospital in which I was to get treatment because of the high-quality medical care there. But I have read articles in current psychiatric journals warning that the side effects of Prolixin and other drugs include *myositis ossificans*.

Though I escaped what I thought persecution by this hospital, I could not shake the depression that now seemed my shadow. Mother convinced me to sign in for six weeks at the psychiatric clinic of one New York hospital, then for two weeks at the psychiatric "pavilion" of another.

We were still hoping to find a solution other than shock or further drugs. We have never given up hope that, magically, one day someone will find the way to true mental healing, à la Jesus, à la Freud, à la anyone.

The psychiatric pavilion was my final hospital. The psychiatrist told mother, "We are sending your daughter to Bellevue. They will help her."

Mother looked him in the eye. She said, "Rosette is not going to spend one more day in an institution. She has had enough punishment."

She took me home.

III

Day by Day

It has been nine years since mother and I started living together knowing it might be forever. We moved to another apartment in the same building but on the second floor. Mother did not want to live with the fear I might hurl myself out of a high window.

Ever since I was thirteen and a half, except for the last three years, I have seen Dr. Blau, even though intermittently at times, at her private office on Park Avenue and 39th Street at $15 a visit. I paid the fee out of the social security disability to which I am entitled because I worked for seven years. I also have Medicaid.

Though I am sure I benefited from Dr. Blau's help, I could never tell her my deepest feelings. I felt ashamed of them and believed if I spoke of them she would never want to see me again. Feelings I might be a lesbian, unfeminine, ugly. My belief I was persecuted by the Rosicrucians. The conviction I was "bad" and did not deserve to live. The delusion that I could talk to God and the devil and hear their voices.

After my second stay at Central Islip, where I was introduced to Mellaril and Tofranil, I needed medication just to keep going. Dr. Blau did not believe in medication and would not write prescriptions. So mother took me, at the same time I was seeing Dr. Blau, to psychiatrists who would prescribe medication. The first four years after Central Islip, I swallowed 600 milligrams of Thorazine a day for a year, then 500 daily for a year, then 400. For the past two years I have used between 100 and 400 milligrams a day, as well as 20 milligrams of Stelazine daily as a stimulant. The Thorazine tends to make you feel lethargic.

At the age of seventeen, when I left Rockland State Hospital, I went to Dr. Blau as a private patient for six months until I flew to Rio. When I returned, I resumed seeing her for two years, until sent to Central Islip, then saw her after my release. Mother would take me to Dr. Blau's office and wait in the reception room. In the last few years, mother wanted to be part of the sessions so she could understand me better. That was the end of my therapy.

Dr. Blau sometimes gave what I called pep talks. She would say, "You are a fine, talented person. Look at Helen Keller's inner reservoir and how she mobilized it. You said you admired her more than any other person. Try to be like her."

Or she would suggest, "Will yourself to get well. Believe in yourself. Trust yourself."

But I could not "will" myself to get better, as Dr. Blau and my mother urged. Something stronger than "will" defeated my will.

I told Dr. Blau, "You say I should will myself not to be afraid. Isn't that impossible? Can someone will himself to paint like Michelangelo? I don't know what I'm afraid of. It is years now that I have been seeing you and I still don't know what scares me. I had a horrible dream containing monsters after I started talking to you about my fears last week. My life is a nightmare and you aren't helping me to understand it."

"Understanding takes time," she said.

She claimed I had too much "interference" from my mother, which prevented me from using my full intelligence. She also said my fears had created the delusions in my mind.

I left Dr. Blau when she semi-retired, but also because mother and I felt she no longer was helping me. I even started to consider her an enemy. One day I accused her, "You want to damn me."

She said, "Your paranoia is destroying the transference."

I knew it was but could do nothing about it; whatever was set on breaking up our relationship was out of my control. I felt so devastated

I wrote her a letter of apology. I said I had never met a more kind or decent person. I added I was ashamed of my hostility, for which she was generous enough not to rebuke me but condone as a sign of my suffering.

I explained I felt belligerent at times to compensate for the feeling that I was not going anywhere, that three years before I had started going backwards, so that "going forward" meant striving twice as hard and I did not know if I could make it. I concluded by saying I was hostile because I did not want to face up to my inadequacies and that I would appreciate another chance with her.

Which, of course, she gave me. But in 1976, when she closed her New York office, it seemed the right time to stop seeing her. I occasionally wrote her how much I missed her. I treasure one of her letters saying she was happy to hear from me and learn I had done "a lot of thinking and real reappraising" of my role in solving my problems. She reminded me once again, "In the end, it is always you and only you, the person involved, who actually and successfully can solve your problems permanently."

She also wrote she was flattered by my statement that I considered her "the chosen one" whom I had permitted to help me but that "if I made myself so important in your battle that it is only I whom you are willing to permit to share your fight, I failed you. I hope that such is not the case. Rosette, it is you who has a lot of fight in you. It is you who can do it."

I could not make a successful transference to the psychiatrists I then saw. I stayed with one for three months, another, two months, a third, four weeks. When they ventured any opinion, beyond giving medication, they said I was unable to separate from my mother not only physically but emotionally and this crippled my natural drive to be independent. I finally found Dr. Aylin Radomisli, a woman psychiatrist I liked very much and felt I could trust.

Mother and I have both led lonely lives, except for each other. I wish I had brothers and sisters for then I might have learned to share mother's love. And I would not have had to bear the full brunt of her anger. I once wrote, "Children who do not have a brother or sister are damned by God for all eternity because they don't have someone their own age in whom to confide their secrets."

I know that my relationship with my mother has been too close.

Once I wrote, "I want to bury myself in you as an ostrich buries her head in the sand and feel no pain ever again." Another time I sketched a girl sitting on a hill gazing at the setting sun, titled it, "Myself—Herself." Sometimes I feel as if I live in a web, a warm, enveloping web out of which I cannot move. Part of me wants to escape but part wishes to remain trapped, knowing mother will take care of me no matter how angrily she sometimes screams at me.

When I went to Cunningham Junior High, I had a classmate named Pearl, a very bright girl, who later became a psychiatrist. One day when we were at the beach, she asked about my mother, intimating there was something wrong between mother and me. Recently I met her while riding on a bus with my mother. She said, "I see you are still with your mother." I felt guilty and afraid that if we renewed our friendship Pearl would feel repelled.

I know I am paying a high price for not being more independent, for not feeling more of a sense of my own identity. I did try to move away from mother. I wanted to share an apartment with Vicky when I was discharged from Rockland at seventeen. I wanted to stay in Rio with Aunt Berta and Uncle Kurt. I wanted to live with a girlfriend from Eastern Airlines, and then to live alone when I started to earn good money.

But mother did not think I was capable of making it by myself. Looking at my record, I am not sure I could have. I felt torn about moving away. I did not want to abandon my mother as too many people in her life had done. Had I not felt conflicted, I would have been able to walk out on her no matter how strongly she protested.

Sometimes I think of mother as two people, one loving, one angry. And of myself as several people. There is the me who, with medication, can handle myself with mother and strangers and in classes at Hunter. Then there is the me who creates nightmares as I sleep and indulges in illusions sometimes while awake. And the me who once in a while has the urge to play the piano or paint. Also the me who, without medication, sinks into such depression life does not seem worth living.

I wish I had known my father but it is a reality of life that I was deprived of him after the age of three and a half, just as my mother did not see her father when she was growing up. Luck probably plays a part in what happens to us, though I don't think of good luck as something special. I think good luck is when you escape suffering—you are lucky if nothing bad happens.

The last day of July, 1975, the postman rang our bell, an unusual event, for he usually leaves the mail in our box in the lobby. He handed me a special delivery letter from Caracas. It was sent by my father's nephew Luis. He wrote that my father died on July 27. He consoled us by saying my father's death "brought him rest from great suffering. In his last four months he had no feeling in his legs, was in a wheelchair, and had to be fed. All because the medicines had ceased to be effective." Just before my father died, Luis reported, he remarked he had paid dearly for the errors he had made in his life, the biggest one being to separate from his wife and daughter. He died with his sister and nephew at his bedside. Luis asked that if my father had ever "acted badly" to us, would we please forgive him.

I felt very sad that my father died in a nursing home, paralyzed from the neck down, after suffering so many years. He knew little happiness, never fulfilling his creative urge to be an artist or architect, always in poor health due to his four-year imprisonment as a young man. My anguish is different. I live under the threat of impending doom. I fear a new Hitler will sweep the world. Or the atom bomb will be dropped on New York City. Or I will be dragged off to a mental hospital out of which I will never emerge.

I have strange fantasies, like being reincarnated into a sphinx. Or I feel deaf and dumb as if living in an iron lung, all emotion deadened, incapable of love for anyone or anything. I am like a runner who has been paralyzed and must learn to walk again. I have a vague desire to get better but the will to carry it out never materializes.

At times my thoughts go in circles like a cat chasing its tail. Intellectually, I have become somewhat of a cripple. There are days I cannot concentrate long enough to read a book or play the piano. I have forgotten how to paint and feel devoid of all talent, as though I had never held a brush in my hand or mixed a soft color.

I am scared even during the day. Though I know the sun is shining, the sky may look dark or eerie blue, filled with foreboding. There are times I do not want to leave the house. Or dress, or wash my face.

I feel there are powerful forces outside me that I cannot fight, as if someone is bent on destroying me. I am blackmailed by someone trying to make my life miserable. I think of Anna, a woman in a fictional story, who could not account for certain periods of the day. A voice in her head told her that the voice's name was Vicky. One day as Anna lay down Vicky's voice warned she had made Anna disappear for an hour and taken over Anna's life. Vicky said this would happen more and more until she had completely replaced Anna.

I cannot stand intensity—the intensity of my mother's love. At times, to combat this intensity, I try not to feel her love. I may be so overcome by unhappiness, estrangement, alienation and lethargy that I even deny hearing her. Perhaps this is due to the medication. Or is it the medication that brings on such withdrawal?

My mother and I are both victim and torturer, exchanging roles every so often. There are moments I feel she wants me to die a violent death. I often think I *was* murdered as a child and reincarnated into a doll.

When she rages at me, though it is not often, I feel a demon in her takes over and I want to smash something—a dish or cup. Sometimes I talk back. But most of the time I ignore her as though she were a complete stranger. I just smoke a cigarette and keep quiet. Or laugh, which annoys her.

Once she shouted, "Why are you such a curse?" Imagine calling your daughter a curse. That got me to speak up. I said, "The nobody inside you is very mean and hateful." I was not attacking all of her, just the nobody part of her, the part that strikes out at me, pressures me.

I love my mother more than I know how to say but at times I have sadistic fantasies of revenge. They make me feel guilty when I think of how much she loves me and what she has done for me even though she may get angry and hit me or scream and accuse me of hurting her so badly she wishes she were dead.

Most of the time we are best friends. We kiss often during the day or cuddle on the couch, except for those moments I do not want her near because she has hurt me. Though I usually feel relaxed with her, comfortable enough at times to tell her how frightened I still am of men, sexually speaking, though I daydream of having sex affairs.

Maybe I am brain-damaged from taking Thorazine all these years. I am sorry I consented to insulin and electroshock treatments because I found out they can cause brain damage. I still have nightmares in which white-coated figures torture me and I wake screaming. You cannot spend all those years in mental hospitals without the images returning to haunt and torture you, reminding you of the pain caused by unfeeling men and women who treated you like an animal.

Sometimes my mind does not synthesize words and their meaning. Or when I finish reading a paragraph, I forget the first sentence. Or I may black out for a few minutes every so often.

Occasionally I make ostensibly illogical comments to my mother like, "I will be Snow White unmutilated by Donald Duck." Perhaps I feel my mother quacks away at me like Donald Duck. And that I wish I were Snow White, not sullied as I often feel. Wish also that I did not think of myself as mutilated, parts of me missing, parts I need to feel whole.

Once mother interrupted as I was reading a magazine and I said, "Carole Lombard's puppy dog is making so much noise I cannot read." Perhaps this was a way of calling my mother a bitch for interfering with my pleasure of the moment. And wouldn't I love to be blond and chic like the late Carole Lombard! I have always envied girls with flowing blond hair and creamy white complexions. I have yearned to look like them. I dream I will someday have a little girl who will be a strawberry blonde.

I told mother one night, "I am going to be interviewed on television about my art. If you don't believe it, you can ask the moon. And I'm going to be photographed naked, after I'm beautiful, by Richard Avedon, who photographed Garbo for *Vogue*. If you don't believe it, you can ask the moon." Mother's face is round, like the moon, so perhaps I am referring to her, the fount of all my wisdom.

There are times I write nonsense, though perhaps some psychoanalyst would make sense of it. I wrote an essay on breasts, saying "the second least pretty of the twenty-four types of pretty bosoms that will exist in the year 2576 will be my mother's future breasts. The third least pretty of the twenty-four pretty-type bosoms will be Greta Garbo's. My daughter's bosom type is number 15 but with pink nipples, not beige. Numbers 18, 20, and 22 will have pink nipples too. But there will never be a bosom type prettier than number 23 (which I don't believe is in existence)."

Sometimes I feel I will die of fear and stress and it is somehow connected to my mother. I ask, What is this spirit in her that can harm me? She hates me when I do not help around the house. I tell her, "I can't." Something inside paralyzes me. It is safer to sit quietly reading or listen to music while smoking.

One morning she asked me to look for my watch, temporarily misplaced. I was reading a movie review in the *New York Post* and kept reading.

She yelled, "Parasite! You'll be the death of me! Go look for that watch." She once told me the parents in Bessarabia called their children parasites.

I put down the *Post,* made a cursory search of the apartment, could not find the watch, and returned to my reading.

She screamed, "Don't just sit there! Get dressed!"

We went to the Metropolitan Museum of Art and on the second floor I stood in front of the Jean Baptiste Carpeaux sculpture of *Ugolino and His Sons.* Ugolino was the political prisoner described by Dante in his book *Purgatorio,* condemned to death. The sculpture shows him naked, surrounded by his four sons, also naked. I announced loudly to mother, "Someday I will have a son who can sculpt like that."

Mother snapped, "If you want to go out with me, talk low. I don't want everyone to hear your dreams."

Then I went to a session with my psychiatrist, at that time a man, told him I daydreamed of having a son. He asked, "What does he look like?"

"Like the oldest son in the *Ugolino,*" I said.

That night I felt so upset I wanted to call Dr. Blau. It was a long-distance call and mother screamed, "Stop spending the money for which I work so hard. You are driving me to my death. What will you do when I die? Who will take care of you then?"

I could not conceive of life without mother—she was right, who *would* take care of me then? On the other hand, I often feel the devil would be kinder to me than she is. I think of the devil as an evil spirit

who reads my mind. He watches everything I do. I cannot look at television or see a movie or read in peace because he is all over me in one
form or another. He wants me to die. Once I drew a picture of my
mother with horns, like the devil.

I wrote a note to myself on September 20, 1978: "I have had
diabetes for four or five years now. This is the tenth time in five years
that my mother buys ice cream or cake for her house even when she
has promised over and over not to. She even asks me sometimes to
have a bite even though she has told me actions speak louder than
words and kisses and you can tell if a person really wants to murder
you more by their deeds than their words."

Another day I left a note "to whom it may concern in case of my
death," saying: "My mother by giving me tranquilizers wants to lobo-
tomize me. . . . She knows I'm feeling more and more like a half-
dead, drugged zombie and yet she continues to medicate me with tranquilizers in such massive doses as to toxify my system. She lies to
doctors in order to obtain large quantities of Thorazine and other medi-
cations. She has enough pills to fill up two empty shoe boxes. Why
does she have the need to 'store' up so many of these pills? Anyone
else in my situation (of being so drugged) would prefer euthanasia but
even if she causes me to have more brain damage, I will not submit to
euthanasia!"

Sometimes a wave of blind terror engulfs me. I feel that God (the
supernatural) wants me to keep my terror a secret or I will be punished
even more. He doesn't want anyone to feel sorry for me. I know only
He can keep me from being afraid but he wants me to know terror. I
ask myself, Will today be the day of terror again?

I feel like the actress Olga in the film *Slave of Love* who found herself all alone in a trolley car without a conductor, speeding 100 miles
an hour with ten men on horseback in pursuit to trap and torture her.
She did not know where the trolley was heading, whether she would
ever get off it, if it would crash into another trolley and kill her, or the
men on horseback would catch her.

I sometimes think of a girl persecuted by a certain sect, who kept
screaming for help, crying out that she would be murdered by this
group but all the people she asked to save her called her paranoiac and
did not lift a finger to help her and she *was* murdered.

Many nights I dream I am standing trial for having committed murder. Two prison officials take me away to the electric chair. In the dream, Hitler is my judge, jury, and executioner but it is really not Hitler. It is someone I know. He tortures me for an hour. The charge is that I have killed someone or taken their eye out. I think of that time in the nursery when I hit little Nell in the eye and was accused of blinding her though she was perfectly fine the next day; and when I bit that girl Susan in summer camp as she tried to strangle me.

One morning after my mother nagged me to clean my room, I told her, "On account of you I may die a terrible death. Why don't you leave me alone? It is your fault my life has been so horrible. You torture me mentally and emotionally, you brought all my bad luck."

Mother feels everything is her fault because she is the one who sometimes explodes in anger. But our house is no one-way street of rage. I have turned on her in a fury. Sometimes I want her to get angry because then I have a reason to rage at her without feeling guilty.

One morning when she woke me and I wanted to sleep, I felt tortured. That night I dreamed I was held captive in a dungeon as sadists beat me. I could not find my way out, one hundred miles of dead-end streets led nowhere. I kept telling myself, "I wish I knew where the gate is so I could leave this hell."

I fall into another kind of hell when she goes out and leaves me alone at a time I need her. I feel she hates me when she deserts me like this. I often feel very close to her, especially when I have nightmares and want to sleep in her bed. I say to her, "If you don't sleep with me, I'll die."

My greatest grief is that I feel a failure because I haven't accomplished anything but only reeled backwards. I read books by learned psychiatrists on how to achieve the sense of identity I seem to have lost. But it is not enough to understand these concepts intellectually. I do not know what destroyed my self-esteem or how to restore it.

I still enjoy classical music, to which I listen much of the day, but I seldom sit down at the piano. If I feel in a relaxed mood I will play the *Moonlight Sonata* though it is difficult to remember it to the end.

I stopped painting in 1966. I once did a life-size painting of myself in the nude and I also painted my mother's face. I sometimes feel I am a camera that has taken millions of pictures of my mother's face. I think she looks like Maria Maddalena Baroncelli painted by Hans Memling, in his double portrait of Maria and her husband Tomaso Portinari, hanging side by side in the Metropolitan Museum of Art. I once had the delusion I painted Maria and I understand why, for she and my mother have somewhat the same eyes, eyebrows and high forehead. I see my mother's face as beautiful, as in the Memling painting. Mother's mother, Rosa, of whom we have a large photograph, also resembles Maria.

I black out what I have painted in the past. As though I have scraped my paintings off the canvas in sadistic fury. For a long time I forgot how to paint. Painting depressed me, it was too much of a mental effort, more difficult than a physical effort. Mother said I was just spoiled. Maybe she was right. Maybe mental illness is just "being spoiled."

The happiest moments of my life are spent at the Metropolitan Museum of Art. I sit in front of serene landscapes and peaceful portraits. One of my favorite sculptures is *Andromeda and the Monster* by Pierre Ettienne Monnot. She is a mythical goddess chained to a rock, a gaping monster rising out of the waters surrounding her. I see the artist as representing his mother as very sexy and sensuous, chained to her by his tabooed love. Sometimes I have the fantasy I will marry a sculptor or architect and live in a town house facing the museum and in the evening hop into our Cadillac just to go the few feet to the museum to hear a lecture.

My mother says I am a born art historian and perhaps someday I will be. When I get my B.A. in Fine Arts perhaps I will even paint again. The subject of my thesis is why there have been no great women artists. I think the art created by women is different from that of men's, both in content and form, and for both psychological and biological reasons. All great art is based on conflict and the mediation of that conflict and I think perhaps men are more conflicted and thus have created the great art of the centuries.

I feel sad when I remember once I was the best student in my class at school. It was taken for granted I would go to a university. I feel worse than if I were born stupid because when you have been stupid all your life you do not know what you miss. I suffer "mental blocks" and would not be surprised if they have become organic, like brain damage, and create this feeling of being "stupid." I also hate myself because I have gained so much weight. It has been difficult to take off ever since I started to put on pounds after the insulin treatment at Central Islip.

I feel I have never bounced back from that hospital experience. I am no longer resilient emotionally, as I was before, when I took traumas almost for granted. Even though physically I had a much easier childhood than my mother or Aunt Berta, emotionally my childhood was worse because of the years in institutions.

My mother blames herself for my unhappy childhood. The truth is that the three of us—mother, Aunt Berta and I—had unhappy childhoods due to circumstances beyond our control. But my mother's love mitigated the otherwise devastating effects of fate in my life. Her childhood was a very hard one yet I have never heard her complain about it. She is a saint, superhumanly good. I wish I could get well and mother could depend on me for a change so I would not feel like a parasite living off her labors and her strengths.

I also love Aunt Berta. I think of her as a second mother. I will never forget that she wrote me on my seventh birthday, "If I ever have a child, I'll love you more than that child." She has not been called on to prove this for she has never had a child.

As I look back on my confused life, I think that just before I went to the final hospital, I faced a crisis. Up to then I was content to work in an office and take home a salary. But one day I thought, Good God, is this how I am going to spend the rest of my days? Going to the office every morning at eight with only weekends to offer a modicum of pleasure and nothing to show for my life? I felt depressed because I wanted more—much more. I wanted to get married or have an interesting career, be an astronomer or microbiologist, if not an artist.

Dr. Blau told me the answer was so obvious she did not know how I could not see it. I never understood what she meant; sometimes she talked to me as if I were Freud. I wanted to be told to *do* something that would change my life. To act was the answer. But she spoke in riddles, made me feel a fool not to understand something so simple as my "problem."

I also like to write and over the years kept a diary for my thoughts and poems. Once I had the illusion I wrote the movie *Last Summer,* probably recalling the three boys who tried to rape me at Forest School. The movie contrasts one girl who is promiscuous and aggressive with another who is shy and passive. The promiscuous girl and her two boy friends are uncomfortable in the presence of the virgin and decide to rape her. I identified with both the girl who was raped and the aggressive girl, as I, a virgin, had envied the tough girls in the gang at the school.

Usually my daydreams are pleasant—it is the nightmares from which I wake screaming. At the last hospital, I woke in terror from a nightmare in which lions were chasing me. Once I drew a picture of a lion who was part snake. I have always been afraid of lions and tigers. Something happened when I was a child, something to do with tigers. I feel a sense of déjà vu about tigers. After waking from the nightmare I wandered around until a nurse saw me and made me a cup of tea. In the state hospitals no one showed concern when I woke sobbing or screaming. Usually I had company as other women in their night terrors moaned, shrieked, or gasped as though strangling.

Once after mother and I returned from a trip to Washington, D.C., I dreamed I had gone back to our hotel but this time I possessed supernatural powers so I could control my mother and when she became furious at me I told her, "You are never going to get angry at me again." But then the supernatural powers disappeared so that when I said to her, still dreaming, "You are never going to get angry at me again," she became angrier than ever.

In a fury I said, "I am going to send the devil to you and he will fix you." She ran away, disappeared into the hotel lobby. Suddenly a monster with eyes of glowing coals appeared in my room. He walked over to me and snarled, "I am the devil! I am going to kill *you.*"

At this, I woke up screaming. I was so frightened I ran to my mother's room and slipped into bed next to her. After a while I felt less afraid and thought, It's only a dream, perhaps I believe that my mother, when she gets angry, has supernatural powers and, to fight her, I too must be endowed with such powers.

Not long ago I dreamed I was prisoner in a concentration camp which had as commandant a very sadistic woman. The camp was located at the North Pole. I tried to escape in the winter by swimming between ice floes but could not find a way out. So I waited for summer when the ice would melt. In the meantime I taught the commandant's parrot to say, "I am a prisoner in a concentration camp. My name is Rosette and the address is the North Pole."

I planned to free the parrot so he could fly away and bring help. But I did not know two things—whether he was able to fly and whether the sadistic woman warden would release her pet. So I told her the prisoners wanted to play a game that involved hitting the parrot with stones but, to do so, he would have to be let loose from her hut.

She agreed to let the parrot free. Just before the inmates picked up stones to hurl at him, I whispered, "Fly." He soared into the sky and escaped.

But I could not fly, I could not escape. I had to remain in the frozen concentration camp, victim of a sadistic woman.

Sometimes I dream not of icy prisons but blazing fires. In one dream I pictured myself attending a class at Columbia University with my mother and Aunt Berta. All of a sudden a roll of toilet paper in the bathroom burst into flames. I yelled, "Fire! Fire!" Realizing this would alarm everyone, I shouted, "Don't panic, don't panic!" I ran outside with my mother as the building started to collapse. Mother wanted to go back to rescue Aunt Berta. I struggled with mother to keep her from the dangerous flames just as Aunt Berta came running out.

Another time I dreamed I was trapped in a fire in our building with my mother and Aunt Fanny. Someone asked what time it was. I said, "Twelve minutes past the end of the world." As I woke I thought of an anthropologist who had written a scatological book about God, and decided God might want to punish him by destroying the world.

I once wrote a poem about God and my mother:

> *I feel bad now even though you love me*
> *I feel bad because I don't love you*
> *I am bad because I don't love you*
> *God doesn't like me when I don't like you*
> *I don't like God when I don't like you.*
> *You should never let me be bad.*
> *I wish I would die before I get bad*
> *The worst thing about being bad is to*

Not believe it about myself and instead to
Believe it about everyone else
Including God.

Sometimes I feel there is someone in me who hates my mother, who makes me want to push her away instead of hugging and kissing her. This person within also is angry at me, does not want me to have any warm emotions like love but wants me to feel cold. I feel very frightened when I am cold inside.

Will I ever be free of the terror that appears in my nightmares? I do not know. Maybe the damage has been too devastating. But, like mother, I will never give up trying. At least I am on my way to the college degree she has always wanted me to have.

After that, we'll see.

One summer at an exclusive girls' camp, I was chosen to play the role of Mimi in *Mrs. McThing,* a play by Mary Chase. Mimi is the daughter of the witch, the title role. In the final scene, Mrs. McThing, not wanting her daughter to become a witch like herself, gives her to a woman who will love her and teach her to be human.

The daughter begs, as one of the last lines of the play, ''Mother, please don't leave me.''

At the thought of never seeing her mother again, the daughter is supposed to cry. But I could not shed a tear. I felt a complete lack of emotion. The fictional situation was too painful, too much like my own life. But in spite of the absence of tears, I was congratulated for playing the part well.

Offstage I have often felt this almost total lack of emotion. This may be partially due to medication, but also to repressed guilt, Dr. Blau once told me. She said my great guilt toward my mother showed in the compulsive act of washing my hands over and over. I was unconsciously expiating the guilt, washing away imagined crimes.

What were the crimes? I had not been a good daughter, obeyed my mother, attended school. I had refused to do what mother expected of me, the things she had done as a girl—work hard, revere knowledge, not kiss a boy until I married him. All things I was supposed to do out of my love for her.

Sometimes it is very difficult for me to show love for mother or respond to her love for me. I have been so hurt I am afraid to feel affection, afraid I will be hurt further if I give any sign I care. So I have built an iron wall around my feelings, turned hard and cold to avoid pain.

There are times I wish I could feel more deeply. Perhaps to feel pain is better than to feel nothing. After all, pain is part of life.

At least I can feel a certain anger toward the world because I have been cheated. Robbed by hostile forces that took away my free will. I have never had control over my destiny—it has been imposed on me by others. I envy those who control their own destiny.

At times I feel I am living the lines in the song *Old Man River* in which the hero tells of feeling sick and weary and tired of living, yet is afraid of dying.

At seventeen, I wanted to die when I felt Alfredo deserted me. I thought I was destroyed, I did not want to live in such agony. Yet I did not suffer then the way I do now, afraid to die. The fear of dying to me is more terrifying than being able to decide to kill yourself and end all the suffering.

It goes on and on, the suffering. A suffering without tears. I want to cry but I cannot dredge up the tears. Along with many of my memories, they are too deeply buried.

Jenny's mother, Rosa Sadovnick Altman, shortly after her marriage in 1910 in Odessa.

Jenny's father, Motel (Mark) Altman, shortly after his marriage.

Jenny's grandmother, Etti-Feige Altman, who was drowned by the Nazis in the Dniester River. Jenny lived with her between the ages of eleven and sixteen in Rishcon, Romania.

Jenny and Rosette, then two years old, sitting in the park in Caracas known as La Plaza de la Concordia, former site of La Rotunda, a prison in which Manuel was unjustly imprisoned for four years by dictator Juan Vicente Gómez.

Jenny's husband, Manuel Spinoza, Rosette and Jenny, in a passport photograph taken October 27, 1944, when Rosette was two and a half.

Jenny, after arriving in Chicago in 1945, to make a new life in a new country.

Rosette at the age of four gets a birthday hug from Jenny on the porch of their Chicago home.

Rosette on her ninth birthday on the boardwalk at Brighton Beach, holding the hundred-dollar doll sent her by her Uncle Sam.

Jenny in Brazil on her birthday, November 10, 1959.

Rosette at sixteen, just after returning from her visit to her aunt and uncle in Rio.

Rosette, at seventeen, gives her mother a kiss.

Rosette at eighteen sharing the joy of St. Valentine's Day with her mother.

Rosette at nineteen, an office worker at Eastern Airlines.

Rosette in a blond wig and Jenny, wearing the new fur coats that Rosette bought out of her earnings.

III

Jenny — Rosette

I

The Unshed Tears

Mother—daughter. Their lives closely intertwined in the day-to-day living they have chosen to solve their dilemma.

If you casually met them you would not suspect the torment of the past. Jenny is a spirited woman, outgoing, maternal, good-natured. She has an attractive, pleasant face. Photographs of earlier years show her to have been very pretty. Her blue-gray eyes often sparkle with vivacity and humor. Occasionally she is wistful, a reminder of the little girl within.

She is intuitive, sympathetic, and thoughtful, generous with her time and showing interest in others. She does not hide her thoughts, you know exactly what she feels. She is intellectually very bright though sometimes uses her intellect, as many of us do, as a defense. In her emotionally traumatic life, her defenses are deeply entrenched. She has the tenacity of the survivor.

Rosette's earlier photographs show her to have been pretty also, slim in figure, piquant in face. She is a sensitive, artistic woman. There is a feeling of reserve about her, though she answers questions frankly and perceptively in a low, warm voice. Like her mother, she is very intelligent. She expects shortly to get her college degree in art history.

The courage, creativity and intelligence of both Jenny and Rosette are praised by Professor Sybil Brinberg, of the English department at Hunter College, who teaches courses in the late 19th and early 20th century American and British drama and world literature, short story and fiction writing. Jenny and Rosette have been in some of her classes, separately and together during the last three years. She says:

"When Mrs. Spinoza and her daughter first discussed with me their desire to write the story of Rosette's life from their separate points of view, I was concerned that the project would be extremely painful for both. In fact, however, it has thus far proved beneficial. To me, their soul-searching is related to the restlessness that has characterized their life-style. From Rosette's earliest infancy, theirs was a desperate shut-tling from one violently unfamiliar and inhuman environment to another. Intensifying their restlessness was their conviction that they had to aspire to the academic goals achieved by some of the illustrious members of their family. Given their extreme economic hardships, modest intellectual goals might have decreased some of the pressures Rosette experienced during adolescence.

"Now it seems that their lifetime pursuit of the 'finer things' is being retroactively justified. Both mother and daughter expect to graduate from Hunter College in June, 1980. Their contribution to this book for which they have received academic credits is an appropriate climax to their intellectual efforts as well as a special source of pride for Rosette. Mrs. Spinoza's account rings with eloquence in her heroic efforts to help keep her daughter well and alive. And Rosette's narrative has an aura of innocence and beauty. Love and achievement, however mangled by misfortune and illness, remain the sustaining forces in their lives."

Rosette speaks with feeling and sometimes flashes of humor about her experiences in institutions, never with excessive anger. Her mother is much more vocal about Rosette's suffering in the mental hospitals. Jenny also is critical of the therapists who "blame" her for her daughter's illness which, she believes, is genetic, caused by biological defects that have nothing to do with the relationship between Rosette and herself.

She thinks perhaps the constitutional defects came from her mother's family. Her mother suffered from such deep depression she tried to commit suicide when she lost her first child and did kill herself after her husband left her. Her mother's sister also spent time in a mental hospital.

Jenny does not believe Freud's discoveries about the psychic functioning of the mind apply to her or Rosette. She says Freud did not observe the poor, working-class people but only the middle class and wealthy.

Several psychiatrists and one psychologist who hold differing opinions as to the cause and treatment of mental illness were asked to comment on Jenny and Rosette's stories. Dr. Robert Cancro, chairman of the Psychiatric Department of Bellevue Hospital, wrote the following:

"This book is a kind of psychiatric *Rashomon*. All of the actors, no matter whether central or peripheral, have their own personal convictions of the 'truth.' Interestingly, it is very likely that none of them would be willing, and perhaps not even be able, to give up his or her vision of the truth in the face of contradictory evidence. In psychiatry a delusion is defined as a fixed false belief. Yet, we find that many 'normal' people, including mental health workers, have fixed beliefs about the origin of mental illness which will not yield to contradictory evidence. Are they, too, delusional? Perhaps.

"As is always the case, all of the versions of truth have some merit. Even the contradictions reveal deeper truths. So is it with mental illness. There is no single mental illness, but many different illnesses. Each 'individual' illness contains many different forms. The variations within a single 'type' of mental illness may be almost as great as the differences between two so-called different forms of mental illness. Two patients with a diagnosis of schizophrenia will differ in their premorbid personality, growth, and development, presenting symptoms, clinical course, response to treatment, and long-term outcome. Yet, they carry the same label. Despite the similarity in label they very likely have different illnesses. It is a small wonder that people become confused.

"The existence of biologic factors in the development of certain forms of mental illness is beyond reasonable doubt. This does not mean that a child is born with a genetic time bomb which will go off inevitably independent of the child's life experiences. It does mean, however, that not everyone is capable of a psychotic illness and that most individuals will never develop a psychotic illness no matter how difficult their life circumstances become. If we are to understand the role of biologic factors, they can be appreciated only by integrating nonbiologic factors into a comprehensive model. The unity of human development in the real world cannot be divided neatly into disciplines such as biology, psychology, sociology. Disciplines are arbitrary ways of looking at reality. Reality is far more complex than any single academic discipline.

"People do not develop, for instance, psychological or medical problems, but rather develop problems in adaptation that we conceptualize in, for instance, psychological or medical terms. Disciplines are ways of thinking about adaptive problems but do not capture the process of that adaptive effort in every detail. Today we know that environmental experiences activate and release genetic mechanisms which in turn influence subsequent experiences. We speak of this process as an interaction between biology and the environment of the organism but the truth is that living is unitary and cannot be reduced perfectly into compartments such as biology and experience. To then take these arbitrary divisions and treat them as if they were real is the height of naïve reification.

"One of the saddest chapters in the history of American psychiatry was the abuse heaped on parents, particularly during the 1950s but even to the present day, for causing mental illness in their children. It is painful enough to have a psychotic child but even worse when you are held responsible for it by the 'experts.' There is no parent who is free of guilt. There is no parent who has been perfect in every way. Every parent fails his child with some regularity. In many ways if this were not the case the child would not be prepared to live in the real world. If you have the misfortune of having perfect parents then you cannot learn to adapt to the imperfections of all the other members of the class homo sapiens.

"Thus it is with Jenny and Rosette. They are imperfect people in real and obvious ways. The relationship between them is complex and in certain particulars unfortunate. This relationship very likely has played a part in the course and development of Rosette's illness. There is no reason to believe, however, that it is the *cause* of Rosette's illness. There is even less justification to add one more blow to the anguish suffered by Jenny and Rosette by this reviewer's opinion as to the origin of the illness, which opinion can be neither tested nor refuted.

"It is a curious phenomenon in psychiatry that if the patient gets better the doctor often takes the credit, but if the patient fails to get better the patient and/or the family frequently get the blame. It would seem, to this observer, that if an individual has the power to cure a patient then that individual must assume the responsibility for the failures of his or her cures. Similarly, if the physician does not have the power to cure then the physician cannot take the credit for those patients who actually improve. This physician has not had a cure since his last reduction of a shoulder dislocation.

"The process of improvement is a complex one involving a variety of factors. There is no isomorphism between etiology and intervention. The pain of cancer can be responsive to a sympathetic tone of voice. The pain of living can be responsive to medication. These observations do not prove that the pain of living is biologic and the pain of cancer is psychologic. It merely proves that people and the process called living are complex. Why certain people improve and others do not is poorly understood. Experience teaches us that certain things can be helpful and others harmful in the process of recovery. This process is difficult to predict and even more difficult to influence. Most patients, even those who suffer from the schizophrenic syndrome, do in fact get better. Unfortunately we do not know why. Given enough time the vast majority of such patients tend to improve. Time remains the greatest healer of all.''

The genetic approach is upheld by Dr. Aylin Radomisli, who started seeing Rosette in September, 1976. Dr. Radomisli is a psychiatrist on the staff of the Payne Whitney Psychiatric Clinic of the New York Hospital-Cornell Medical Center, and is also in private practice. Born in Turkey, where her father was director of Turkish railroads, she first lived in Istanbul, then went to the University of Lausanne in Switzerland for her medical degree. She had psychiatric training in this country at Roosevelt Hospital and Columbia University's College of Physicians and Surgeons.

She believes Rosette was ''born with the seeds of her illness,'' that ''it is biological, not environmental, though the environment may have helped precipitate what was there." Interviewed in her office about the nature of Rosette's illness, she said, "There is no evidence to blame the environment for such severe mental illness. In my opinion, the theory that blames the mother is obsolete."

Though psychoanalysts are still adhering to the environmental theory, which sees the cause of mental illness as due to the relationship between child and parent, she says, "I see such explanation as a remnant of the prescientific era when people did not know the cause of a disease and had to explain it in some way such as 'evil spirits.' The cause of severe emotional illness is still not known. The unknown is terrifying. It's better to pin the answer on something and the mother, as the most powerful figure in the child's life, is the innocent target."

She is "dismayed to see how fashionable it still is to blame mothers for their children's psychiatric illness. I am not saying mothers do not ever harm their children. They do. But they do not cause mental illness. And it does not help to place a load of guilt on the mother."

She believes the cause is purely biological, that "more and more evidence seems to prove this. One sign is that the patients respond to medication. Another is the studies that show mental illness is genetic, not environmental."

She claims it is "putting the cart before the horse" to blame the mother. "Professionals who blame the environment study the sick young adult, then look at how his mother and father treated him in the past," she says. "But the reason such a child was treated differently was because he was mentally ill. Mental patients do cause anguish and anger in parents, do elicit overprotection. The blame on overprotective mothers keeps the patient postponing his responsibility."

Psychoanalysts "confuse correlation with causality," she says. She adds that "normal children grow up in the most bizarre homes, mistreated by parents, while others, brought up under ideal circumstances by supportive, loving, giving parents in the best manner possible, become mentally ill."

Jenny reacted to Rosette because of her illness, Dr. Radomisli says. "Jenny has been overprotective because Rosette needed it. It's not that Rosette became sick because of Jenny's overprotectiveness but that Jenny became the ego that Rosette lacked. She had to supply her with the strength Rosette didn't have."

She describes the relationship between mother and daughter as "symbiotic but not destructive." She explains: "Some symbiotic relationships should be encouraged—where mother and daughter are giving certain things to each other that are important. Jenny is full of strength and energy, uses all her resources and the resources around her. I see this as a fortunate symbiotic relationship."

Dr. Radomisli prescribes medication for Rosette which, she says, Rosette needs to function. So far, according to Dr. Radomisli, Rosette has responded well to Thorazine. As yet she has shown no side effects such as the involuntary shaking which may lead to Parkinson's disease, though she has put on weight, one adverse side effect. She will always need medication, says Dr. Radomisli, who also prescribes Stelazine to counteract the sedating effect of Thorazine.

In the three years Dr. Radomisli has been seeing Rosette, she has "improved quite a lot," Dr. Radomisli says. She notes, "Rosette's self-confidence is higher. She functions better intellectually. Jenny has helped her gain self-confidence by getting her to study for her B.A. Her creativity has flourished. She wants to paint again and play the piano. She is interested in literature, rereads the classics.

"Socially, she is less withdrawn. She used to be completely self-centered but now she is interested in people. She is lively and contributes to an exchange. She is a thoughtful friend and companion."

In her weekly session, Rosette talks about her feelings. There is much repressed anger in Rosette, Dr. Radomisli reports, some tied to the belief people can read her mind and control her thoughts. Of Rosette's occasional delusions, Dr. Radomisli says, "I do not try to analyze them but to decrease their impact. I'm doing supportive therapy. I give her the extra support she needs.

"My goal is not to separate her from her mother but to make it possible for her to have some independence so that when her mother is gone, she will be able to live alone. She will always be functioning at a marginal level though she is very intelligent. She is also very sensitive, very perceptive. She senses my moods, picks up thoughts, pinpoints my character traits, has insights that amaze me. We have a good relationship. She knows I like her. She doesn't see many people. I'm happy if I can help her in any way."

There are times Rosette "lives in a world of her own, isolated by her fantasies and delusions," according to Dr. Radomisli. "The richness and complexity of her fantasies reflect Rosette's intelligence," she says. "Her private world enables her to survive in spite of the psychic pain of her illness, while Jenny enables her to cope with the real world.

"On the other hand, Jenny's intelligence is a practical, functional one. It probably took this form out of necessity from the moment she had to face the world as a child without much help. She continued to do so throughout her life and now does it for Rosette. Jenny desperately tried to provide for Rosette when the doctors and hospitals could not and I believe she did as well as possible under the circumstances."

Upholding a different philosophy, Dr. Blau, who for twenty-one years, on and off, saw Rosette as a patient, believes her illness caused "by the interplay between mother and daughter which started the day the daughter was born." Interviewed on the telephone, Dr. Blau (a pseudonym) said that "every life has its tragedy, life is an intertwining of tragedies," and that her heart "went out to both mother and daughter because of their lives of misery."

In her opinion, Rosette is "a truly fine, relating, warm human being, suffering because of the pathology. She is very sensitive underneath all her defensive layers. She is lively, very talented, writes well, paints."

In treating Rosette and trying to help Jenny, "it was like fighting in a sick room for someone who is desperately in need of help," Dr. Blau observed. "I tried to find their strengths and to mobilize the strengths, in order to help them ease their pain. Pain makes for an unproductive life."

She said that both mother and daughter suffered childhood depression and "the child and the mother" are still fused in Jenny. She called Jenny essentially "well-meaning" but caught in a desperate need to help her daughter and, at the same time, keep Rosette from separating from her.

Warning that "the human psyche is a very complex thing and to try to make it simple is to do us all an injustice," Dr. Blau commented that both mother and daughter were caught in their own fantasies, distortions of reality, illusions, and dreams, "with many ambivalences— not just one ambivalence."

Both mother and daughter have been desperately in need of help and the only facilities available have made their plight even more desperate, she pointed out, in that the public mental hospitals could not possibly meet their needs. "The needy people who are poor are cut short," she put it. "State hospitals are limited financially and otherwise. What do they have to offer? The people who work there are limited."

Rosette, according to Dr. Blau, "sent out messages telling of her suffering at the onslaught of her pathology. She indulged in nebulous acting out [at the Forest School] as a way of asking for help to ease her pain and suffering. She felt confused and embarrassed as the pathology crept up on her."

Because of Rosette's inability to express anger and her great need to deny any hostile feelings toward her mother, she believes "love can take the place of anger" as a way of fighting her anxiety, Dr. Blau said. She expressed it: "For Rosette, to be closed in her own world was not as threatening as facing the real world or her own anger."

Dr. Blau pointed out that she would not prescribe medication because she does not believe in medication as treatment for mental illness. She said, "I tried to help Rosette reach her own self, a beautiful self, without medication. I tried to treat the interfering elements and cash in on the strengths. I addressed myself to the real child, tried to work with her."

Dr. Walter A. Stewart, a training psychoanalyst and former treasurer of the New York Psychoanalytic Institute, author of *Psychoanalysis: The First Ten Years* and *The Secret of Dreams,* comments about Jenny and Rosette:

"The life histories presented in this book offer a detailed clinical picture of a not unusual interraction between a mother and daughter. The material mostly speaks for itself; yet I would underline certain aspects of the relationship between the mother and daughter which led to their disturbed relationship.

"The mother summarizes her difficulties in the second sentence of her chapter: 'I love her more than life itself . . .' but the quality of this love was suffocating. The daughter was an extension of the mother—the mother's second chance in life. The 'condition of love' was that the daughter's success in life would make the mother's life acceptable. The rage that emerged when the daughter failed in any way to live up to the mother's need showed the demanding nature of the love.

"Jenny complains that she frequently felt deserted and unloved, angry, and suicidal, and states she regrets that she had not drowned as a child. Much of her way of mothering she learned naturally from her own mother, who once shouted at her, 'I wish you were dead!' Jenny's mother was suicidal and finally killed herself. Jenny's experiences with her depressed, suicidal mother led to her own dramatic way of living.

"The early feeding relationship between Jenny and Rosette (named after Jenny's mother, Rosa) was prototypic for the rest of their lives.

"In the delivery, Jenny's bladder became affected and she had a difficult time but says, 'I thought it was worth all the agony.' Implied also is the debt the baby owed her in return. The breast feeding was on schedule; toilet training accomplished by six months. This rigid control reflects lack of empathic understanding by the mother of her daughter. It led to the baby's rebellion and then to the ambivalent closeness of mother and daughter, who became locked into a sadomasochistic merging relationship which prevented the child from becoming independent (from achieving what Dr. Margaret Mahler named 'separation-individuation'). Each exploited, loved, and hated the other. Jenny's love was primitive and based on an identification but showed no regard for the person as separate from her own needs.

"The love between Jenny and Rosette showed the worst quality expressed in the saying 'Do unto others as you would have others do unto you.' This clouds the separate interest of self and the other. This way of relating precedes a more mature understanding, in which you do unto others as you understand their needs and wishes and can balance that against your own needs. It is less sacrificial, more understanding, less guilt provoking, and allows separation-individuation. Clearly the danger of separation was frightening to Rosette and she begged her mother never to leave her.

"Typical of Rosette's character is the scene when she and her mother are reunited after three weeks' separation, during which Rosette had been placed with the Daughters of Zion nursery. The mother 'cried hysterically' while the daughter hardly seemed to recognize her. The mother indulged herself in a spasm of grief, guilt, and self-pity. This entirely ignored and at the same time overwhelmed the little girl, whose own feelings received no recognition.

"In the mother's report I cannot recall one time when she helped her daughter to come to terms with reality. Instead, she used her as a narcissistic extension and exhibitionistic replacement. For example, she took pride in the fact Rosette was 'the most stylishly clad child of the ninety-nine families in the building.'

"In adolescence Rosette became sluggish, showed habit deterioration, and spent hours daydreaming, which reflected her inability to deal with sexual conflict. She could not concentrate, probably because of the overwhelming nature of her sexual and aggressive fantasies. Her mother's heterosexual interests disgusted her. This distaste affected Rosette's own crippled sexual development, which was damaged by the close symbiotic relationship with her mother. The mother who had never felt a 'deep passion for a man' was unable to convey to her daughter the joys of being interested in men. Rosette entered into her heterosexual life with no guidelines, no judgment, and no joy. It is not surprising after 'almost rape' and a suicidal attempt after a transient love affair that she gave up her heterosexual impulses and went back to the ambivalent and limited mother-daughter relationship which she could handle.

"When one thinks of the implications of this type of stage-door mother-daughter relationship, the most interesting aspect of it is what it excludes: separation of mother and daughter—a sense of self-identity; awareness of the other as separate and different; awareness of the other as disappointing, but not all bad; awareness of the other as a sexual rival.

"The mother couldn't cope with the defects which had emerged in her daughter. She struck her and blamed her for not fulfilling her expectations. If the daughter had been more fortunate, she would have objected to her mother's demands and gotten away from her much earlier. She didn't have the strength to follow her own interests and became an angry, defiant child. The mother naturally saw this as 'laziness and defiance' and not as a collapse.

"The mother's third chapter details the horrors of Rosette's psychiatric care. I believe the earlier mother-daughter relationship made Rosette virtually untreatable. Any effort to be helpful to her and impose some restrictions re-aroused the fear of engulfment and loss of her own fragile identity.

"By this time her emotional life was based on an idealization of her mother. Her anger at her mother for the poor maternal care was projected onto the outside world which she felt mistreated and misunderstood her. Her therapists magnificently supported the reality of the abandonment and the misunderstood feelings; but one should not underestimate the therapeutic challenge involved in the wish to help someone who has faced so little reality, and most of that traumatic. Her mother had no way to help her, nor did her incompetent therapists.

"The mother sees, quite correctly, that all the statements by Rosette's therapist accused *her* of the crime. They surely were clumsy, inept, inadequate, and cruel in their efforts to be 'helpful.' The mother, in response, made their jobs harder because she was deaf to the idea of 'no fault' illness, as were the therapists. She confesses she had some major problems in being a mother. Her ignorance I can understand and forgive. Their ignorance I can only understand. The report of their pompous, harsh, indifferent, and cruel attitudes rings true. Physicians are trained to ignore the patient's suffering, to be self-confident and autocratic. They must travel a long way before they can accept the suffering, the guilt, the ignorance by which we run our lives, without responding with moral disapproval and a sense of superiority.

"Jenny tried hard, did her best, and it wasn't good enough. She couldn't benefit from any insightful comments, hearing them only as condemnation. She retaliated by accusing the therapists of not helping.

"Is she being self-deprecatory or is she accurate about having major defects as a mother? I think the latter is true. Her correct insights to her troubles are no help to her. She admits her imperfections but then manages to ignore them. She thinks of her relationship with her only child as good. She writes, 'I am proud that Rosette has turned out so fine a woman. I tried to instill in her a sense of honor and decency . . . I forever stressed the importance of a good education. I had an obsession about study and discipline.' Jenny manages to ignore the tragic failure of her daughter to develop into a real person. Her so-called insights into the difficult relationship between her and her daughter are limited. Jenny could not tolerate understanding any fault of her own because of the intense self-hate it aroused. She defended herself by arousing in the therapists their criticism of her in response to which she could then feel wrongly accused.

"The resolution of the human impasse between Jenny and Rosette is documented in the mother's last chapter, 'The Compromise.' Jenny became the almost good-enough mother and Rosette became the infantile child.

"The doctors' efforts were to make some sense out of a difficult and complicated situation. Jenny managed to ignore those comments of the doctors which might have been helpful. She clearly intended to have her own solution, in which she lives in a 'mutually gratifying atmosphere' with Rosette. This 'mutually gratifying atmosphere' includes her screaming, 'I'd rather have died in a concentration camp than endure what I am living through with you.'

"As Jenny's second sentence in her opening chapter gave insight into the pathology of her relation to her daughter, so the first paragraphs of Rosette's chapter give us insight into her torments. She reports a dream about going to the baker and being threatened by a tiger. Her dream reflects her wish to eat and her fear of being eaten. You will recall she had great difficulty in being fed as an infant and almost starved to death.

"As Rosette became more mature, the exclusiveness of the mother-daughter relationship broke down. The mother's control lessened. Rosette needed control.

"The tragedy of her life was that she was offered inadequate help, though she and her mother may well have had difficulty in accepting any help which would have threatened their relationship. Rosette was partly defiant, but more, she was ignorant of how to handle anything beyond the dyad of mother-daughter. She could not become part of a peer group, make a heterosexual relationship, or understand loving or being loved. She had fantasies of throwing a child into a fire so it could feel loved and warm.

"Rosette's chapters reveal very little that is not already known. There is insight which is not useful; her cliché views of her relationship to her mother reflect an avoidance of regression. She is a damaged, frightened woman for whom the outside world of reality is mainly a threat—Hitler's return or an atomic bomb. This of course reflects her relationship to her mother. The mother is seen both as the threatening outside world and as a protector against it.''

The fifth therapist to comment on Jenny and Rosette is Dorothy Bloch, psychoanalyst, in private practice in New York. Former dean of the Training Institute of the National Psychological Association for Psychoanalysis (founded by Theodor Reik), she is author of *So the Witch Won't Eat Me: Fantasy and the Child's Fear of Infanticide*. She wrote:

"I have discovered from my treatment of patients that any attempt to understand the pattern of life must focus on discovering the unconscious fantasy that may be directing it and the frequently early terror that required that fantasy in order to establish some sense of safety. It was only when I began to define the unconscious fantasy that appeared to be controlling the lives of Jenny and Rosette and to speculate about the terror that produced it that the puzzling character of their relationship began to assume some degree of clarity. If there were any doubt about the pervasive role that fantasy may play as an instrument for survival and a defense against the fear of infanticide, their story must surely dissipate it.

"I have found that children universally defend themselves by self-deception and fantasy against their fear that their parents will kill them, and that the intensity of their fear depends on the degree of violence and of love they have experienced as well as on the number of traumatic events that have occurred in their lives. That they may have such a fear becomes apparent as soon as one considers their vulnerability and the kind of thinking with which they emerge from infancy. It has been called 'magical' because of their tendency to endow their thoughts, feelings, and wishes with 'magical' powers. Unfortunately that process leads them to blame themselves for whatever happens and therefore to anticipate punishment. When, in addition, they do encounter intense anger and violence, their terror becomes intensified. In order to establish a feeling of safety, they therefore idealize their parents and deceive themselves into believing that everything is their own fault, so that whenever they change and become 'good' they will be loved. That fantasy does not usually disappear without therapeutic help, but frequently retires to the unconscious where it may continue to direct the lives of adults.

"When we consider Jenny's life in the light of this concept, the degree of her terror and the requirements of the fantasy that can defend her against it appear monumental. It would be hard to conceive of a more traumatic or terror-instilling childhood than hers. The effect on any child of a mother's death would be devastating enough, but the impact of a suicide is beyond reckoning. In Jenny's case, the circumstances surrounding the tragic incident could only magnify Jenny's guilt and the accompanying terror. The night before the suicide, her mother had tried to embrace Jenny, perhaps in farewell, but Jenny, not understanding this unusual display of affection, rebuffed it. That rebuff set in motion the waves of 'indescribable guilt' that never subsided.

"From Jenny's brief references to her childhood, it appears that even before her mother's death, she had already developed considerable feelings of guilt toward her mother and a considerable degree of terror. When parents don't care for a child and absent themselves for varying periods of time, the child frequently interprets the parents' behavior as proof of his or her 'badness' or unworthiness to be loved. The child may also develop a pattern of behavior that justifies the parents' feelings.

"Jenny had to deal not only with the absence of her mother, who had to leave her with nursemaids from the age of one month, but also that of her father, who was away for months or even years at a time. In addition, a letter of Jenny's reveals that she had responded to the violence that was used in her home with her own violence and she states elsewhere, '. . . my mother hurled at me, "I wish you were dead!"' and another time, 'May your children do to you what you are doing to me!' It therefore didn't require her psychotic Aunt Ana's comment after her mother's suicide, 'You're very spoiled—you killed your mother,' to establish Jenny's guilt. The warnings about what she was 'doing' to her mother as well as the significance she ascribed to her rebuff of her mother's embrace had already taken care of that.

"Abandonment must surely have been a major source of Jenny's terror. Even before her mother's suicide, her father had already introduced her to that experience. She reports that when she was eleven and a half, she stood with her mother and her three-and-a-half-year-old sister, Berta, as her father departed on a train into exile with a woman twenty years younger. 'Nobody shed a tear,' she writes. Although that was his final farewell, he had exposed the family many times before to the absences that could last anywhere from three months to several years as he sought positions in distant villages.

"Following the abandonment by her parents, Jenny also had to face the desertion of the only other meaningful adult in her life. She said of her Aunt Fanny, '. . . she brought up Berta and, to a lesser extent, me.' The magnitude of the shock of this additional loss can scarcely be grasped. Fanny had lived with the family and may have played a more continuous mothering role than Jenny's mother, who was away teaching for many hours a day. Since Jenny's father was also absent for long periods, Fanny was left in charge. Her leaving may therefore have had an even greater impact on Jenny than her father's. Jenny was already acquainted with his character, but it may have seemed to her that Fanny had a choice and chose to leave her and her sister. Berta was taken in by her mother's sister Ana, but 'Nobody wanted me,' writes Jenny. One can try to imagine the feelings of an eleven-year-old as she set out alone on a journey to a grandmother she had seldom seen and whose welcome she had no way of anticipating, but Jenny reveals very little.

"Her description of her perilous journey when she was sixteen, across Europe and the Atlantic to Brazil, clutching the hand of eight-year-old Berta is the only evidence we have of what she really felt about these traumatic events: 'In Europe I possessed the fear,' she writes, 'she might wander off and not knowing the language of strange countries would be unable to find her way back to me. So I held her by the hand, slept with her in the top bunk of the ship which barely held one person, and did not leave her alone on deck for a second, fearing she might fall into the ocean. This was the first time I was aware of the devastating fear of losing a loved one, a fear so intense it drives every other thought out of mind.'

"Their solitary state, surrounded by known and unknown dangers, and Jenny's awareness that they were seeking refuge with a father who had already abandoned them once, must have heightened their need to cling to each other. Had Jenny some assurance that she would find security at the end of her journey, her fear might have been alleviated, but, as she discovered when she arrived, 'My father seemed as unconcerned as ever about the fate of his two daughters.'

"A listing of the traumatic events in Jenny's life would be incomplete without mention of the climate of political terror in which she lived. From the age of eleven and perhaps earlier, that terror was her frame of reference. The sense of danger that commenced with her father's exile and her mother's loss of her teaching position, followed by her suicide, culminated in the violence that forced Jenny to flee from Europe and resulted in her father's death at Auschwitz, the destruction of a major proportion of her family, and the drowning of her grandmother by the Nazis. She became preoccupied with her role in their deaths—if only she had responded to her mother's embrace, or said goodbye to her father when she left Paris; if only she had borrowed money to give to the Nazis . . . if only she had written to her grandmother. . . . To her already monumental sense of guilt were now added the feelings of many survivors. 'If I were to summarize in one phrase how I have felt all these tormented years, I would say an indescribable guilt,' she writes.

"A major source of Jenny's guilt, however, relates to Berta. Although Jenny's overwhelming concern about losing Berta during their voyage to Brazil appears, under the circumstances, to be a natural response to a terror-instilling experience, like many instances of intense concern, it may simultaneously conceal its opposite. On an unconscious level, Jenny possibly wanted nothing more than to get rid of Berta. The information gleaned from both Jenny's and Rosette's disclosures, as well as what can be surmised about the character of the sisters' early relationship under conditions that could only have fostered intense rivalry, make clear how impossible it would have been for anyone in Jenny's position to have wanted Berta.

"Jenny was in the difficult position of having been born the middle child where the older was a boy and the younger another girl. Under normal circumstances that would have presented her with serious problems, but the fact that her older brother died at the age of two, before she was born, and precipitated her mother's first suicide attempt made him a rival with whom she could not compete. There may be no more formidable task for a child than to supplant an older dead sibling. Where the second child feels loved, he or she can usually master the challenge of competing with a frequently idealized child. Where the second child is a different sex and feels rejected, however, the rejection may often be explained on sexual grounds. In view of the effect of her brother's death, it would only have been natural for Jenny to feel that if only she had been a boy, like her dead brother, she also would have been loved.

"To have discovered after the birth of Berta that it was possible to be a girl and still be loved, even if only by an aunt, may have come as a shock. Fanny's preference for Berta emerges very clearly from Jenny's story. When Jenny's father was at home, Fanny shared the narrow couch with Berta, who was 'beautiful.' In telling about Fanny's response to Rosette, Jenny also states, 'Aunt Fanny seemed to love Rosette as she once loved Berta.' The jealousy that any child would normally feel under those circumstances could only have been exacerbated when a home was found for Berta but not for her. It may therefore have required all the repressive powers Jenny possessed to bury the bitterness she may have experienced at finding herself in charge of such a rival. Part of Jenny's intensity in holding on to Berta may therefore have been a reflection of a wish that was intolerable to her—to lose her. Jenny was undoubtedly relieved at getting rid of Berta at the earliest opportunity when her father arranged it, though she was the one to suggest the foster family. The absence of any reference to their feelings at parting, Berta to live with strangers and Jenny once more to make her way alone in a strange country, suggests the possibility that Jenny's anger and jealousy of Berta may have created feelings of guilt about sending her away even though it may have been what was best for both of them.

"Until Jenny fled from Europe, there is no suggestion of the nature of the compelling fantasy that Jenny was apparently forced to act out following the escalation of her terror resulting from Nazi violence. At a point where being killed is no longer merely a fear, but appears to be an imminent threat, a fantasy no longer functions as a defense. In order to provide a sense of safety, it then has to be acted out. It is only when Jenny's fear reached a point of heightened intensity under the threat of Nazi violence that she began to act out a fantasy that until then had remained hidden. From then on, it is possible to discern the fantasy in the tragic events it secretly brought to pass.

"In attempting to define the fantasy that has directed Jenny's life, it might be helpful first to identify her most serious trauma. Although there are many to choose from, there can be no doubt that her mother's suicide, for which she blamed herself, was the most severe. She had already experienced the threat of this mother who hurled at her the words, 'I wish you were dead!' As I have found to be true in my treatment of patients, the death which Jenny felt she had caused did not seem to register in her unconscious. The 'crime' against her mother that resulted in her mother's death appears only to have intensified Jenny's fear of being killed by her. Since, as a child of eleven, she would have assumed it was her 'badness' that had caused her mother's suicide, being 'good' apparently then became her unconscious preoccupation. To please her mother, to make her mother proud of her, became the obsession of her life.

"The first intimation that Jenny is acting out a fantasy comes after her marriage. Although marrying Manuel, who could help her escape from the Nazis, was undoubtedly a step toward safety, it may also have been the first step in her acting out. She reports that he was like her father, but we have no way of knowing when Jenny's unconscious plan began to take shape to please her mother, perhaps by becoming her champion and avenging both her and herself. When her child was three and a half, the age of Berta when her father abandoned the family, however, she reenacted that early event, this time reversing roles.

"Recalling the day she left her husband, she writes, 'I was reminded of the day we saw my father off at the Khotin station. Only now I was the one breaking up the family.' She had waited many years to get back at her father, and now she did so symbolically—and tragically. She gives only a perfunctory reason for abandoning her husband but the fact that Rosette was Berta's age at the time confirms the suspicion that a fantasy is involved. That it is Aunt Fanny to whom she turns, bringing Rosette to her at exactly the age of Berta when the traumas started, is still further confirmation.

"An important element in Jenny's fantasy of how to win her mother's love was provided by Aunt Fanny's announcement the day after the tragedy that her mother's dying wish was that Jenny secure a high school diploma. When she began to act out her fantasies that wish became expanded indefinitely to encompass ever higher education for both herself and Rosette. Getting an education became Jenny's mission but then assumed dimensions that could be explained only by its fantasy purpose. Wherever possible and against enormous odds, regardless of cost either to herself or Rosette, she has devoted herself to its fulfillment. When she moved from Chicago to New York, after working all day, and in spite of having to take care of a house and a child, she went to school three nights a week. More recently, when both she and Rosette attended college classes, the fantasy surfaced. 'My mother would have been proud of me,' she stated.

"A still earlier fantasy of how to win her mother's love, it appears, also began to be acted out after her marriage to Manuel. Jenny's assertion that 'it's a man's world,' which had so many determinants on both a psychological and a realistic level, may very well have had its origin in her early experience in coping with the image of her dead brother.

"It is very likely, however, that Jenny's father was the more important source of her bitter conviction about 'a man's world.' The knowledge that he could go off with another woman and leave his wife and two small children in a situation that soon led to suicide must have festered for many years before it erupted in actions that finally expressed the intensity of the emotional impact of his behavior. Early in her marriage she began to act out a fantasy of a masculine identity—that is, an identity of aggression and effectiveness. She took a factory job as a cutter that was usually held only by men because it involved the lifting of heavy bales, and when she became pregnant, she refused to acknowledge her physical limitations and caused bladder difficulties.

"If the accumulated terror of Jenny's early years and the fantasy that she required in order to feel safe are kept in mind, it is possible to approach her relationship to Rosette with some possibility of understanding it. Although the four significant people during that period provide the various components of the fantasy, it is her mother and Berta who dominate. There are times when Jenny becomes aware of some confusion in her way of perceiving Rosette. 'I insist on treating her like a healthy person,' she states at one point. Earlier, she has replied to friends who attempted to impress her with Rosette's reality, 'She's just lazy and defying me.'

"The tragic fact is that Rosette became the instrument for the expiation of Jenny's 'crimes.' It is not only the 'crime' against her mother, but also the 'crime' against Berta that appears to have destroyed Jenny's peace and made inevitable her unconscious use of Rosette to defend her against her fear. Jenny's traumatic voyage with Berta and her acceptance of Berta's living with strangers appear to underlie her obsession of keeping Rosette with her. Of the former experience, she writes, 'This was the first time I was aware of the devastating fear of losing a loved one, a fear so intense it drives every other thought out of mind.' By itself that statement might seem to explain Jenny's frustration of every attempt on Rosette's part to lead a separate life, whether it was to share an apartment with a friend, go on trips with her fellow airline employees, have lunch with co-workers, or, finally, to get married.

"At times, Jenny appears to have some awareness that Berta figures somewhere in her obsession. In her many efforts to understand her role in Rosette's illness, she writes, "I loved her more than any parent loved a child. I have always had a terrible fear of losing her. It is like the fear that seized me when I took Berta to Rio.' Elsewhere she states, 'At all times of the day and night, I must know what she is doing, even what she is thinking.'

"I suspect, however, that the intensity of her preoccupation also has foundations other than merely the terror of that voyage. It is notable that Jenny glides very casually over the disclosure of her actually getting rid of Berta shortly after their arrival in Rio. Her real feelings and Berta's about the separation are therefore left to speculation. Berta's interpretation of Jenny's feeling toward her and Rosette is contained in a letter to Jenny. 'You don't love her either,' she states. Jenny also provides a glimpse of her feeling in a letter to Rosette. 'I shall never forget as long as I live the day Berta came to this country. . . . Berta and I didn't get along at all, but I was very proud of the fact that she loved my child so much because it proved in a way that she loved me too.' That is as illuminating as anything in Jenny's writing of her painful feelings toward Berta, compounded of both a yearning for her love and guilt over her treatment of her.

"We get some inkling of what that treatment was when Berta was a child in another reference to her in a letter to Rosette after Jenny's first visit to a psychiatrist. 'Whether he will be able to help loosen up this state of complete amnesia I get when I am angry at you and sometimes other people, I don't know,' she writes, 'but we will both try to see what causes this anger . . . I love you so much, I hate myself for hurting you . . . but I cannot help myself. It is a sickness within me . . . I know just how much harm I have caused you, my poor darling, how scared you were of me when you were very young and how much I would upset you. . . . Even Berta suffered from my anger when she was a child, when she visited us the first time in Chicago and when I was in Brazil. In this I am like Fanny.'

" 'The devastating fear of losing a loved one' takes on a new dimension in the light of Jenny's abandonment of Berta. It is scarcely conceivable that when Jenny returned to Paris soon after, leaving eleven-year-old Berta with strangers on a strange continent, she did not experience some feeling of guilt about deserting her, even though she probably had little choice. As the threat of Nazi violence made it necessary to flee from Europe, it is possible, as so often happens with traumatic events, that Jenny unconsciously may have experienced this new development as punishment for her 'crimes.' I would guess that with the acting out of her fantasy that followed, her guilt over abandoning Berta became intensified. She therefore defended herself by returning to the earlier experience when she had not allowed Berta out of her sight for an instant, as though to demonstrate to her mother what a 'good girl' she really was. Throughout the following years she has continued to act out that image by sacrificing her life for Berta via Rosette. If only she could establish that she was a worthwhile person and deserving of love, then perhaps her mother could forgive her, and—irrational as it may seem—return from death.

"That Rosette developed asthma, a suicidal depression, and finally became severely disturbed, followed inevitably from her mother's suppression of her needs in the service of her obsession. The story of Rosette's illness is an object lesson in the consequences of repressing aggressive feelings. As each new attempt to enforce her conformity to Jenny's fantasy increasingly restricted her freedom, her rage escalated. By itself, that would not necessarily have led to the tragic emotional developments depicted by both her and her mother. The problem was that all of Rosette's defenses were designed to contain her anger. In order to defend herself against the magnitude of the terror inspired by Jenny's rages, and without any other parent to turn to, Rosette had no choice but to bottle up her own rage. Starting with the pressure on Rosette to excel at school, and probably even earlier, and proceeding with all her efforts to keep Rosette by her side, Jenny employed the same verbal and physical abuse that she had been the victim of during her childhood. The violence that Rosette learned from Jenny, just as Jenny had learned it from her mother and Fanny, necessarily had to be turned against herself. On those occasions when her repressed rage became unmanageable she attempted suicide. Although the direction of Rosette's rage may have been partially determined by a fear of retaliation if it were leveled against Jenny, it may also reflect Rosette's perception that Jenny was all she had and that she was loved as well as hated. For Rosette to give up her strong defense, her terror would have to be sufficiently reduced to allow her to experience and to express her anger.

''Other aspects of the relationship of Jenny and Rosette follow automatically from the pattern imposed on their lives.

''Once normal needs are stifled and harnessed to the tyrannical requirements of an ever-present past, they necessarily erupt wherever they can find an outlet and assume whatever forms are available. In the isolation imposed by Jenny's need for expiation, the instinctual feelings that ordinarily find expression outside the family were naturally directed toward the only other person present. For Jenny and Rosette to have found normal satisfactions of such needs, it would have been necessary for Jenny to have received help in understanding the early events of her life and in experiencing the unbearable feelings they provoked. She would also have needed assistance in curbing the acting out of the anger she had learned within her family and in developing an appreciation of the extraordinary qualities that have helped her to survive. If she had been helped to work through the severe traumas of those early years, with the consequent resolution of her feelings of guilt, she would have been free to direct her considerable energies to finding gratification in her present life apart from Rosette and her dedication to being a student. Her separation from her daughter would then have freed Rosette to give up defenses she no longer needed and to pursue her own life.

"As I read the stories told by Jenny and Rosette, I could not help being moved by their tragic implications. What appears so obvious even to a cursory reader seems to be shrouded in mystery for them. Even more distressing is the realization that from the age of thirteen, Rosette either attended special schools, was a patient at mental hospitals, or was in private treatment, and that her mother was also exposed to psychiatric or psychological help. That this could go on for over twenty years, at the end of which the mother can still ask, 'What did I do wrong?' and the daughter state, 'My problems are all of my own making,' is a sad comment not simply on the depth of their problems but on the effectiveness of the help they received and the kind of care available to people with little means. I also could not help marveling at the strength and the devotion of this mother who, through all her confusion, beset by problems she has not been helped to understand, has persisted in her efforts to live in a way that she hopes will bring happiness to herself and her child."

One important question must be asked: Did the treatment Rosette received in the many institutions to which she was committed or to which she went voluntarily harm or help her—did anyone aid her in understanding her conflicts, lessen her anguish, make it possible for her to move emotionally away from her mother?

Dr. Blau tried, but she seems to be the only one. Through her help, Rosette gained a slight sense of self-esteem. But therapists at other institutions revealed the inadequacies of our underfinanced state mental hospitals, especially where young people are concerned—ironically, those for whom there should be the most hope.

It was punitive of psychiatrists at Central Islip to have prescribed for a twenty-year-old, especially when Rosette was not outwardly violent but depressed, sixty-two insulin shock and six electroshock treatments. During one of the latter she came to consciousness too soon and felt "electrocuted."

When something is "done to" the brain or body, rather than allowing the person's intellect and emotions to take part in changing the course of his emotional illness, lasting change is often difficult, if not impossible. A mind that has received the blows of electroshock, insulin shock, or heavy medication is a mind that remains crippled.

Because they do not have enough money or qualified professional help, our public mental hospitals cannot offer what is called psychodynamic psychotherapy, the help that most effectively eases mental torment. Such treatment, based on psychoanalytic theories, is costly and lengthy, and our city and state mental hospitals are too restricted financially to use it. The psychiatrists in these overcrowded, understaffed hospitals cannot give much time to a patient but have to rely on the temporary easing of violent symptoms and suicidal depression by drugs and shock. In most cases this does not "cure" depression or violent feelings but obscures even further the deep sources of distress.

What of our private mental hospitals where those who have money or health insurance may go for help? The living quarters are far more comfortable, the food more palatable, the nursing care of high quality. But even these hospitals vary in the type of treatment they give. Some, like Austen Riggs in Stockbridge, Massachusetts, and Chestnut Lodge in Rockville, Maryland, provide long-term, intensive therapy based on psychoanalytic theories. Many however do not have sufficient modern psychotherapeutic resources and may resort chiefly to medication.

The public is often confused as to the difference between a psychiatrist and a psychoanalyst. Only about ten percent of the nation's psychiatrists have studied for an additional three years at one of the twenty-six institutes accredited by the American Psychoanalytic Association, during which time they also undergo their own analysis. Jenny mistakenly believes all the psychiatrists who saw Rosette were psychoanalysts. They were not—except for Dr. Blau.

The depressing atmosphere of the mammoth state hospitals caused Rosette additional suffering. There was no one to help her realize that her adolescent rebellion and occasional sexual acting-out hid a fear and anger she could not face. And in both private and public institutions she was occasionally the victim of cruelty: the obese nurse who slapped her, the near-seduction by a male aide, the sadism of the German woman doctor. At the age of sixteen, already terrorized by her fantasies, she was brutalized in another way when sent to an adult ward at Rockland where her lullaby was the shrieks, sobs, and screams of seriously disturbed women of all ages, and where she saw a nurse's aide order a patient beaten, and had a friend who was seduced by a lesbian nurse's aide.

Jenny believes, as do a number of psychiatrists and a large part of the public, that severe emotional disturbance is biological, caused by "constitutional defects" or "genes." A few psychiatrists attribute schizophrenia to the consumption of "cereal grain glutens." They cite as proof that schizophrenia is less frequent in societies that eat grains other than wheat and rye. Would that the explanation of mental illness depended on a loaf of bread!

The public is all too willing to accept the "constitutional" approach and demand a "magical" cure. It is unable, because of what Freud called "resistance," to think of mental illness as a developmental process, years in the making and years in the easing. There is no swift, short-cut method of lessening the pain of the mind. It takes work on the part of the patient and the therapist before the dangerous feelings that have interfered with mental functioning are faced and conflicts resolved.

It is simple to understand how we grow physically and intellectually. But it has been difficult for mankind to accept that we also develop psychologically. Freud discovered from his patients and his own look within what he called "the great secret." This was the existence of "psychic reality" as contrasted with outer reality.

Psychic reality is composed of the fantasies in daydreams and night dreams that add up to our hidden wishes. Psychic reality may at times dominate us as we feel "out of control." Rosette retreated more and more into psychic reality when she found outer reality too harsh.

The psychic reality, or inner world, of Jenny and Rosette erupted in their behavior and in the dialogue, spoken and unspoken, between them. Inner reality dominated the day-by-day, month-by-month, year-by-year emotional development of Rosette, dependent only on Jenny for the ways she would meet the challenge of the world.

All the therapists Jenny and Rosette consulted called the relationship between mother and daughter "symbiotic." This close relationship is natural for the newborn child in order to survive. But if such attachment continues much beyond the first years, it is bound to cripple the child emotionally and stir feelings of intense anger as his drive for independence becomes blocked.

Rosette put these angry feelings into words: "Someone has controlled my destiny. I have had no free will."

Jenny says sorrowfully: "I have destroyed my daughter. If I were a judge, I'd sentence me to jail." She refers to allowing her daughter to be sent to institutions but unconsciously she may be speaking of her own part in unwillfully helping to form Rosette's illness.

The story each tells is a cry for help. Mother and daughter are trapped in the past, confused, seeking salvation. They feel there is no exit, yet they have not given up hope.

There are those who "blame" the person who is mentally ill. But it never helps to "blame"—either the self or a parent. "Blame" does not ease emotional illness. To "understand" is more useful. In this case, to understand Jenny, then Rosette, and how each tried to adapt to the world and to one another in order to survive.

As we understand Jenny's suffering, all "blame" vanishes. She could do no differently in terms of the severe emotional blows dealt her as a child and growing girl, as Dorothy Bloch eloquently points out. Berta summarized this poignantly when she wrote, "We never were children. We were born and immediately after we became old."

Jenny received little understanding of her life from the many therapists she saw. A large part of her salary went and still goes to therapy for both Rosette and herself, yet not one therapist has helped her face the devastating losses in her life—losses against which she has had to erect powerful defenses.

She is filled with such hidden sorrow she can say, "I wish I had drowned as a girl in the beautiful Dniester River I loved so much." And, "When I read that a refugee ship sank within sight of the haven it sought and all those aboard drowned, I wished I were on it." She maintains her "manic pace" perhaps to avoid facing feelings so devastating they drive her, at times, to wish she were dead. She is victim of a lifelong depression she denies.

This denial also encompasses deep anger and grief, feelings inherent in unfulfilled mourning. Repressed anger and grief have haunted her every move. Jenny has never permitted herself to mourn the losses of a life where abandonment was the norm. Where, as Virginia Woolf put it, "All my dead ones are inside me and these dead ones are tearing me and calling me."

TOO DEEP FOR TEARS

Before Rosette's birth, Jenny paid no attention to traffic lights as she crossed the streets of Caracas, not caring whether she lived or died as she invited a car or truck to strike her. Such depression was bound to be deflected onto her baby, a burden Rosette has had to bear. She was supposed to make up for all the losses Jenny suffered.

What were these losses? The most overwhelming occurred when Jenny's mother, Rosa, killed herself. Jenny, in effect, was orphaned at eleven. Six months before, Jenny lost her father when he walked out on his family for a younger woman.

There was also a far earlier loss that haunted the family—Jenny's brother died of pneumonia two years before Jenny was born. Jenny's mother was so stricken she tried to kill herself. Jenny's father, an irresponsible man with hardly a thought in his head but satisfying his own childish whims, wanted at that time to end the marriage. He wrote in his diary that he no longer loved his wife. But somehow she persuaded him to stay and bore him in this "loveless" environment two other children, both girls.

The effect on Jenny, the older, of taking the place of her dead brother was undoubtedly traumatic, especially as a member of a Jewish family where traditionally the boy is worshipped, the girl treated as inferior. Jenny assumed an overwhelming psychological burden following in the wake of her dead brother. She was expected by her parents to make restitution to them for having lost a son, to *be* the vanished boy. Jenny says she wished she had been a man, that "it's a man's world, as I early realized."

Throughout her life she has unconsciously acted like a man. It is as though Jenny made her mind up when she was eleven, when her mother killed herself, that she had to go it alone. She says proudly, "I have never asked anyone for anything. I depend on no one but myself."

Jenny was never able to trust a man. Her father could not make an adequate living, often leaving the house for months—once for four years—to lecture and tutor children in far-off cities. Her mother taught school to pay the rent and buy food, just as Jenny later worked when Manuel failed to provide for his family. Her images of femininity and masculinity were confused by the models in her home as she grew up.

And as her mother did to her as a baby—turn her over to a nurse—thus Jenny did to Rosette.

As most daughters do, Jenny unconsciously followed in the footsteps of the woman who formed her image of femininity—her very depressed mother. A woman who thought so little of herself that, waiflike, she walked to the railroad station to see her husband off to Brazil accompanied by another woman, leaving her and their two children penniless and deserted.

But Jenny, not wanting to die like her mother, fought against becoming so deeply depressed by acting like her father and denying all depression. Jenny flew out into the world in flight from her grief and anger. Her flight probably saved her life. If she had remained in Khotin or Rishcon no doubt she would have been slaughtered by the Nazis along with her grandmother.

Jenny also never trusted a woman. She professes complete love for her mother, "a saint," denying all hate aroused by a woman so depressed she killed herself when her husband abandoned her. One might ask what kind of mother would leave two little girls to face the world alone? Only a woman whose depression was so severe it obliterated even her deep maternal instinct. She doomed Jenny and her little sister Berta to wander the earth feeling deserted, in the shadow of their mother's early death by her own hand. Berta is more realistic than Jenny in that she realizes the tragic effect of her mother's death on her two daughters.

Jenny describes her mother as coming from an emotionally disturbed family of four daughters whose mother died at an early age. One of the daughters spent time in a mental hospital. Depression *is* handed down from a mother to a daughter not through genes or constitutional weakness but in the creating of a psychic aura suffused with the repressed sorrow and rage of unfulfilled mourning. An aura that contributes to severe emotional disturbance from generation to generation. An aura that, in this instance, led to Rosette, the end result, a young woman so depressed she had to resort to illusions to bear her sorrow and frustration, and several times tried to take her life.

As Rosette lifted the bottle of iodine to her lips at the first institution, she mirrored the fatal act of her grandmother, Rosa, an act undoubtedly described to her by Jenny. Rosette *became* Rosa in the sense she was the target of many of Jenny's unconscious feelings about her mother—feelings of hate for the mother who walked out on her forever, who deprived her of the emotional sustenance she desperately needed in childhood, who deprived her of a father. These feelings Jenny may deny but they have not vanished. Hurt and hate do not lie quiet or disappear. In distorted form they have been inflicted on Rosette, overpowering Jenny's strong maternal desire to protect her child.

Jenny's outbursts occurred sporadically when she would explode at what she thought Rosette's irrational behavior. Jenny did not often threaten her daughter. But a parent need say only once to a child, "I wish you were dead," and the child never forgets. Jenny remembered only too well the time her mother hurled these words at her.

As Rosa conveyed her depression and her masked feelings of anger to Jenny, so Jenny did to Rosette. A small child is acutely receptive to a mother's moods. Jenny also communicated to Rosette the feeling, "You shall never leave me, as my mother did, and my father, and my older brother, and Berta, and Aunt Fanny. I will have total control over you as I did not have over them. I will make sure *you* stay by my side forever. I will take care of you and love you as I wish my mother had taken care of and loved me."

Someone mourning excessively for a beloved dead person can maintain the illusion of total control over "killing or not killing" the one who has died, for whom he has substituted a living person over whom he does have control, according to Dr. Vamik D. Volkan. He presented this theory in his paper, "The Night of the Living Dead" (the title is taken from a film in which the dead are pictured as eating the living in order to exist). The paper was delivered at the annual meeting of the American Psychoanalytic Association in December, 1978, in New York.

Jenny unconsciously used control of Rosette as a link to her dead mother. Just as Jenny's mother used the control of Jenny as a link to her dead mother and dead son.

"This designation of the living daughter as uniquely precious will lead her to crystallize in later life a pathological grandiose self," stated Volkan. Jenny often calls Rosette "precious," treats Rosette as her whole world, the focus of all her affection and fantasies. This has made Rosette feel, in Volkan's word, "grandiose." Rosette still sees the world with a child's eye, herself as its center.

Out of Jenny's myriad intense conflicting feelings of love and hate for her mother and father, out of her early losses of a mother and father who themselves were emotionally disturbed, came Jenny's excessive need to be close to Rosette. Jenny, like many other women, became a mother who had never received enough mothering. She was not able to meet her daughter's need for protection and emotional nourishment because she had never received protection or emotional nourishment from her very depressed mother.

Jenny was victim of what psychoanalysts call "soul murder," originally August Strindberg's phrase. This probably takes place to some degree in every family, for a mother is bound to have feelings of both hate and love for a child. No one of us is capable of pure love. But because Jenny's emotional deprivation was so deep, she in turn unconsciously inflicted on Rosette an emotional deprivation that thwarted Rosette's natural psychic and sexual development.

Dr. Blau told Jenny it was her duty to help Rosette grow up and become independent. "But how can I do it?" cries out Jenny, realizing she is helpless, prisoner of her past.

She has tried to do her best. She read countless books on how to bring up a child—unfortunately some based on the fad of the moment. At times she acted naïvely and unwisely but there was no one to show her a more reasonable way.

She believes she has protected Rosette. She confuses *protection* with *possession*. The fantasy that to control a child excessively is giving "love" and "protection" is perhaps one of the great illusions of all time. The sacrificing mother who will do "anything" for her child, who emotionally binds the child to her long after he should become free, not only cripples the child with guilt but denies the child's right to his own body, both sexually and for the expression of anger. Love sets free. Love does not aim at control. Jenny loved Rosette "not wisely but too well," with the passionate, possessive love of a child for a mother rather than the mature, supportive love of a mother for a child.

As we understand Jenny's life we realize how deeply she suffered as a child. But we have to start somewhere to show specifically how severe emotional illness may come out of the relationship between mother and child. Though many a mother of a severely emotionally disturbed child prefers to believe the illness "inherited" or "constitutional," for then she can deny her part in its development.

When Rosette was born, Jenny thought her baby would bring love into her life. But this is not a child's function. A child brings new responsibility and the sacrifice of some of the parents' needs as they establish a model of maturity.

Jenny wanted Rosette to be all she was not—the brilliant student, the artist, the concert pianist, the ballet dancer. She unconsciously thought of Rosette as a part of herself. Some mothers continue to think of their baby after birth as they did the fetus—an extension of their body, to do with as they will. Such mothers cannot countenance the slightest display of disobedience or anger on the part of the child. To some degree every mother will unconsciously use her child to satisfy her needs. But the less she does, the happier the child.

Because Jenny had great difficulty allowing Rosette to separate from her, Rosette felt merged with her mother. A shadow of Jenny. Sometimes Jenny did not even let Rosette finish a sentence, cutting in and speaking for her, as though Rosette did not have a self. Rosette speaks of feeling like two or three personalities, not a unified one.

In a sense Rosette's illness was the result of both spoken and unspoken wishes in her own and her mother's mind. What Jenny wished Rosette to be influenced what Rosette became, though sometimes this worked in reverse when Rosette was able to rebel. Torn by intense love and intense repressed hate, Rosette at times thought her mother a "devil." She could not see her mother as a human being entitled to her own fears, angers, and desires. It is difficult for a daughter who does not mature emotionally to be objective about her mother.

We can trace Rosette's losses, grief, and anger as starting in the nursery, the place where, as Freud said, the seeds of murder are sewn. The desire to commit suicide comes out of the repressed wish to kill someone beloved. A child, because his survival depends on the loved-hated parent, may turn his angry wishes on himself.

As an infant Rosette was excessively lonely and frightened. Her feelings of being deserted by her mother and the natural anger that followed started in her crib at Caracas, just as Jenny's anger during her infancy at being left by a mother who went to work probably started in *her* crib.

One of the first severe emotional (and physical) blows Rosette suffered was frustration of her hunger. Jenny tells how, in accordance with the books on child care then popular, she fed Rosette only every three hours. At times Rosette cried because she felt starved but had to wait to be fed. Jenny recalls finding Rosette so apathetic she would refuse to nurse.

When Rosette was one month old, Jenny returned to her job. But she continued breast-feeding her baby as the maid carried Rosette across the street to the factory where Jenny worked. At the age of four months, Rosette went on a hunger strike.

This was her first attempt at suicide. She was expressing a murderous rage at her mother for leaving her six days a week during the first months of her life. Her angry protest at being abandoned worked. From then on, Jenny spent two hours at home during her lunch period trying to force food into Rosette, who accepted a mouthful every twenty minutes.

Her current nightmares of fleeing raging fires may be interpreted as expressing the intense early oral rage aroused by her frustrating experiences in breast-feeding. Rosette told Dr. Blau that at times she imagined someone biting her breasts and felt actual physical pain. This may have been projection of her wish to bite her mother's breasts when, as a hungry baby, she was denied milk. Freud said the infant's experience with feeding is ''a crucial factor in his personality development and integration.''

Dr. Leo Stone recently stated: ''There is no unconscious human impulse to which fire gives expression so thoroughly as it does to the ravenous oral, devouring impulse. Fire is uniquely fitted to express, in fact or intrapsychically, the central archaic sphere of oral destructiveness.'' These comments appear in his paper, ''Remarks on Certain Unique Conditions of Human Aggression (The Hand, Speech, and the Use of Fire),'' in the *Journal of the American Psychoanalytic Association* (Vol. 27, No. 1, 1979).

He points out, ''The human infant is exposed to the breast for a relatively long period and his earliest intense frustrations, ranging from

an irreducible ('ideal') minimum to the very severe, occur in this con-
nection.'' The child may be exposed not only to the sight of succeed-
ing infants nursing at his mother's breast, but may suffer severe punishment for the aggressive use of his teeth in biting. He may also be
''the target of unconscious adult oral ravenousness.''

Dr. Stone presents the theory that ''the cannibalistic devouring impulse (varying in intensity) is one of the earliest and most powerful dynamic forces of the human unconscious, that indeed it may have con-
stituted one of the fundamental conditions (if not *the* decisive
condition) for its development.''

The need for Rosette to go on a ''hunger strike'' in the first few
months of life shows how furious she was at her mother for the strict
feeding schedule as well as for deserting her six days a week. This
was immediately followed by too early toilet training at six months as
Rosette was forced to hold back her wish to urinate and defecate except at certain hours and in certain places. Dr. Stone also points out
that a fantasy of burning fires also serves to release a repressed wish to
urinate freely as a way of putting out the fire.

''Most frequent dreams connected with fire are enuretic dreams,''
he says. ''The fire is invoked as a dream mechanism to permit the
urination based on other than sexual causes—for example, the rebellion against harsh sphincter training.''

Rosette's oral rage was also shown when she *bit* the girl in camp
who attacked her rather than hitting her in retaliation. Biting is the earliest, most primitive way of destroying someone.

A second blow to Rosette's psychosexual and emotional development was the very early toilet training demanded of her at six months,
far too severe a burden to be placed on any infant. The normal age for
complete toilet training is two years. To force a child to be toilet
trained at six months is likely to create an intense anger that may per-
vade his whole life. Too much rage occurs too early, as well as too
much guilt at the rage. Too intense a desire to please the mother develops too early, a result of too much fear of losing the mother's love.
Jenny's expectations were gargantuan all along the way, as no doubt
were her mother's in relation to her.

A consistent relationship with a mothering person is essential for the
first three years of life, according to psychoanalysts. Jenny did take off

six months and spend them caring for Rosette, a very important act in easing her daughter's emotional pain. Dr. Henri Parens says, "We all retain yearnings for the mother of symbiosis. We must learn to tolerate the pressure. The degree depends on how traumatizing our early life experience." Jenny, by staying home these six months, helped ease Rosette's trauma.

Rosette was "a good little girl" when she complied with her mother's demands to become toilet trained. And throughout life she was her mother's "good little girl" but at the price of the loss of some of her identity. The mother who makes such a strict demand so early in a baby's life is apt to be the mother who makes strict demands throughout the child's life, as Jenny unknowingly did of Rosette, both in her education and her sexual behavior.

Rosette's choice of her favorite painting as "Echo and Narcissus," based on the Greek myth in which a young girl's body disappears and all that is left is the echo, sums up how she feels about herself. Her body has vanished, she is merely the echo of her mother.

Just as the threatening "tiger" in her life was both her mother and the raging animal instincts within herself as she wished to fight back what she saw as destruction. Children project on animals their own dangerous impulses.

Rosette suffered another significant loss at the age of three when she virtually lost her father forever. Not only did she lose the second most important person in her life but his loss meant that Jenny would now focus many of her feelings for her husband on her daughter. Freud spoke of a divorced or separated mother's "libidinal shift" from husband to child, meaning love in all its aspects—passionate, tender, ambivalent—and the maternal seduction this implied.

A wife who leaves her husband or is left by him may use her child to meet emotional needs formerly supplied by the husband. Or she may try to work out unresolved conflicts with him by displacing them on the child. In either instance, the child suffers, as Sidney H. Grossberg and Louise Crandall point out in their paper "Father Loss and Father Absence in Preschool Children" published in *Clinical Social Work Journal* (Vol. 6, No. 12, 1978).

"A mother who has experienced the loss of her spouse can become excessively concerned about her child's health . . . may also feel the child is a burden or a detriment to her prospects of remarrying or having a career . . . may see the child as a constant reminder of her failure as a wife,'' the authors state.

The child's normal intense ambivalence toward the mother, one of love and dependence versus hatred, ''can turn into an intense fear of being devoured by the omnipotent mother now that the father is not present to act as a buffer in the mother-child relationship,'' they add.

The mother's attitude toward the absent father, and her feelings toward men in general, are important to the child, who lacks the daily opportunity to experience a ''real relationship'' with a father that would correct distortions provided by the mother.

For fifteen years after Jenny left Manuel, she blocked him out of her life. Then, ''out of fairness'' to Rosette, she invited him to the United States. This fifteen-year interval, to Rosette, must have seemed like one long denial of her father. Yet even in his absence he played an important role in that Jenny's angry feelings about him—an irresponsible man who lived in a world of daydreams just as her father had done—were conveyed to her daughter.

With the loss of her father at the age of three, Rosette was left to bear the brunt of all Jenny's feelings. There was no father to share the love and the hate. When Jenny shouted at Rosette that she wished she were dead, Rosette had to stifle her rage to keep alive the hope that she could win her mother's love, for she had no father either as buffer or alternate love. In Rosette's mind, Jenny was too dangerous and powerful to oppose; Rosette depended on her too desperately. Consciously, Jenny asked Rosette to be a ''good girl,'' kind and thoughtful to everyone. But unconsciously, Jenny asked Rosette to be a daughter, son, lover, husband, mother, father, sister, aunt, grandmother.

The depth of Rosette's dependency on her mother and her fear of abandonment—equating it with death—was shown in her extreme reaction the evening Alfredo failed to show up for a second date. The average girl of seventeen would not try to kill herself if a man she had seen only once disappointed her. What could Alfredo, a man she did not know beyond a one-night stand, possibly mean to Rosette? He was important only as he symbolized the mother of childhood. He reawakened her feelings of being deserted at a time she was unable to cope with desertion—in infancy when her mother left her to go to work and again at the age of three, when she was forced to live alone in the Chicago nursery. She said recently, explaining why she took the overdose of pills, "It wasn't really Alfredo. I thought my mother was not going to show up, that she would leave me alone in South America forever." To a child, if a parent vanishes at a time of need, it feels like death—what Rosette sought when she swallowed the sleeping pills.

Thus where there is no father, a child may have a very difficult time becoming independent of the mother. Rosette suffered what psychoanalysts call a "hostile dependency" on Jenny. She repressed her anger in order to remain close to her mother. And Jenny, because of her own unresolved dependency on her depressed mother, responded to Rosette's natural attempts to become free with excessively strong expressions of fear, anger and control.

"When a mother has fostered too intense a tie with her child and does not encourage autonomous functioning—when she continues to do things for the child though it is no longer appropriate or inhibits independence, when the child believes that to separate from her would mean loss of her love, this creates an inhibition of independent assertion," states Dr. David Krueger in his paper, "Anxiety as It Relates to 'Success Phobia': Developmental Consideration," presented at the annual meeting of the American Psychoanalytic Association in December, 1978, in New York.

"When the mother spares the child the pain of ordinary experiences of trial and error, the ensuing emotional component in the child is the belief that he cannot do these things which have been done for him by his mother, that he *needs* an object functioning for him—that he is inadequate," Krueger points out.

Any atmosphere of physical or verbal violence, or hostile competition, results in the anticipation of attack or retaliation, and this inhibits aggression, he adds. The inhibition of aggression, in turn, undermines self-confidence and esteem and results in a chronic feeling of inadequacy. This is how Rosette felt whenever she saw Jenny as engulfing, controlling, and manipulative, needing Rosette to sustain and comfort her.

Psychoanalysts are studying how a child separates emotionally from his mother and the fantasies that exist in the child and the mother that either impede or aid his psychosexual development. How infants take the steps—literal and psychic—that enable them to separate has been noted by Dr. Margaret Mahler. She calls this psychic process within the child "separation-individuation." She divides it into four phases.

The first is the "differentiation phase." It occurs about the age of six months as the infant becomes aware he and his mother are two different entities. This is followed by the "practicing phase," as he dares to tentatively try physical and emotional separation. The third, the "rapprochement phase," occurs from age twelve months to twenty-two months. The child toddles away from his mother, asserting his independence, then returns to make sure she is there. The fourth, or final stage, is called "on the way to object constancy." The child establishes a feeling of "basic trust" in his mother so he no longer needs her presence to feel she loves him. Her image in his mind is enough to sustain him. If a child does not have enough trust in his mother to proceed on his way to "object constancy," he will have difficulty becoming independent.

A mother can either help or hurt her child as he takes his first steps away from her. She helps him develop and enjoy his rapidly growing capacities, skills, and abilities if she is able to treat him as a person outside her "self" and allow him autonomy. But a mother who becomes anxious and angry when her child asserts himself conveys this anxiety and anger to the child. She increases his fears of separation by making him feel she will withdraw her love if he achieves separation. Thus the child believes that to move away from his mother and gain his own identity means she will no longer love him. And he feels guilty at trying to become independent.

Jenny unknowingly added to her daughter's guilt by sleeping in the same bed with her from the time Rosette was three and a half, when they lived in the porch bedroom in Chicago, until she was thirteen. In later years Rosette sought to sleep with her mother whenever she woke from nightmares or felt afraid of sleeping alone. Jenny should not have encouraged or allowed this.

Even though nothing sexual occurred—Jenny would not have permitted it—the fantasies, and the ensuing guilt aroused in Rosette must have terrorized her as she lay night after night, year after year, physically close to her mother. We are all primarily sexual and aggressive beings.

Jenny grew up in a family where it was natural for two members of the same sex—her aunt Fanny and her sister Berta—to share the same bed. Jenny, between the ages of eleven and sixteen, slept in the same room with her grandmother, and lived with roommates in Rio and Paris for four years. It never occurred to her, in the face of poverty, she might be harming her daughter when they shared one room.

There can be a seductive relationship between parent and child without any sexual act taking place, says Dr. Gregory Rochlin. The child may be seduced not only "out of his wits," as he resorts to fantasies of desire and revenge, but also "through his wits," in that the seduction is mental, not physical.

The fantasies in Rosette's mind, both conscious and unconscious, aroused by sleeping so near her mother all those vulnerable years, must have been overwhelming. Her defenses against her wishes to seduce her mother or be seduced by her, probably were strong, her rage deep.

Some depressed mothers try to escape depression by the use of "sexualization," according to Dr. Stanley J. Coen. He says: "A depressed mother may come alive by creating a sexually seductive atmosphere between her and her daughter. No bodily stimulation need be used. The daughter is made to feel special, precious, the one and only.

"Underneath these feelings however lie intense feelings of depression, deadness, unresponsiveness, loneliness, rage and humiliation. The daughter may feel sexually exploited by her mother but this is better [to the mother] than no response at all."

In his paper, "Sexualization and the Choice of a Sexual Mode of Defense," presented at the December, 1978, meeting in New York of the American Psychoanalytic Association, Coen states that sexual pleasure, a basic directing force in mental life, may be used defensively. The mother uses her "sexualized wishes" as a way of expressing her own childhood unmet need for love.

A threatening maternal image may be transformed by a daughter into an omnipotently protective, paternal one, Coen adds. Rosette, to ward off her hostile impulses, consciously thinks of Jenny as the "good, loving mother." And Jenny, by feeling seductive and dominating, does not have to face the picture of herself as a weak, helpless, and frightened child.

Rosette tried to break away from her mother and experiment with some sort of relationship with a boy, first, after running away from the private school for a sexual experience, then in Brazil, through the brief affair with Alfredo. Several times she expressed the wish to move out of the apartment and live with a girlfriend but she was not strong enough to defy Jenny. The part of Rosette that still wished to be her mother's baby triumphed over the part that wished to be free. Also, as Jenny realized, because of the depth of Rosette's illness, it was unlikely she could successfully live on her own.

Because of her missing father, Rosette had difficulty loving a man. A daughter must first love a father, someone of a different sex, so she can eventually transfer these new feelings to a man outside the family. For her to achieve this psychic task, she must have the understanding and guidance of both her mother and father. Her relationship to her mother however is the first and most important one of her life. On it all other relationships will be based. Their success or failure will be determined by the quality of her first love—a love that develops from the day she is born.

The consequences of severe conflicts in the early years of life include "a pathological development of oedipal conflicts, not an absence of them," says Dr. Otto F. Kernberg in his article, "Object Relations Theory and Technique," appearing in the *Journal of the American Psychoanalytic Association* (Vol. 27, No. 4, 1979).

"I believe that the controversy regarding the predominance of oedipal versus preoedipal conflicts in regressive conditions, or when early ego distortion or lack of development of the definite tripartite intrapsychic structure [id, ego, and superego] exists, really obscures some of the significant issues," he said.

He reports that not even in the most severe emotionally disturbed person "have I ever been able to find a patient without evidence of crucial oedipal pathology; the question is not presence or absence of oedipal conflicts, but the degree to which preoedipal features have distorted the oedipal constellation and have left important imprints on character formation."

Rosette's erotic feelings for her father never crystallized. They were too dangerous, distorted by her intense earlier conflictual feelings about her mother and father. She had never seen her mother in a man's arms, except for early memories of Caracas, and even then Jenny and Manuel were not very ardent, according to Jenny.

When Rosette walked into the kitchen at Brighton Beach and saw her mother, naked from the waist up, being caressed by a strange man, the shock was severe. Up to then Rosette believed her mother belonged only to her—no brothers, no sisters, no father—just she and her mother against the unfeeling world.

We can trace Rosette's failure in school, and her rebellion against her mother, from that moment on. She felt deeply wounded, betrayed. She retreated more and more into the world of fantasy, read magazines, listened to music, chain-smoked.

Her hidden anger at her mother emerged in oblique fashion at the first institution where she learned to freely use the word "bitch." When she hurled this epithet at the obese nurse who deprived her of cigarettes, she was unconsciously applying it to the woman she felt her first tyrant.

Jenny established what may have been the most mature relationship of her life with Victor, able at long last to become friends with a man. At this time she was a very attractive young matron, with a husky, appealing voice, a keen sense of wit, and a desire to keep on the go.

Realizing Victor was becoming a permanent fixture on the scene, Rosette retreated even more deeply into her private world. At the same time, out of a sense of defiance and rage, she allowed herself some expression of her natural, intensifying sexual desires. She indulged in romantic adolescent fantasies about Benjy, her first boyfriend, then Alfredo, though by the time she traveled to Brazil she was possessed by the delusion that if she enjoyed a man's body it must be because he had "supernatural powers." What she thought passionate love was deeply suffused with sensual feelings from an earlier time of life—the sensual feelings a child has for its mother. Rosette's fear of sexual penetration by a man was so great she could not permit herself to enjoy sex.

The fantasy that "supernatural powers" are in control is possessed by those who blame God, the devil, or occult spirits for their own wishes and acts so they do not have to feel guilty. The supernatural powers represent the mother and father of childhood. To a frightened, angry child, the parent looms as so monstrous, so inspiring of awe, that he *is* "super-natural." The child whose parents are "natural" is not terrified of them. If the parent is psychologically or physically cruel, he may remain "super-natural" to the growing child, who may then believe, as an adult, that his parent has the power to see everything he does, know everything he thinks, just as a baby believes his mother knows his every thought and wish. When Rosette accused her co-workers of reading her mind, her mental functioning was that of an infant in regard to his mother.

Rosette had the fantasy there was a Rosicrucian society whose members could read her mind and that if she belonged to it she could read the minds of others. This makes sense in terms of her childhood wish to be as powerful as her mother so she could fight back. The "ros" in Rosicrucian is part of her own name and that of her grandmother, making the Rosicrucians a sort of familiar and familial society.

What we call "delusions" make sense to the one who suffers them. Rosette's fear of stepping on the grass because she might "hurt" the individual blades reveals her sensitivity to pain and the feeling she had been stepped on and hurt. She spoke of "trampling" on the heads of people in association with stepping on the grass, also showing a wish to hurt those who had harmed her.

As Dr. Blau pointed out, Rosette's guilt over wishing her mother dead showed itself when she kept washing her hands obsessively. The washing away of the imagined blood on her hands so that, as Rosette explained, "my mother won't die," shows her unconscious wish that her mother *would* die. Rosette has never dared face her anger except in dreams, safety valves for her deepest wishes, wishes too shameful and embarrassing for her conscious mind to accept.

The fantasy of drowning runs through the lives of both Jenny and Rosette. Jenny nearly drowned as a girl while swimming in the Dniester. Her grandmother *was* drowned in the Dniester by the Nazis. Jenny told of wishing she had drowned in that river as a girl, or along with the refugees fleeing Hitler, who died when their ship sank within sight of South America. Rosette describes how she nearly drowned in a lake as her mother talked to a friend on the beach.

In another kind of death, Rosette may have unconsciously felt she was being "electrocuted" when she was forced to undergo both insulin and electroshock, and threatened with a drug that was experimental. At a time she desperately needed understanding and help, she received only further emotional floggings, in addition to physical ones, when given or threatened with such punitive treatments. Her enforced isolation in one institution after another, as her deep loneliness and despair intensified, aroused agonized memories of the Chicago nursery. In a sense she has been destined to repeat, over and over, the pain of those early days as an infant in Caracas when she existed apart from her mother, knowing only desultory caretakers.

Rosette attempted at first, earnestly and successfully, to be the overachiever Jenny wished her to be. She learned to play the piano, studied ballet, listened to classical music, applied herself to art. She skipped one grade in grammar school, another in junior high. But unconsciously she dared not become a "success" at anything. To succeed meant to separate from her mother.

Rosette defended herself against the wish to become independent by giving up the goal of success. She failed in school, failed as an artist, as a ballet dancer, as a pianist. She also gave up on being a woman, realizing Jenny disapproved of erotic feelings, ready to punish any expression of them. After Rosette experienced her first sexual act, their relationship cooled for a while. Jenny feared Vicky would lead Rosette into promiscuity. Rosette did not dare "expose" herself sexually, artistically, or any other way, for to her this meant losing her mother's love.

A child's failure to meet a parent's too high expectations makes the child feel inferior and devoid of self-esteem. What self-confidence Rosette had seemed to evaporate when she could not keep up at school. She was not helped by the inconsistency of Jenny's feelings—violent rage one minute, apologies and protestations of love the next. A child is always confused when a parent draws him close in intimacy after heaping curses on his head. The child never knows whether to expect an embrace or a beating.

When Jenny attacked Rosette as "bad" and "irresponsible" and slapped her because she would not go to school, this verbal and physical assault made Rosette fell guilty because of her repressed wish to fight back. But this wish appeared symbolically in such physical symptoms as her asthma attacks and later in the suicide attempts. As though she were saying, "It is a far, far, better thing I do to take my own life than the life of the woman who has sacrificed so much for me, even though I feel she is destroying me."

For the most part, Rosette has denied her natural aggressive impulses toward Jenny. According to Dr. Hyman Spotnitz, author of *Psychotherapy of Preoedipal Conditions,* the severely disturbed person turns his aggression on himself, "placing himself in a psychological straitjacket to prevent being aware of his aggression or acting on it."

A child may sacrifice his own emotional health to protect a parent. He may feel like killing the parent but instead destroy his own ego by deadening his feelings of hate. He does not realize it is normal to hate as well as love, that the expression of hatred at times may be a psychological need, a natural desire pressing for outlet.

"No person really lives in an emotionally healthy way until he has developed the capacity to give balanced expression to love and hate," says Spotnitz. "We need to recognize the problem is not hate itself but its expression in harmful ways."

The word "parasite," which Jenny called Rosette, is used to describe a fetus, a "parasite" in the mother's body. When she was pregnant, Jenny probably considered the fetus within as a parasite, feeding off her, which most mothers do, according to psychoanalysts, because of conflicting feelings about having a baby. Jenny also spoke of her mother calling her a parasite. Jenny wanted Rosette, but, married three years to a man she supported and with whom love was never ardent, she may have had ambivalent feelings about having a baby. She probably thought of leaving her husband before Rosette was born, wondering how he would ever support her, much less a family. The baby's birth had to be a burden, tying her down for life, as it turned out.

Rosette has paid for the denial of her fear and anger at her mother, which appears in her fantasies as she calls on the "devil" to punish her mother. She is asking the devil to provide reassurance against her fear of being annihilated by her mother's anger and fear of annihilating her mother if she should ever let go.

Rosette wrote her mother from the first institution: "I was so happy after our last visit . . . don't you think we're improving, we don't scream at each other as we used to. Of course I'm not perfect and I never shall be but I can try to be near-perfect. It might take some time but I'll reach it."

What an illusory goal—leading only to misery, guilt, and rage, a vicious circle. To be perfect is to be inhuman, an impossibility. That Rosette thought this necessary for her to win her mother's love tells of her great fear of her mother and the fantasy that if she could only change, her mother would love her.

That Rosette believed she had to be perfect to win her mother's love, that she could never give up this illusion, is part of the tragedy of her life. Both she and Jenny contributed to the fantasy of the eternal "good little girl."

Both Jenny and Rosette tried valiantly to fight for their share of happiness in the face of overwhelming odds, as the passions of each clashed at times in terrifying battle. Seldom did either give in to grief-stricken feelings.

Jenny recalled that one day Rosette cried "as I have never seen her cry," as she looked at the photograph of a small boy trying to be brave as he marched off to a concentration camp and death. For the moment Rosette was able to identify with a victim of oppression, allowing her deeper feelings to break through.

Jenny and Rosette have not been able to shed the tears that must flow so they can know the depths of their torment and the distorted fantasies by which they have lived in order to survive their agony. No one thus far has helped them realize life would be far more bearable if they could look into the complexity of the self.

In the long run, there is only the self. A self that must face honestly, if there has been too great a psychic injury, the causes of that injury. And go on from there. Blaming no one. Accepting life as the challenge it is.

For Jenny and Rosette, this would mean the shedding of many, many tears.